Catholic
VOICES

Tom Thompson, 'Annunciation with distant town'.
Acrylic on wood panel, 84.5x132 cm, 1993. Detail on front cover.

Catholic
VOICES

Best Australian Catholic Writing

Editor
EDMUND CAMPION

Aurora Books
David Lovell Publishing

First published in 1996 by
Aurora Books
300 Victoria Street
Richmond Victoria 3121

in association with
David Lovell Publishing
PO Box 822
Ringwood Victoria 3134

Front cover :
Tom Thompson, 'Annunciation, with distant town' (detail)
Design by David Lovell
Typeset in 11/14 Bembo
Layout by Scott Howard
Production by Sylvana Scannapiego
Printed and bound in Australia

National Library of Australia
Cataloguing-in-Publication data
Catholic voices: best Australian Catholic writing.

ISBN 1 86355 053 4

1. Church and social problems - Catholic Church
2. Catholic learning and scholarship. I. Campion. Edmund.

261

Acknowledgements:
The articles reproduced in this book were all published elsewhere in magazines,
journals or newsletters. Acknowledgement of particular sources is given in the
introduction to each piece. Each article is reproduced with the permission of the
author. Every effort has been made to trace individual authors. We apologise for any
case where this has not been possible.

Photograph Album by John Thompson and Small Town by B. A. Breen are from
Australian Voices, published by Penguin, Australia; the section of Driving Through Saw
Mill Towns by Les Murray is from his Vernacular Republic published by Angus &
Robertson. All appear in 'Diary of a Country Priest' by Pat Kenna, and are reprinted
here with permission.

CONTENTS

INTRODUCTION

Once upon a time the chief job of the religious roundsmen of the daily papers was to cover Sunday sermons. Their big day was Monday, when the papers would carry columns and columns of sermons. Each Sunday, on his way out to open a church or school, Archbishop Duhig of Brisbane would drop his speech in to the *Courier-Mail*, where it would appear the next morning. That was a long time ago.

Those were the days when Catholic writers were deferential to bishops. Episcopal words and pictures dominated the church press; and the opinions of bishops were treated with the respect elsewhere reserved for St Augustine. If laypeople had doubts about the sagacity of their leaders, they kept these thoughts private. Very occasionally you might hear the voice of the toad beneath the harrow. Most of the time, however, loyalty to the church encouraged a strict Sicilian observance of the code of *omertà*. Such subservience was reinforced by a feeling that we Australian Catholics were living in an unfriendly society. With the *Sydney Morning Herald* and the *Argus*, to say nothing of the history departments in the universities, ready and willing to attack our church, we kept our secrets to ourselves.

In 1958 two remarkable fortnightly magazines appeared in the newsagents: the *Observer* and *Nation*. Frank Packer had set up the *Observer* to engage the full talents of Donald Horne; and for a time it functioned under the umbrella of Packer's lowlife *Weekend*, which Horne also edited. After three years the *Observer* merged with the *Bulletin*, when Packer bought that antique property for its real estate holdings. *Nation* was different in kind. Its founder and editor, Tom Fitzgerald, was a financial journalist whose ambition was to start such a magazine before he turned 40. His only asset was a suburban home, which he mortgaged in order to bankroll his dream. In the same spirit, his writers worked for nothing, happy to engage in a venture that, with the *Observer*, was changing the face of Australian journalism. Look at the Australian press before and after the fortnightlies and you will notice immediately how successful they were in their objective. They opened public life to fresh ideas and more robust debate; they were sceptical in their assessments of the would-be great; and they had a pretty, irreverent wit.

Both fortnightlies were interested in religion. Donald Horne, as his three volumes of autobiography and other books make plain, was a textbook secular humanist, a child of Sir Henry Parkes and Sir George Higinbotham. Nevertheless, as a public intellectual he recognised the force of the religious idea in Australian life; and he set out to explore it in a candid way. Tom Fitzgerald, on the other hand, came from a strong Catholic background. A regular communicant with a personal devotion to images of Jesus (as he told Ken Inglis), he had taken charge of the religious upbringing of his younger brothers and sisters, who remain observant, even fervent, Catholics. He read Catholic newspapers and was a founding member of the Australian Catholic Historical Society. When he married, his bride was a daily communicant. By the time he started *Nation*, however, all that was in the past. By then, in the objective canonical sense of the word, Tom Fitzgerald was an apostate. Whatever the reasons for this, it did not abbreviate his interest in the church—to the end of his life he liked to hear news of Catholic scholarship, especially about that deep well, John Henry Newman—and he opened his pages to anyone writing intelligently about religion. Like Donald Horne, he thought it bad journalism to ignore something of major concern to many Australians.

When it came to religion, the two fortnightlies found a school of young writers who were catching some of the new waves coming from the universities. By the beginning of the 1950s, university chaplaincies were resonating with the insights of Joseph Cardijn, whose Jocist movement became the key lay element in 20th century Catholicism. In part this university phenomenon grew in opposition to B. A. Santamaria, whose interest lay in colonising the university in the service of extraneous objectives. It is a melancholy fact that Santamaria, the most significant Catholic layman in Australian history, has not succeeded in nurturing intellectuals or independent writers. Why this should be so, is an open question. By contrast the Jocist-style chaplaincies produced an abundance. Jocist movements developed critical intelligences which, while being rooted in Catholicism, were comfortable with the liberal ethos of the universities. In the chaplaincies, undergraduates were formed to use their intellects as critical tools at the service of both the gospel and the university. It was a servant, rather than a colonising, Catholicism; one which energised the life of the mind; and so produced writers. A decade before the formal opening of the second Vatican Council, here was the Vatican II generation stirring to life in Australia.

The harbinger of change was an attractive university paper, *Prospect*. Produced by the circle which formed around Vincent Buckley, it appeared in 1958 and made an immediate mark. 'There is no contradiction in being both Christian and intellectual,' the first issue announced. Subsequent issues made good on this claim by taking seriously the questions of the day, that is, by not acting as if there were an easy solution to every problem—if only one could locate the relevant papal encyclical. Here was a paper which was neither clerical nor overtly ecclesiastical; and yet it was manifestly Catholic. Outside their own ranks it attracted writers as diverse as A. D. Hope, Ian Turner and Sam Lipski. Half-way through its seven years, it printed a list of financial supporters; the names included two archbishops (O'Brien and Young) but also Donald Horne and Manning Clark. In true Jocist style, the early focus of *Prospect* was on university, educational and cultural matters. Gaining confidence, they then began to publish material more nearly related to the church. It is worth noting that they won their colours first as lay intellectuals before claiming attention in the household of the faith. Today these essays read like rehearsals for Vatican II.

The appearance of the fortnightlies gave them a forum. Too young and unknown to win space in the metropolitan dailies, and suspicious of the clerically controlled diocesan weeklies, they found room to grow on the pages of *Nation* and the *Observer*. Mostly they wrote under pseudonyms, to protect their friends and mentors in chaplaincies and seminaries. The pseudonyms of those years—A. J. M. Sayre, Lachlan Edmunds, Matthew Vaughan, Elliot Vaughan, Lacordaire, Peter Hunt, W. O'Hara were some of them—are worth a separate study. Odd as they may seem now, pseudonyms were a necessary precaution then. For open discussion of its doings bewildered the hierarchical church, which struck out randomly at those who were perceived as enemies. Not enemies, but questioners. The blind giant clumped around, seeking ways to contain the damage. A priest who had been to school with Fitzgerald called in and asked him to lay off. When *Nation* wrote about the Knights of the Southern Cross, batches of copies went missing in the mail. And when the magazine wrote about Bishop Muldoon's attack on a visiting nun's theology, the North Sydney newsagency cancelled its order for the magazine. Later, when one of these youngsters had joined the *Sydney Morning Herald*, A. R. E. Thomas, a bush bishop, telephoned the editor, J. M. D. Pringle, to warn him against the dangerous radical.

To understand why this novel journalistic freedom was so shocking one had to go back to the atmosphere of the pre-conciliar church. The

Catholic press was thriving. Each state had at least one weekly paper, while some dioceses supported their own weekly or monthly papers as well. Religious orders maintained magazines which promoted the order's spirituality and interests. There was a plethora of other publications, such as the serious quarterly *Twentieth Century* ('of literary and academic interest'), founded by Melbourne laymen and taken over by the Jesuits when it fell on hard times, the *Catholic Worker* for political and social comment, *Sursum Corda*, a review for religious, *Australasian Catholic Record*, a clerical journal which went into every presbytery, and *Catholic Documentation*, an archive of papal statements. Lay apostolate movements had their own publications: *New Youth* for young workers, *Rural Life* for farmers and *Rising Tide*, published by the Young Catholic Students Movement. Below this hyperactive surface, uncollected by librarians and so now lost to historians, was a dense network of little magazines and newsletters, such as *Waysider*, the organ of Catholic bushwalkers, or the roneoed adventures in print of the university Catholics.

The first thing to strike one about this commonwealth of publications is its size. By any standards it was enormous, not only in the number of different titles but also in its circulation figures. In 1961, the year before the council opened, Sydney's *Catholic Weekly* was selling some 60,000 copies per week, the Melbourne *Advocate* about half that and its rival *The Tribune* 20,000 copies. Equally impressive were the circulation figures of the monthly magazines. The *Messenger* sold 45,000 a month, *Annals* and *Harvest* 32,000. *Catholic Missions* outstripped them all, with something like 140,000 subscribers; but since copies went to all paid-up members of mission aid societies, this figure is dubious. Another mission magazine, *Far East*, however, claimed 63,000 subscribers; which may be right because this was the best written of them all, a favourite with many nuns, who signed up their classes as subscribers.

Another thing to strike a taster of these papers and magazines is their dutiful tone. In the diocesan press bishops and the pope were given acres of coverage, their pronouncements printed without analysis or comment. Throughout these papers it was all good news. Controversy entered when some opponent of the church needed to be rebuked; this was usually done by a masterly cleric. Dr Rumble's *Question Box*—'Question: Do you know of any good in Luther? Reply: Intellectually, not much'—was popular. Elsewhere, confident experts made mincemeat of objectors. The most magisterial of these writers was the *Advocate's* D. G. M. Jackson, who filled a page of international affairs each week. Many of the features came from the Catholic press agency in Washington DC (USA) and were bland and processed. Typical of them might be a series on Catholic shrines in Europe or an article on some dead Catholic worthy. As with many other papers of that time, there was a children's page to encourage youthful writers and artists. Social pages chronicled dances and balls, outings òf the many alumnae associations and weddings, weddings, weddings. The sports pages gave news of inter-parish competitions, the *Catholic Weekly* even running to a weekly column by a prominent footballer. From front page to back, the diocesan press mirrored the church of its time: secure, confident, unquestioning and deferential.

Occasionally an individual voice stands out, such as the *Advocate's* P. I. O'Leary. When he died in 1944 at the age of 56, he had won the respect of Australia's literary community. They took up a subscription and a memorial book of his essays eventually appeared. Although O'Leary wrote for every department of the paper, it was his full-page articles on literature which made his name. He believed that literature was for Everyman, not for the elite. Like many journalists, he wrote against the clock; but his work was never shoddy. He introduced *Advocate* readers to Donne, Yeats, Joyce and Hopkins. Another whose name survives from this weekly pressure chamber is Carl Kaeppel, who died two years after O'Leary. He appears in Manning Clark's memoirs as an anti-Semitic teacher and certainly he was a man of the Right. He said he had become a Catholic because the church seemed to be the only body capable of preserving the values he cherished. In his final years, he wrote a weekly education column in the *Catholic Weekly*, providing in-service training for harassed teachers in Catholic schools His range of subjects was astonishing, from ancient history to mathematics; and he never condescended to his teacher readers, treating the silliest request with courtesy. The magnanimity of this polymath lent personal distinction to the *Catholic Weekly*.

When it came to the magazines, they sought their readership among eager, even enthusiastic, Catholics, who looked for encouragement and insights into the spiritual life, Like the diocesan press, the magazines mirrored the church of the time, which was attentive to authority, mathematical in its piety and did its praying by the book. Attendance at mass and frequent reception of the sacraments were its distinguishing marks.

The writers tended to be impersonal, they rarely wrote of what they themselves had learned of temptation or grace. Instead, they relied on approved authors and traditional experience. Nevertheless, bonds of friendship grew between readers and writers of the magazines. Even imaginary authors, like the *Far East's* 'Mickey Daley', who wrote a comically ill-spelled chronicle, made lots of friends. On the *Messenger*, Father Eustace Boylan sj fielded the doubts, crochets, scruples and worries of his troubled readers, who found him a kindly literary pastor. Many years later, the historian K. S. Inglis was the first to see that the *Messenger's* 'Editor's Chair' pages were a rich source of Australian history, for they revealed some of the tensions devout Catholics experienced in a pluralist culture. Later other historians would come along who realised that there was more to be learned about people's history from these magazines than from episcopal archives. For the archives reflected bishops' concerns; while the magazines spoke of the people. Librarians, too, began to see their importance as a source for the study of popular religion in Australia. So a valuable historical resource is being saved for future scholars.

The single most popular writer in the magazines was 'Miriam Agatha'. A pupil-teacher in the Townsville Mercy Sisters convent school, whose real name was Agatha Le Breton, she sent her first story to the *Messenger* at the age of 15. For more than 60 years she contributed stories and columns to the magazine, for most of that time as editor of the children's page. People, including bishops, went on reading her long after they had ceased to be children. It is not hard to guess her appeal, for she wrote about an innocent world of faith-filled boys and girls who loved their church. Her children kept the church's seasons of the year, made visits to the Blessed Sacrament at their parish church, saved pennies for the overseas missions, were attentive at school and helpful in the home. Year by year, she passed on the culture of Catholicism to new generations of boys and girls. Her writing was simple and she never failed to explain hard words. At the end of her life she was writing much the same as she had done decades earlier, although modern times made her warn young readers about the dangers of traffic on their way to early morning mass. 'Miriam Agatha' rarely said much about herself. She once wrote that when she was growing up her favourite writing paper came from cutting up off-white sugar bags—thus revealing the poverty of her home life. And she unconsciously revealed her own childlike candour when she told readers that she still sometimes laughed and even cried as she was writing. Apart from that, she hid behind her work, which remains as a source for the spiritual history of her times.

If, as I have said above, the *Prospect* writers were early pointers to Vatican II, others do not seem to have caught the signs of the times so accurately. A few months before the council opened, the Australian bishops put their names to a joint pastoral letter written for them by Thomas William Muldoon, a Sydney seminary teacher recently made bishop. Scouting rumours that a central aim of the council would be the reunion of separated churches, Muldoon's letter said that such speculation was 'unauthorised'. The question of reunion, he wrote, was fundamentally a question of 'home-coming' for fellow Christians separated from the See of Peter. The council, he predicted, would consider ways and means of facilitating and hastening their return. It was as if some Rip Van Winkle from the sixteenth century Council of Trent had come awake and begun to write pastoral letters. Implicit in every line of this pastoral was the assumption that the bishops owned the church and that only bishops had a right to critical intelligence.

As this Australian pastoral was being digested, a little book was streaming out of the shops and working its way into the discussion. This was *The Council, Reform and Reunion* by an unknown Swiss theologian, Hans Küng. A product of the modern historical approach to theology, Küng knew that the church had been conditioned and bruised by time. It was always in need of a clean-up. Nothing shocked many of his readers so much as this. Brought up to think of the church as never-changing, they lived in an imaginative world best described as non-historical orthodoxy. Their church was ruled by wise popes who handed down directives to the bishops, who passed them on to a compliant laity. Nothing much changed in this church: the mass was much the same as it had always been, the lifestyles of the clergy were no different from one century to the next; it was a church outside history, outside time. Change was a Protestant word. These people kept Dr Rumble busy answering questions about Küng's little book.

Jim Kelleher's reaction to Küng was typical of a vast middle territory of Australian Catholicism before the council. A good journalist, with experience in Hong Kong before becoming editor of the *Catholic Weekly* in 1942, he belonged to the loyalist lay organisation, the Knights of the Southern Cross. In 1961, looking back on 20 years experience, Kelleher wrote: 'Although the directors and staff of the *Catholic Weekly* have always regarded themselves as the servants of the Archbishop, it is an extraordinary fact that not one single policy directive has ever been given to the paper by the Cardinal or the chancery office'. Such harmony may not have been as remarkable as the editor seemed to think, since the church was unlikely to have chosen a maverick to edit the diocesan paper. Jim Kelleher was the sort of layman the Sydney archdiocese knew it could rely on. He liked bluff, manly priests noted for being street smart and dinky-di. Such priests were as puzzled as he was by the need for an ecumenical council; the church seemed in pretty good shape to them. Kelleher's comments on Küng expressed their viewpoint. The book might be erudite, but why was a priest denigrating the church in public like this? Only clerics and a few scholarly laymen would read the book, perhaps. But think of the harm when under-instructed Catholics read news magazines reporting that a priest had written about 'fallible infallibility' and of new sympathy for Martin Luther among Catholic scholars. As for saying that *every* area of church life needed renewal—'Father Küng voices a number of criticisms which are frequently expressed by Protestant writers'. The winds of change were unlikely to come close to Jim Kelleher's *Catholic Weekly*.

The next year showed how true this might be. At issue was whether the Knights of the Southern Cross could be discussed in the *Catholic Weekly*. *Nation* and the *Observer* had already run articles on the Knights, scoring in particular their code of secrecy. In recent months, however, KSC leadership had allowed a few bland references to appear in the Catholic press, thus acknowledging their hitherto clandestine existence. Then came the death of Dr Horace Nowland, top Knight and prominent Sydney medical man. Kelleher wrote a long obituary, including a comment that the Knights were 'widely misunderstood, mainly because of ill-formed, distorted and even malicious articles in a few periodicals'. To this, two journalists, members of the *Prospect* circle, wrote a rejoinder, which anatomised the systemic secrecy of the Knights and the sectarianism of the order. Of course their letter was not published. So they wrote to the chairman of the board, Bishop Freeman, to protest at the lack of free discussion in the sole organ of the archdiocese of Sydney. That got them nowhere. *Prospect* supported them; and some sentences from *Prospect's* editorial may be worth preserving here for their historical significance:

> The present suppression is the latest act of a whole history of intolerance that is generally unknown, although widely

suspected. To be precise, the Editor and Board of the *Catholic Weekly* have kept out of their pages any discussion of the issues that have anguished Australian Catholics in recent years. Indeed, a perusal of the Letters column of this newspaper over the last twelve months gives the impression that the real issues facing Australian Catholics are school uniforms, youth clubs and dirty advertisements in the daily press.

The *Prospect* Catholics traced their lineage back to Acton and John Henry Newman, who had run open journals one hundred years earlier. Douglas Woodruff's introduction to Acton's 'Essays on Church and State', printed first in the *Dublin Review*, had alerted them to the connection, particularly his lambent phrase that the closing down of Acton's *Rambler* and *Home and Foreign Review* in the face of episcopal disapproval was 'a story of the lay apostolate cut short'. When Newman was struck down by enemies in the church he said that he took his punishment willingly because he knew that one day soon the values he stood for would find a place in the church. *Prospect* thought that day was coming now, with Vatican II. They were linked to Newman and his times through people like Edmund Bishop, the historian of liturgy at the beginning of the twentieth century. In those days too there were people like J. M. Kelleher. Edmund Bishop once said, they always asked 'Will this disturb the simple faithful?'; never 'Is this true?'.

The advent of television increased the power of the controllers. To enhance their respectability in seeking licences to the new channels, people like Frank Packer invited the churches onto their boards. In response the churches got easy access to the new medium. Catholic programs were controlled by central committees and only approved people with approved views went to air. If a channel wished to make a program about the church, clearances from the committee were necessary A priest who was requested by a program maker would be told that he was to enunciate only church doctrine and not to offer his personal views. Otherwise, he didn't go on. This chimed in with the mentality of the time, for priests were then forbidden by canon law to publish without their bishop's permission.

But what about nuns? Were they under similar control systems? In earlier times such questions had scarcely arisen. Now, however, nuns in great numbers were beginning to encounter tertiary education and soon some of them might want to speak for themselves. Late in 1966 a Boston

Sacre Coeur nun, Mother Gorman, a specialist in psychology, came to Australia for some conferences. The *ABC* got to hear of her and invited her to discuss theology on a program it called 'X = GOD'. Mother Gorman said that the concept of deity was hard to express in modern symbolic language. This puzzled a Sydney catechist, who complained to the bishop in charge of media, T. W. Muldoon. He fired off an intemperate letter which made plain that the gravamen of her sinning was that she had spoken on TV without permission: 'Mother Gorman had no permission from ecclesiastical authorities to speak of any doctrinal matters in the archdiocese. It has been made known that Mother Gorman is not welcome again in this archdiocese. Both she and her stupidities and ignorance and error and near-heresies are in fact banned from the archdiocese.' Acting with his customary vulpine suavity, Cardinal Gilroy moved swiftly to limit the damage. He was too late. Sydney laity organised a protest meeting—the first in over a century—to deplore the lack of free speech in the diocese and the press had a field day. For the controllers it was a public relations disaster. Today the episode survives as a chapter in Tom Kencally's first successful novel, *Three Cheers for the Paraclete*.

Readers of that novel may be aware that the real-life model for one of its main characters was Bishop Muldoon. Whether the bishop learnt anything from the Mother Gorman incident may be doubted. Shortly afterwards, the editor of Brisbane's *Catholic Leader*, Brian Doyle, published a call for greater freedom in the church press. Doyle was a very talented journalist, an honours graduate in philosophy from the University of Sydney, who had worked under Jim Kelleher at the *Catholic Weekly*. In the early days of the Santamaria movement, he had warned Kelleher that when the movement's secrecy was blown, as was inevitable, he was not going to be the one to tell the necessary lies in the *Catholic Weekly's* pages. Now he drew attention to the deficiencies in the 'good news only' policies of the Catholic press. It was better for Catholics to read about church problems, such as the loss of priests—the word, as common then, was the harsh pejorative 'defections'—in their own papers than elsewhere. Why not treat readers as grown-ups? If some might be upset by the appearance of unpleasant news, there were others who were equally disturbed when such news did not appear. Hear, hear, said historian Bob Scrivener, an organiser of the protest meeting. It doesn't apply to me, said the *Anglican's* Francis James, I made complete editorial freedom a condition of my taking the job. 'The difficulty many of

my colleagues in Sydney face is that their journals are owned and controlled by the central organisms of their churches.' Not so, said the editors of
Australian Baptist, *NSW Congregationalist* and the *Methodist*: we are free to
publish what we wish. And Bishop Muldoon? Elbowing for time to let this
annoyance pass, he said that Brian Doyle's article needed much reflection
and study before an objective judgment could be made. 'My immediate
reaction is that it is not a matter of what is reported but of how it is
reported. There is a tendency in the Catholic press to imitate the sensation-
alism of the secular press instead of putting news in its right perspective
and educating readers to a balanced view of things.'

It was already too late for that sort of spin doctoring. After two years of
the council, a new weekly paper had appeared in the USA which transformed
the English speaking press around the world. This was the *National Catholic
Reporter*, produced by lay people in Kansas City, perhaps an unlikely place for
such activity. There was intense interest in what was happening inside the
council, which Vatican news management was powerless to control. Major
world dailies and news magazines had their best people in Rome and no one
could stop them getting the stories that mattered. The *Reporter* was part of this
phenomenon of the free press. By treating the news simply as news, without
deference to eminent persons or vested interests, they sent a powerful message
to the rest of the Catholic press. Instead of the suppression of unpalatable news,
they tried to get the facts out to their readers, because they believed that each
member of the church was responsible for the life of the church. This was the
core of their manifesto: everyone 'owned' the church, not just the pope and
the bishops. An adult church required more news, more open discussion,
more freedom of expression.

One of the first signs that the *National Catholic Reporter's* manifesto
was catching on was the freeing up of the Letters pages in the diocesan
press. Theologian Karl Rahner had pinpointed the Letters pages as a critical area for free speech in the church. Suppression of nonconformist views
had been as normal in the diocesan press as in Soviet newspapers. Now
signs of change began to appear. Michael Costigan's *Advocate*, already the
opinion maker on the Australian scene, led the way in encouraging robust
debate. From this distance in time the *Advocate's* pages are beginning to
look like a primary historical locus for studying the reception of Vatican II
in Australia. It is good that they are being microfilmed, thus making them
available to scholars outside Melbourne.

Another such locus is the *Annals* magazine, edited by Paul Stenhouse MSC from 1966. It had had a long career as a devotional magazine with missionary interest—the Missionaries of the Sacred Heart were the first Australian order entrusted with a specific missionary territory by the Vatican, eastern Papua, in 1929—and its readers loved the stories of 'Miriam Agatha' and Constance M. Le Plastrier. Now Stenhouse brought Vatican II ideas into play. Using modern design and layouts, he projected council themes towards the schools. Hungry for new catechetical material, schools placed bulk orders for the magazine; and the circulation of *Annals* outstripped that of the national news magazine, the *Bulletin*. Implicit in Stenhouse's approach was discussion about religion; discussion meant differing points of view; and that meant freedom of choice. Already the church was a long way from the catechism class and religion by rote.

Two years after Stenhouse took over at *Annals*, two young Melbourne priests began their own magazine, *Priest Forum*, to reprint overseas material. 'We see this newsletter', they wrote, 'as an extension of the program of the Second Vatican Council to the grass roots level.' Soon they found that local discussion and Australian applications of overseas thinking were crowded onto their pages. They began a series of interviews with priests, men in the parishes who were consciously trying to make Vatican II work. Although the editors were thought of as radical (they opposed the Vietnam war), all points of view got a hearing in their magazine. *Priest Forum* was the only Catholic publication in Australia to give space to all sides of the *Humanae vitae* debate. They didn't bash bishops, as radicals are wont to do; nor did they get caught up in trivialities such as questions of clerical dress or pay scales for the clergy. Unlike their Sydney contemporary, *Report*, a newsletter which filled the censored gaps in the diocesan press, they refused to get excited about how bishops should be selected. One of the outcomes of their magazine was the founding of the National Council of Priests, peak body of the rank and file clergy. *Priest Forum* lasted only a couple of years but that was enough. It was a voice from the church of its own time and, in speaking, it helped to renew that church for the future.

By then, other voices could be heard. To a historian, what is most remarkable is how the new spirit caught up and energised venerable devotional publications like *Madonna* and the *Messenger of the Sacred Heart*. Perhaps the most unexpected signal of change was the fact that the *Messenger* even found space for an article saying something complimentary about

Martin Luther. In the past, despite individual names and faces—Eustace Boylan, Mary Agnes Finn, 'Miriam Agatha', Constance M. Le Plastrier—all these magazines had institutional voices. They served institutional person-alities, who preferred their spiritual and intellectual navigation to be done by others. Their maps were the ones already published and authenticated. Now individual voices began to be heard, telling of what they had discov-ered on journeys without maps. Still recognisably Catholic, they spoke in their own voices of what they themselves had found; not what someone in authority had told them was there.

The best example of this is prayer. Apart from public prayer, known as the liturgy or worship, Christians have prayed privately from earliest times. We know that the favourite private prayers of the earliest Christians were the Sign of the Cross and the Lord's Prayer. These were prayers they used constantly throughout the day. Over the centuries this practice of repeated daily prayer persisted; only the formulas changed with taste and fashion. In 1925 'Miriam Agatha' gave some advice to her young readers in the *Messenger* that seemed timeless: 'As you go to and from school, as you play, as you dress, as you lie in bed waiting for sleep to come, you could offer these short prayers'. This was advice she would repeat many times in her long writing life. In essence it was no different from advice given in the third century by Tertullian or the spiritual regimen adopted in the thir-teenth century by the lay tertiaries of St Francis of Assisi. Another constant feature of 'Miriam Agatha's' advice to young readers was her insistence that they count how many prayers and penances they had performed. She sug-gested that they keep the count up to date in little notebooks. Such count-ing appealed to juvenile imaginations, it added an element of play to their religious lives. It also fitted easily into the prayer style of the contemporary church, which was mathematical. Decades of the rosary, the nine First Fri-days devotion, the 40 days of Lent, indulgences—everything had a number attached to it.

A major part of the shift in Catholic life which historians conven-iently label as Vatican II was in this area of private prayer. More historical work is needed before one can confidently chart what was going on. Observable changes in the public prayer of the church included the Englishing of the mass, the heightened prominence of the Bible and the declericalising of worship. What impact these changes made on the private prayer life of the faithful is still conjectural. What is clear from reading the magazines, however, is that change certainly did extend to private prayer. Repeating the biblical 'teach us to pray', people began to want to go beyond formulaic prayer and launch into meditation or contemplation. Adepts of the inner life now found audiences for their experience. Whereas the magazines had formerly spoken of prayers (in the plural), now they wrote more about prayer (in the singular). In time learners felt confident enough to report on their own experience of prayer; and so the magazines began to be written by their readers. The result is that we now have in these magazines a unique archive of contemporary popular religion.

It was not only on prayer that one heard the personal voice as a hallmark of contemporary Catholicism. No longer institutionalised believers, people made the story their own. This personalising of the Catholic story seems to have freed many of them to risk telling their deepest thoughts. So insistent were these voices of discovery and affirmation that they have silenced the merely polemical, editorial, disputatious or theological which might have been considered for this anthology. That is why all of life—not only prayer—seems to crowd into the limited space of this book. But it is life written from individual Catholic angles of discovery.

I started out unsure of what I should find. My principal repositories were the Mitchell Library in Sydney and the Veech Library at the Catholic Institute of Sydney, now at Strathfield. The treasures stored there were overwhelming; and I blessed the librarians who had had the foresight to preserve such a rich heritage. What one library lacked the other might supply: *AD2000*, *The Grail Newsletter* and *Anawim* at Strathfield, *Harvest*, *Magdalene* and the *Catholic School Paper* at Macquarie Street. I tried to read everything; although I found that the tone and direction of some magazines made them wrong for this collection. For similar reasons there are few selections here from the 'secular', or non-church, press. My first rule was to look for what seemed to me to be good writing. Under this rule much of what I read in devotional magazines proved to be unusable. Nevertheless, I did find there a mountain of material which met the highest literary standards. The Christian Brothers are famous as educators of some of our best Australian writers. One might argue that the traditional Catholic school system, language-based and grammar-conscious, has made a similar distinctive contribution to our literature. The wealth I discovered in periodicals allowed me to ignore splendid writing already available in published books, such as B. A. Santamaria's deathbed scene in his life of Archbishop Mannix or

Patrick O'Farrell's description of Galong cemetery in *The Irish in Australia*. As for fiction, I decided to exclude that too, on the grounds that Australian writers of distinction who favour 'Catholic themes'—Thea Astley, Gerard Windsor, Desmond O'Grady, Thelma Forshaw are some of them—already have collections in print, with, one may hope, more to come. Equally, there are no poems in this collection because two excellent contemporary anthologies of Australian religious verse already exist, Kevin Hart's *Oxford Book of Australian Religious Verse* and Les Murray's *Anthology of Australian Religious Poetry*. What is here, so far as one can determine, now appears in book form for the first time. The publisher has made every effort to contact the writers for permission and to give each his or her due. Future editions will right any wrongs.

I dedicate this anthology to the late Peter Condon. We arrived at the University of Sydney in the same week early in 1951, enrolled in the faculty of Arts. There is a fragmentary memorial to him in the *Oxford Literary Guide to Australia*, which quotes a sentence from my book *Rockchoppers*: 'Peter Condon used to say that the "real" University of Sydney was on the [State] library steps'. The quotation always elicits from me a smile of nostalgia, for it summons up those careless days when we had all the time in the world to talk and talk and talk. We learned to write in those days too, working on the university paper, *Honi Soit*. The next year he became co-editor with Meg Cox. Here his father intervened, insisting that he give up the editorship and enrol in Law. This was a hopeless misdirection because Peter was passionate about journalism. You can read what he thought about the press in the 1954 *Hermes*, the university magazine which we edited together. After a job on a building site in Tasmania, he found his way to the *Canberra Times*. In midnight sessions he had often spoken of a national magazine he would one day attempt. Now, in Canberra, he began to speak of it again. He began to gather collaborators, resigned his job and announced a title: *Home and Nation*. It was not to be. Driving to Canberra from Sydney, he crashed his car. No one else was injured but Peter Condon was dead.

Edmund Campion
Catholic Institute of Sydney
Easter 1996

LACORDAIRE
In the Tinsel World

This sharp piece of writing initiates the modern era of Australian Catholic letters. It remains the best profile available of Cardinal Gilroy, a man whose 'false placarded smile', as the poet James McAuley wrote of him, protected him from close analysis or disinterested assessment. When it appeared, the Cardinal told a friend that the article worried him, not for personal reasons but because it put the church in a bad light. He inquired whether the author was a practising Catholic.

People soon guessed the identity of the writer, who was to have a distinguished career in publishing and the media. The profile's appearance in Nation *in October 1959 alerted Catholics to the magazine's existence. It became one of the publications those interested in the church and unofficial ecclesiastical views began to read regularly. The* Nation *editor's introduction has been omitted here.*

A reporter once asked Cardinal Gilroy what was the most serious crisis facing the Western world. 'Mortal sin', he answered, and the reply is typical of the thinking of the man who has had to weather nearly 20 years of the most intense political activity of the Catholic Church in Australia. Almost immediately after his consecration as Archbishop of Sydney in 1940, he faced the task of meeting the brilliance of one of the best politicians ever to become a bishop, Archbishop Mannix, and of his Movement, the first really strong group of Australian Catholic laymen to organise politically on a nation-wide scale. Though Dr Mannix's militant ideas on the church and politics will be, if they are not already, defeated, the Cardinal will have little positive claim to the victory. The wily old Melbourne prelate will have been defeated by his excesses and by age: his own; and more importantly that of an Australian church no longer made up of poor, home-looking Irishmen ready to accept the strident political aims of churchmen of the type of Cardinal Moran, the first Irish bishop to play Labour politics on a scale comparable to that employed by

Dr Mannix. To the Cardinal will fall an inheritance of middle-class, cohesive, minority-minded Catholics who wince at the public spotlight of Tammany politics but are not above touting its benefits — strictly in private.

It would be wrong to attribute this inheritance as having been entirely gathered by the Cardinal. A long succession of mediocrities in both the clerical and the lay state have failed to give luminous intellectual calibre to the church in pace with its external development. Yet, as Archbishop Mannix himself described the Cardinal in an otherwise biting congratulatory speech on his return from the Rome Consistory in 1946 as the first Australian-born cardinal, he has 'the same (comparing him with the English convert, Cardinal Newman) consuming zeal for the salvation of souls and the extension of God's Kingdom on earth; the same inborn gentleness which is extremely strong; the same natural unlaboured dignity which wins respect without loss of affection; the same gracious urbanity that fits men for any position to which they may be called'.

The Cardinal was born in the Sydney slum of Glebe in 1896. At St Benedict's Church, Broadway, there is a plaque commemorating the fact that in this church Norman Thomas Cardinal Gilroy, Archbishop of Sydney, was baptised, confirmed and made his First Communion and confession. Like many Catholic priests, the Cardinal looks to his mother as the dominant influence in his life. One of ten children of a pious Irishwoman, his mother held the Gilroy family together after the Cardinal's father, a tailor's cutter, had lost his flourishing business through 'too great an appreciation of social life'. In a brief autobiographical sketch—'The Tinsel of the World'—the Cardinal said: 'My mother's was the deepest faith it has ever been my privilege to encounter. It never faltered; it was exercised constantly; it related to everything. Early in life God blessed me with the realisation that her attitude was right. It has ever been my ambition to learn well the lesson she taught, hardly ever by precept but constantly by example'.

Another model was a Marist Brother at Kogarah school, where the boy received brief training after attending convent schools. 'The Marist Brother who was my teacher during my last year at school, in the thirteenth year of my age, was a positive hero in my eyes. He seemed to have all the qualities of an ideal man. After a lecture he gave concerning the religious life, he asked the boys to consider whether they would not like to dedicate their lives to God as members of a teaching order. The idea appealed to me very strongly. Both my father and mother, although not very enthusiastic, were inclined to agree to the plan of my going away to become a Marist Brother.' However, the unexpected opposition of Mrs Gilroy's mother saved the boy for a cardinal's hat.

He left school at 14 to be a PMG messenger. At 18, after he had worked in Bourke and Narrabri as a telegraphist, World War I broke out and he was eager to join up. He arranged special leave from the PMG and joined a transport ship as an assistant wireless operator.

The young Gilroy who shipped out from Melbourne on His Majesty's Army Transport A45 on 2 February 1915 was just over 19. When he returned to Melbourne on 9 October of the same year, he thought of that trip as the most educational and valuable of his 20 years' existence. The nine months, however, signified no spiritual rebirth. He seems to have departed the same conscientious communicating Catholic as he returned. If anything, the trip made him more worldly. Good Friday in that April came upon him suddenly—he forgot the preceding season of Lent. The world about that he observed included whimsical details: his own prostration by sea-sickness; the fact that the ship's vet had mislaid the Epsom salts, with the result that five horses died; the drubbing and dubbing during King Neptune's ceremony at the crossing of the Equator, where he was pleased to find that he got off the lightest of all of the ship's company. He found his first sight of the Indian Ocean pleasing because of its tranquillity; he watched the 'mangrove' trick at Colombo and toured around the Cinnamon Gardens, the European quarter at Colombo, pleased at its wealth. In Egypt, he went to see the pyramids and the Sphinx, carefully noting their height and length and the date when they were built. His observation wasn't too close at times; he was surprised that Good Friday should be observed as a close holiday in Alexandria, apparently ignorant of the fact that Friday is the Muslim sabbath.

If his curiosity was limited, it didn't shrink from the unpleasant. He observed a riot started by New Zealanders and Australians in the native quarters of Cairo that April in which houses in the native quarters were burnt down, and, after the landings at Gallipoli had taken place, he calmly noted talk of the mutual desecration of the dead which the Turks had begun and the Allies reciprocated. Gilroy's transport stayed in the Gallipoli vicinity for under three weeks. His ship doesn't ever seem to have been hit, though shells flew past her. Passing through Alexandria and Gibraltar— Alexandria he did not like and Gibraltar's GPO was only the size of a provincial NSW post office—he reached London. Piccadilly, Trafalgar, Leicester Square—these were the streets he had read about and was now walking through. In London the former Marconi student visited the headquarters of the Marconi organisation assiduously, and the pious Catholic went to Westminster Cathedral. Among the town's entertainments, the 'Empire', then the leading music hall, took his fancy.

Sleeping sometimes aboard ship and sometimes in town, he seldom had to miss his Sunday morning mass. He might even visit a Catholic church on a weekday to talk to the priest and go visit a local Catholic club in his company. In his leisure hours, he read and compiled statistics on the warring countries' revenues, expenditures and merchant navy tonnages. In the second half of July, his ship the 'Hessen', now renamed 'Bulla', was on the way to Australia again and in October he took off the uniform of the merchant navy. If he was pleased with this most educational period of his life, he might also have been slightly relieved that it was behind him. In an odd hour in that spring, he had pencilled a humorous sketch. A merchant sailor was leaping away apace from a black devil with tail and three-pronged fork. The sketch bore the legend: 'I'm after you, NTG.'

Returning to the PMG in 1915, he was sent to Lismore where he kept a wartime resolution of weekly reception of the sacraments and daily mass. Then came the turning point brought about by the unusual action of a priest asking the name of a person in confession:

'The confessional of the administrator of the cathedral in Lismore, who was also the Vicar-General of the diocese, became my goal every Saturday night. As I was a regular visitor there over several months, my voice must have become known to the confessor. One night after imparting absolution, he surprised me with the question, "Is that you Mr Gilroy?" The next question completely amazed me. "Did you ever think of becoming a priest?"

'The ensuing pause must have surprised him. It was not easy for me to answer that question. A quick analysis of my thoughts eventually produced some sort of reply. "Yes, Monsignor, but I deliberately put it out of my mind."

'"Why?"

'"Because of my complete unworthiness and unsuitability."

'"No man could be worthy of the priesthood," the monsignor said, "but still God calls men to that office. The training over many years in the seminary may produce suitability."'

The subsequent years followed the fairly usual pattern of Australians on the way to being bishops. He spent two and a half years at the minor seminary, St Columba's College, Springwood, and, although not an outstanding student, was sent to Urban Propaganda College, Rome. With hard work and some extra coaching by fellow students, he got his doctorate of theology, and in 1924 returned to Australia a priest to work as a secretary in the Apostolic Delegation, Sydney. Seven years later he returned to Lismore as secretary to the Bishop and Chancellor of the Diocese. By 1935 he had proved himself an extremely competent administrator and his consecration as Bishop of the far-flung diocese of Port Augusta in South Australia caused no surprise, especially, as the former Vicar-General of Lismore, Monsignor McGuire, (at the time Bishop of Townsville) whom the Cardinal has referred to as his 'greatest benefactor', was a leader of the movement for Australian-born bishops which was gaining force.

But his appointment as coadjutor of Sydney in 1937 was a different matter. Sydney, of course, is the senior archdiocese, and several thought that somebody more than a good administrator was needed. As Dr Mannix said, 'Perhaps people thought it (Port Augusta) was not a milestone on the way to the Sacred College. But God has his own way of working out his designs'.

Several years before, the scholarly Irish theologian, Dr Sheehan, had been appointed coadjutor with right of succession to Dr Michael Kelly, Archbishop of Sydney. As time had gone by the intellectual Archbishop Sheehan found himself more and more out of gear with the bricks and mortar outlook of Dr Kelly, known affectionately as 'Michael the Builder.' Finally, in 1935, Archbishop Sheehan forwarded his resignation to Rome. For two years he heard nothing, then suddenly Rome notified him that it would accept his resignation. Unfortunately, by this time Archbishop Sheehan, although not himself a well man, felt he could stand the Sydney scene for the few years longer that the old and ailing Dr Kelly was likely to last.

Rome thought differently. The movement for Australian-born bishops had continued to gain force, and was, anyway, in line with Rome's traditional policy of indigenous clergy and bishops for missionary countries where possible. But it had to act quickly to stop Archbishop Mannix and his fellow Irish bishops rallying and forcing into the open the shabby circumstances of Archbishop Sheehan's removal. The three or four weeks necessary to arrange for the consecration of a new bishop would have allowed this to happen, so Rome had to announce the appointment of an existing Australian bishop. Here Bishop Gilroy's long years in the Apostolic Delegation bore fruit. He was well-known to Rome, and, as a proven administrator, he had the apparent qualities needed to consolidate the growth of the Sydney Archdiocese.

As an administrator he follows a decentralised policy. If a parish needs a new school, convent or church, it must raise the money itself as no help will come from St Mary's. There is an apocryphal story of a priest, who was going to start a new parish, asking the Cardinal for financial aid: 'Why yes, Father', reaching into his soutane, 'here's a shilling, I believe that's the fair these days'. Although not too happy about innovations in other fields, the Cardinal has not been frightened of new methods of raising finance: housie; art unions, giant or otherwise; and recently, the radically new methods of American fund-raising organisations. While he is careful with church finances, he is very sparing himself. He doesn't own a car, but is driven everywhere by his secretary and others who are paid taxi mileage. He doesn't drink or smoke and tries to persuade his clergy to follow him in this as he believes it results in greater efficiency. One of his relaxations is an occasional night of cards—Five Hundred is a favourite—with a group of older parish priests.

The Cardinal drives himself hard. Although he does not conform to the picture of a scholarly bishop and is more at ease with a ledger than a book, he sets himself a severe round of communion breakfasts, church-openings and confirmations which archbishops often leave to their coadjutors. Public speaking has been difficult for him and in his early years as archbishop he got the help of an old priest expert in rhetoric to give him lessons. Now, when he grasps a problem, he is able to state it to better effect in words than on paper.

During the Cardinal's pilgrimage to Lourdes last year Pope John, then Cardinal Roncalli, patriarch of Venice, persuaded him to stay an extra day there to attend a meeting of all suffragan bishops called to discuss migration to Australia. A fluent Italian speaker, the Cardinal addressed the meeting, and the Patriarch was so impressed that he gave the Cardinal place of honour in Venice's famed Corpus Christi procession. Six months later when Cardinal Roncalli was Pope and Cardinal Gilroy, in company with the other Church Princes, went up in turn to receive the Kiss of Peace from the new pope, John XXIII leaned over and tapped the Cardinal on the chest, 'Who would have thought this six months ago, eh?' But the most impressive thing about the Cardinal is his holiness. Six hours a day are given to prayer. He would be one of the few cardinals in the world to spend up to five hours every Saturday in the confessional. He played a major role in founding the Priests' Eucharistic League, members of which devote an hour daily to adoration of the Blessed Sacrament. He is tireless in encouraging the reading of scripture, and in August the First Australian Biblical Congress was held under his patronage. The religious attitudes of the Cardinal have not moved too far from the simplistic ideal of his boyhood. A prominent convert receiving instructions from him asked for books. 'Read the penny catechism, it's all in the catechism.' And, when Sydney's main Catholic library appealed for help to hold its premises, he nevertheless allowed a firm mainly interested in selling religious objects to take over. In his holiness there is a personal humility of great appeal.

As a pastor the Cardinal shies off innovations. He is much happier with the fun-loving Catholic Youth Organisation, which limits its activities to church halls, than with an organisation like the Young Christian Workers, which has broader aims than creating the right social chances for Catholic marriages. In his parish visitations, whether it is Kings Cross or Springwood, the Cardinal's first interest is the parish register. He picks out a name at random and asks when a priest has last visited the home. He has no time for the outlook that questions the Middle Age concept of the parish as the unit where people are born, raised, work and recreate.

The Cardinal has high standards for his clerics and the bishops he has appointed to general pastoral duties. Surprisingly enough, in view of his own background and early ambitions, he will not accept a candidate for the priesthood who has, as clerics phrase it, 'an unstable background', or one who has started in a religious order. He keeps fairly rigidly to seniority in his parish appointments and rarely selects younger priests, however promising, to run parishes. The bishops he has raised, like Bishop McCabe, of Wollongong, and Bishop Toohey, of Maitland, naturally enough reflect his own qualities. His accountant's outlook keeps him clear of sentiment, however, in his pastoral judgments. Even his old benefactor, Dr McGuire, whom he made Archbishop of Canberra and Goulburn in 1948, was firmly persuaded to retire five years later, despite his own protests, when the Cardinal decided he could no longer satisfy the demands of a growing diocese. Aware of his intellectual limitations, the Cardinal has always had a penchant for advisers or 'experts' to whom he can delegate authority. There is probably no other bishop who has delegated so much to one of his priests that the priest can be confused with the bishop as *the* spokesman for the diocese, as has happened with Dr Rumble.

With his own priests the Cardinal cultivates an aloofness, partly to avoid favouritism and partly because he has, in his own words, 'a positive abhorrence of social life' (the latter helps explain his equal isolation from the laity). This aloofness, combined with a fallible judgment of men, has made for his most damaging decisions. At another time mistakes like appointing a bishop, who even by Australian standards is poorly educated, to be senior member of an educational board; or a convert-theologian interested largely in scoring off non-Catholics as a spokesman, might only have been held as painful, isolated weaknesses. But the same uncertain judgment caused the Cardinal to be led by the ebullient Santamaria when the Melbourne barrister turned from law to politics; and later to select as his advisers two bishops successively who have proved controversial appointments: first Bishop Lyons and then Bishop Carroll.

In the early Movement period the Cardinal was content to follow Dr Mannix in the hierarchy's political moves. In those days the Movement's line was in key with the Cardinal's vague thinking on the situation. There has long been a strong school amongst church ecclesiologists who maintain that 'when politics lays hands on the altar, we attack politics,' ... that the church can organise politically when her fundamental liberties are being attacked.

Towards the end of the war, therefore, when some observers feared a Communist takeover attempt, the Catholic bishops were prepared to close the stable before the horse bolted. Mr Santamaria, already known to them as head of Australian Catholic Action, came to the hierarchy with a scheme to cripple Communist trade union strength: in every union, workshop, office, district, there should be a Catholic cell to oppose and, eventually, eliminate Communist power. Thus was the Movement born.

The work of the 1940s was within the Cardinal's ken. The Movement was parochial: the half-dozen ordinary Catholics meeting in a suburban presbytery, watched over by a young curate; the opening prayer; the pledge to secrecy—juvenile and ineffective perhaps, but in those days taken seriously—the hand raised, 'I pledge myself accordingly'; fumbling their way through a gospel discussion; vaguely trying to meet the central organisation's increasing demands for snooping, character assassination, electoral

results; patiently being bored by young men from Headquarters who out-
lined the latest crisis to minds already obsessed by recurring crises, economic, political, agricultural, international (after a time they began to ask,
'What crisis is it this week?'); finally the chaplain's summing-up and closing prayer, and then a discreet exit from a side door, in case anyone was
watching—and behind it all a feeling that it must be all right, somehow,
because they were doing it for the bishops.

It was the growing organisation emphasis of the Movement that be-
mused the Cardinal as it did the bewildered laymen. The outstanding result
of the new organisation drive was the invention of the Industrial Groups
(although Jim Ormonde still recalls that it was his motion that set up the
Groups, Movement men for years have been boasting that they planted the
idea in his mind in a Sydney saloon bar session). And the groups changed
the Movement's direction. By 1950 Santamaria was saying 'If, in the next
ten years, we can effectively control the situation, prevent the development
of new communities of a fundamentally anti-religious type and build communities which effectively assist our Christian and human objectives, then
I submit that we are doing in a short time what European Catholic Action,
through no fault of its own, can accomplish in a way different only in a
long time ... In all this the fight against Communism is simply a side issue'.

The Movement had come a long way from the early hit-and-run
days. National headquarters in Swanston Street, Melbourne, housed a massive collection of secret files, collected from all over the country. These had
flowed from the hundreds of parochial groups turning in regular reports
on local meetings of the ALP, Parents and Friends Associations, RSL, etc.
... who was there, what they said, how they voted, attitudes culled from
their conversation and so on. These were invaluable to the Movement newspaper, *News-Weekly*, down the hallway from Santamaria's spacious office,
although another 'front' office was kept elsewhere to fool the naive.

In the face of the widening ramifications of the Movement and with
a touch of concern at the increasing power of Melbourne, the Cardinal
realised Sydney had to exert a more positive role. It was for this purpose
that he appointed the readily available Bishop Lyons, originally a Victorian
who had been transferred to New Zealand as Bishop of Christchurch and
had been obliged to resign his see after trouble with his priests. Bishop
Lyons did his job well, so well that early in 1954 when complaints about
the methods and implications of the Movement's political activity began to

gather force the Cardinal was able to say to two objectors, 'But I never knew this. Why wasn't I told?' On top of it, there was Santamaria's purposely nebulous information to the hierarchy. There is, for instance, the story that a country professional man tells of his visit to Melbourne at this time. Headquarters was in a terrific flap as preparations for the invasion of the ALP were under way. After discussing the new venture with one of the staff there, he was shown the letter which had been drafted to inform the hierarchy of it all. 'But', he exclaimed after reading the letter, 'this doesn't say anything about the ALP.' The reply was quick, 'Well, of course, you have to phrase these things the right way for the bishops'.

By the time Bishop Lyons was removed from control in early 1954, Melbourne had already seen the Rome light mirrored by its Australian Ambassador, Archbishop Carboni, and had nominally given the Movement over entirely to lay control. Succeeding to Bishop Lyons as the Cardinal's Movement liaison was the Sydney canon lawyer, Monsignor Carroll. Bishop Carroll, as might have been expected, proved to be more interested in legalities than in underlying principles. Though aware of the juridical implications of Archbishop Carboni's public thrusts at bishops wanting to retain control of the Movement, Rome had not then definitely spoken and Bishop Carroll decided that his first job was to take the Sydney echelon of the Movement out of Melbourne lay control and restore its direction to the Sydney clergy. Relations between Sydney and Melbourne were smouldering when suddenly Evatt attacked. Santamaria took Melbourne out of the ALP into the political wilderness, or what Dr Mannix called a 'moral victory'.

The Sydney Movement, however, by now fully restored to clerical control, resolved to carry on its existence inside the Labor Party, and one of its objects, whether fully known to the Cardinal or not, was to enjoy the plums of office: Premier, Lord Mayor of Sydney, etc. This was the original split. Driven by different interpretations of political expediency, both sides found themselves taking up the theoretical positions which seemed to favour their political objectives. By 1957 Bishop Carroll had helped the Cardinal make a final gaffe. He persuaded the Cardinal that there were no Catholic principles to stop the hierarchy being directly involved in politics—a stand which even Santamaria had repudiated—and prepared a case for the Cardinal and himself to take to Rome the same year. Rome pointed out that the argument was shot through with doctrinal errors (fallacies which at least one Sydney priest had pointed out when Bishop Carroll showed it to him), and re-affirmed its earlier stand to depoliticise the Movement.

Today, Sydney Archdiocese makes no formal attempt to direct state politics. The city is mercifully free from Mannix-like public directions to Catholic voters at election time. In the last state elections the *Catholic Weekly* abstained from editorial comment and even refused to accept advertisements from any political party. So much has been gained for the forces of sanity against those of sectarianism. Even on this plane, however, the quality of the church as a force in general society and the quality of the mental life of its adherents have been too much sacrificed to an anti-intellectual bias. And there remains a lower plane—the plane of the Catholic Masons—where part of the church's prestige is still thrown into petty struggles to maintain a largely Catholic Labor Government.

How does the Cardinal fit into this? In his June quarterly meeting of his Sydney priests, stung by recent newspaper attacks, he felt that the record could be set straight by merely reading three Rome documents: the first a ruling by Rome to the Australian hierarchy on laymen and the church in politics; a further statement by Rome in reply to the Cardinal's request for clarification of some points of the first statement; and part of a rescript from Rome replying to a request by Archbishop Mannix himself for a clarification of the first ruling. But instead of the Sydney reappraisal of the Movement being shrouded in secrecy and expediency, the Cardinal should have made a clear statement of principle. His failure to speak out is explained in part by his sincere fear of giving further public evidence of a split in the hierarchy and causing more scandal. But a hangover of vague loyalty to the Labor Party for its help to Catholics leaves him looking at politics in the light of how they will affect the sacramental mission of the church rather than as an end in themselves for the general good. So, on the few occasions when he has thought on political matters for himself the results are naive. A former Sydney seminarian tells how the Cardinal gave the students a talk after returning from the Lourdes pilgrimage. 'In Italy there is a lot of trouble from anti-clerical politicians … Portugal … Salazar, a deeply Christian statesman, he goes to mass and communion every morning … Spain … General Franco knows that his country is poor and always will be poor, but he doesn't mind because, as he says, "after all Christ loves the poor".' It would be ridiculous to see in these words a Machiavellian desire to maintain an iniquitous status quo. In fact, they point again to the

Cardinal's weakness and strength: an extremely simple view of temporal affairs combined with 'a consuming zeal for the salvation of souls and the extension of God's Kingdom on earth'.

G. C. DAVY
Guests of Patrick White

*Like other Christian Brothers, George Columba Davy taught the
sons of the poor and lived in poverty himself. After some years in the
schools—his pupils remember him with gratitude to this day—he was
sent to the teacher training college to be master of Christian Brother
scholastics. There he blossomed as a Renaissance man: others built
buildings; he built men. Something of his special quality is captured in
this slow-starting account of an afternoon tea with Patrick White. The
reader cannot fail to notice Brother Davy's easy familiarity with
modern Australian painters and writers. The article also gives glimpses
of the usually hidden kindness of Patrick White. It appeared in the
May 1964 issue of* Our Studies, *the in-house journal of the
Christian Brothers which Brother Davy edited.*

I n January of this year the writer of this article, together with twenty-
four scholastics from Mount St Mary, Strathfield, had the interesting
and unusual experience of being the guests of Australia's leading literary figure, Patrick White. The visit was made possible through the kind
offices of Mrs L. C. Rodd (better known as novelist Kylie Tennant).

A prior phone-call to Mr White to arrange the details of the visit
brought the caution that we might be disappointed by the proposed meeting and that 'readers who build up a picture of a writer through his works
are often disillusioned when they meet him in person'. White was quickly
reassured that we were prepared to take that risk.

Patrick White lives in Castle Hill, a locality which, in its fictional
guise of 'Sarsaparilla', might well become through White's novels, plays and
short stories what Hardy's Wessex is to English fiction or Faulkner's
Yoknapatawpha to American. 'Dogwoods', as the rambling White home-
stead is called, is situated no more than a few hundred yards from our own
St Gabriel's School at Castle Hill. The house is set in a six-acre property of
carefully tended garden and bush. Thick trailing hedges, drooping trees and

wide, cool verandahs give the house an air of quiet detachment— the ideal retreat for the deeply meditative man that Patrick White in fact is.

Although 'Dogwoods' was, at first glance, everything that one might have expected from a reading of the novelist's works, we were certainly not prepared for the overwhelming impression gained as Mr White, always relaxed and gracious, invited us inside. We at once found ourselves surrounded by a magnificent display of modern Australian paintings. In each room all the available wall space had been pressed into service to accommodate the collection. By the time our visit had come to an end we had good reason to think that White's pictures mean almost as much to him as his own writings.

The pictures stimulated much interested and animated conversation before we settled down to talk about literature. Among the works on display I noticed impressive canvases by such well-known Australian painters as Sidney Nolan (White pointed out his three Nolans with obvious pride), De Maistre (a masterly painter, neglected in Australia but acknowledged, White was pleased to note, in England where he has received the commission to paint the Stations of the Cross for Westminster Cathedral), Dickerson (a large and typically glowering canvas), Gleghorn, Coburn, Gleeson (here White made the observation that no less an expert than Sir Herbert Read considers Gleeson the most skilful Surrealist painter in the world today), Fairweather, Perceval and many others.

As we stood admiring the large Fairweather painting in one of the bedrooms, White was asked about his obvious interest in modern art, to the apparent exclusion of other types and periods. He explained this by saying, 'I think we ought to try to understand the art of our own day. Collecting "old masters", apart from the cost of such a hobby, is very like living among antique furniture'. Later he indicated that the painter who gave him most satisfaction was the great French Fauviste, Georges Rouault.

Patrick White obviously enjoys buying pictures and is not above the satisfaction of gambling on his own taste. He takes no expert advice in making a selection and confesses to some modest self-congratulation if a picture, through the vagaries of fashion or for any other reason, proves subsequently to be of unexpected value. He made the interesting comment that, if he finds that a particular painting has 'receded into the wall' he replaces it with another. However, one was left in no doubt that White is a discerning patron of the considerable group of gifted and vital painters at work in Australia today.

Evidence of a recent visit made by White to the monastic settlement of Mount Athos in Greece was seen in his fine collection of Greek ikons, including one of Our Lady painted in 1339. Some of the ikons were contributed to the collection by Manoly Lascaris, a Greek who lives with White at 'Dogwoods'. They are in fact the only inhabitants of the large house. White is unmarried and together with his Greek friend attends to the care and maintenance of the house and property. Incidentally, we had noticed on our first entering the house how clean and orderly all the rooms were in spite of the absence of any female help.

At the rear of the house we came out into a well-kept informal garden where our attention was immediately caught by a large metal sculpture by Clement Meadmore, an exercise in welding representing nothing in particular but creating 'patterns of space'. White admitted that it is not always easy, even for the discriminating lay man, to distinguish in works of this kind between the gimmick and the genuine work of art.

A further mark of White's thoughtful hospitality was the afternoon tea set out on a table under the trees. He and Manoly had spent some time that day preparing the dishes which clearly owed much to Greek culinary practices. For some of us at least it took some faith and courage to respond to White's pressing invitation to partake.

White, who is now 52 years of age, spoke to us of his first attempts at creative writing at the age of five. Before he was 12 years of age he had written three or four plays, arranged in acts and scenes. He regretted that he had not preserved some of these juvenile pieces, although he has no desire to resurrect his early attempts at poetry. In answer to a question, he said that he never re-reads his own novels except when it is necessary to check through foreign language translations of his works.

He reads comparatively little fiction, but when pressed for an opinion of his Australian contemporaries in that field he did not hesitate to name West Australian, Randolph Stow, as the most promising of the younger group. He spoke with considerable enthusiasm of two New Zealand fiction writers — Janet Frame and Maurice Shadbolt.

Manoly explained that White lives a very ordered, almost monastic life. His regular daily horarium includes periods of writing in the middle of the night and the late afternoon. Household chores and sleep are fitted into the intervals between writing sessions. White does not lecture, open art shows or attend conferences. (He even got Kylie Tennant to collect his

£500 Miles Franklin Award.) He has no TV in the house and rarely listens to radio. However, it would be wrong to conclude that he is by instinct a hermit. He explained to us that he finds that writing absorbs his powers so completely that there just isn't time for other things.

Having read somewhere that White has a natural aversion to writing, I was interested to hear his explanation of this curious fact. 'I very much dislike writing', he said. 'Perhaps it is because we tend to hate what we are compelled to do, and I feel this compulsion to write. Even in times of mental dryness I have that continual urge to complete what I have started.' Once the general plan of a work is set and the characters and the plot are moving, writing then becomes for him an exhausting search for the right word. Manoly informed us that at times White will spend weeks wrestling with a single phrase. The finished product of all this relentless searching was once described by Professor A. D. Hope as 'illiterate verbal sludge'. When one of our party, with questionable tact, quoted Hope's words, our host was quite unruffled and dismissed the reference with a faintly tolerant smile.

When the sources of imagination and invention show signs of drying up, White has recourse to music, which has a liberating effect on the mind. 'It loosens something in me', he explained, and he made reference to Flaubert who found the same freedom in music. (It was Flaubert who once wrote to a friend, 'You don't know what it is to stay a whole day with your head in your hands trying to squeeze your unfortunate brain so as to find a word'.)

At present White is writing the libretto for an Australian opera. The music is being written by the young Australian composer, Peter Sculthorpe ('The only Australian composer who excites me', said White). To those familiar with the baroque elements in White's prose style, his remark that 'Opera gives me an opportunity to be flamboyant' will come as no surprise. White also has in hand at present a collection of his short stories which is due to be published shortly. A further play, *Night on Bald Mountain*, was in preparation at the time of our interview. (It has since had its premiere during, but not as part of, the Adelaide Festival—a circumstance that drew some wry comments from the dramatist.) White explained that this diversity of interests made it possible for him to say more easily in one medium whatever he might find difficult to say in another. In this way he was sure of 'getting it out of my system'.

White went into some detail to explain his manner of writing a novel. 'I see the characters first', he said, 'and then construct the plot around them. I can never think up plots. A character may live in my mind for years and then that character gets together with other characters and the plot begins to grow round them. At the commencement of the novel I already see how the characters are going to develop, although they certainly do change in your hands as you proceed. All this is worked out in my own mind; I don't discuss my work with anyone.'

Thinking that White might have some Catholic associations, I remarked on the accuracy of his references to Catholic life and practice. He said he had never had any associations with Catholics but had observed them closely, as he observed all people closely. Some readers had assumed that White was in fact a Catholic. Others were equally sure he was a Jew. He recalled with some amusement having received a letter from a rabbi who, after reading the remarkable character study of Himmelfarb in the novel, *Riders in the Chariot*, asked bluntly 'Are you one of us?' White explained that he was brought up in the Anglican faith but that now he owes allegiance to no 'organisation'.

A rich and varied symbolism is a feature of White's writing. In answer to a further question whether he consciously strives for a symbolism based on nature, he replied tentatively, 'Yes and no. The symbolism comes naturally, although you are conscious of it. I think in colours'. It was clear from further remarks that he had been strongly influenced by the French symbolists with their correspondences of sounds, colours and forms.

After reading *Voss* and *Riders in the Chariot* I was sure that White must have made a close study of the habits and the psychology of the Australian Aborigine. His reply to a question on this point was therefore all the more surprising. 'No, I have never made any systematic study of the Aborigines. I've never met one.'

White's novels share many of the features of the modern psychological novel. He explains that he frequently uses various modifications of the 'stream of consciousness' technique in order to penetrate more deeply the motivation of his characters. The understanding of human motives is for him the essential inner reality that the novelist must seek.

Voss has been the most successful of his novels. It was the choice of two Book Societies, but, as White was quick to point out, that fact says nothing about the true value of the novel. *The Tree of Man* had had great success in England and America. When asked for his own opinion of the best of his works he replied without hesitation, 'The Aunt's Story'. Of his work in general he added, 'When a writer has completed a work, he likes to think it is good. However, after some time he realises how inadequately he has conveyed his thoughts and prefers not to have written such books. I consider some of my early novels in this category'.

Voss has also been, in some respects, the most controversial of White's novels. Having in mind that some mistaken ideas are current regarding the germinal idea of this novel (some seeing in it only a fictionalised account of the last expedition of the explorer, Leichhardt), I asked him to explain how the novel took shape in his mind. He said that he had planned it during the War when he was serving in the Western Desert and had time to think of Hitler's megalomania. Also during the London blitz he spent many nights in the midst of the raids reading the journals of the Australian explorer, Eyre. From these two sources came the idea of creating a character who would combine something of the two characters, Hitler and Eyre. An explorer who was also a megalomaniac, in other words. It was only some time later that a study of the explorer, Leichhardt, showed that the latter did in fact have some of the qualities of White's fictional hero.

Patrick White has become one of the most important figures in the sudden revival of Australian drama that came with the appearance in 1955 of Lawler's Summer of the Seventeenth Doll. Controversy has surrounded the launching in recent years of all three of White's plays, The Ham Funeral, The Season at Sarsaparilla and A Cheery Soul. When the last-named had its first production in Melbourne last year, there was a clamour to 'Close the theatre!' Asked to comment on the fact that his plays always seem to provoke audiences and critics, White made the acute observation that the dramatic portrayal of middle-class life is never well received by Australians. 'We have an interest in low life', he said, 'and in some forms of high life but we resent the portrayal on the stage of situations and characters that come too close to ourselves.' He agreed that this was largely the reason for the comparative failure of Lawler's The Picadilly Bushman which White considered better than The Doll. Theatre audiences will, it seems, accept Collingwood, but hands off Vaucluse!

White is sharply aware of the difficulties involved in writing successful drama. The major problem, in his view, lies not so much in the characters or in the dialogue as in the action. 'Getting the thing you want to take place on the stage just as you yourself see it—that's the problem. Of course', he went on, 'the Greeks had a way of getting over this, by having much of the critical action take place off-stage. It would be interesting to try to devise an Australian "Greek" play.'

By this time we were afraid we might be tiring our host, and, of course, there was the possibility that this invasion of 'Dogwoods' by such a platoon of The Cloth could already be taking shape in a fertile mind as one of the more bizarre scenes in a future story. It was time to leave.

Standing on the roadside overlooking one of the pleasantly domesticated slopes of 'Sarsaparilla', Mr White bade us a gracious farewell, with a word of encouragement and good will for the scholastics, who were about to commence their work in the schools.

KEN COOK

God may not be dead but he could quite easily be bored stiff

The swingeing wit of this polemic by the late Ken Cook makes it attractive. Its appearance in The Family Apostolate Bulletin *in Advent 1967 was a signal (if anyone was listening) that not everybody thought all change was for the better. Organ of a middle class lay movement in Sydney, the bulletin expressed the hopes and expectations of the Vatican II generation in transition. By 1967 the little red* Living Parish Hymn Book *was to be found in most schools and parishes. Published in 1960, it looked forward to a church where people participated in the liturgy by singing. Its artistic and theological standards were high—but apparently not high enough for Ken Cook. Novelist and script writer, he may have filled bored moments during bad sermons by researching this article.*

Let the loud and harmonious song of our people rise to heaven like the roar of the ocean waves, and let them give proof by their melodious voices that they are indeed of one heart and soul, as befits those who are brethren and children of the same Father (*Mediator dei,* n. 206).

The song of the few people who ever actually do sing in church rises to heaven like the sound of water trickling down a rusty drain rather than the roar of ocean waves, so is one entitled to wonder what that proves?

'Yawning noises' probably best describes what passes for singing in most Catholic churches in Australia, funny little sleepy sounds that people seem to hope, in fact believe, are pleasing to Almighty God. They must believe they are pleasing to Almighty God, because nobody could imagine for a moment they could be pleasing to human ears.

Which raises an interesting point: why do Catholics believe so ardently that God has some partiality for things which any ordinary human being would run a mile from? Why did Catholics create those masses of paintings and statues and set them up prominently in so many churches? Any reasonable archaeologist of the future might guess that they were there to scare away devils; but they weren't. They were there to please God, among other things. To a certain extent this phase seems to be passing in that, in the more avant garde parishes, we have on the whole done away with the portrait of the wan and effeminate Christ gesturing vaguely at an extraordinary organ of beetroot colour suspended at his breast in defiance of all possible biology.

But a new offence to God is creeping into the churches by way of the hymns which we allege we sing these days. In fact, of course, they are just the old hymns being revived and sung in the mass. But what we have not realised is that many of these hymns are the artistic equivalent of the statues we are so diffidently, and slowly, weeding out.

We seem to be assuming that so long as the hymns contain enough impossibly pious matter the atrocious rhymes will be pleasing to God. In much the same way, of course, we developed the Pellegrini art form on the assumption that so long as we were portraying God, or a saint, it didn't matter if we made them look like something rather unpleasant that had been left too long in the water anyway.

Now perhaps God for his own mysterious reasons does like to hear the English language massacred and does enjoy looking at travesties of himself in painting or sculpture. This could be so, but there is absolutely no proof of it and consequently no moral reason why Catholics should not adorn their churches with splendid works of art or, more to the point at the moment, sing hymns with good lyrics expressing realistic possibilities. Surely one can assume at least that God wouldn't mind?

In fact, one could possibly argue that by singing the sort of hymns we sometimes do, we are crediting God with such a total lack of humour, apart from aesthetic sensibility, that a rigid moralist could well accuse us of at least venial sin.

Let us, as a sort of spiritual exercise, assume for a moment that God has at least the normal reaction to the absurd, the dull, and the inept as the average, moderately well-educated man. What then would be his reactions to the rhymes and images offered by the *Living Parish Hymn Book*.

Possibly something like this:

To Hymn
Number 1: In which the translator Catherine Winkworth has the temerity to rhyme heaven with given.

Reaction: As well for C. Winkworth that there are many mansions in hiven.

To Hymn
Number 7: by J. H. Newman.
Firmly I believe, and truly,
God is three and God is one,
And I next acknowledge duly
Manhood taken by the Son.

Reaction: Thou has not many sins committed
Because at heart thou art a trueman
I therefore overlook your verses
But you're damn lucky, J. H. Newman.

To Hymn
Number 20: **Martyrs**
No force could make his (her) mind relent
No racks, his (her) resolution bent;
Fearless of death he (she) sheds his (her) blood,
And wades to heaven through the flood.

Reaction: Let him (her) wipe his (her) feet.

Hymn 22: **Virgins**
They, whereso'er their footsteps bend,
With hymns and praises still attend;
In blessed troops they follow thee,
With dance, and song, and melody.

Reaction: HELP!!!

Hymn 23: **Holy Matrons**
A valiant woman we proclaim,
Whose *constancy her sex belied*

Clear as the sun her virtue's fame,
And as the earth itself is wide.

Reaction: We firmly reject all imputations of anti-feminist bias.

Hymn 24:   Sword that can pierce the inmost soul,
Stripping whatever thoughts are there,
Cut to the marrow of our minds,
Enter our hearts and lay them bare.

Reaction: Pass us our scalpel.

Hymn 69:   Who, wounded with a direful spear,
Did purposely, to wash us clear
From stain of sin, pour out a flood
Of precious water mixed with blood.

Reaction: Theology, like verse, distorted,
We fear we have been misreported.

And so it goes on. Of course, many of the hymns were written a very long time ago and no doubt much of the ludicrous element is due to different understanding of expressions. But it is still ludicrous, isn't it?

One wonders whether we haven't developed the idea that anything is good enough for God without wondering, even for just a moment, whether the actual form of expression, or at least the common humanity of concept, shouldn't at least be no worse than what we enjoy and understand ourselves.

And pursuing the idea just a little further: does God really like incense, and would his reaction to the spectacle of five hundred small children being confirmed rapidly, one after the other, be greatly different, except in degree, from that of the average parent?

PETER RUSHTON

A convert looks at the post-conciliar church

Peter Rushton was an Anglican priest who became a Catholic in 1956. Since he was married, there seemed little hope that he could resume his priestly ministry in his new church. In 1969, however, Archbishop Guilford Young of Hobart ordained him to the Catholic priesthood. There was a slight sensation in ecclesiastical circles and some newspaper interest. The Newman Society at the University of New South Wales invited Father Rushton to address them, and printed his text in their journal, Discussion. *From there it was reprinted in the November–December 1969 issue of* Compass.

For some time after I was received into the Catholic Church in Bristol, in 1956, Protestant friends frequently asked, 'Are you happy? Are you still as sure?' Sometimes one could almost detect a fleeting glimpse of disappointment when one answered, quite categorically, 'Yes!' It was not charity that restrained me from adding Cardinal Newman's reply to a Protestant who couldn't believe he had made a sincere and convinced decision: 'Would I leave a land flowing with milk and honey to return to the desert?' … I hadn't discovered the quotation at the time.

Today, I am still being asked the same question. But there is a difference now. It is usually asked by Catholics! The form of the question varies, but the gist of it is this: 'You must find things rather strange now …' This is the opening gambit. I try to raise one eyebrow, in what I hope is a quizzical look, to encourage my inquisitor; meanwhile I think to myself, 'Not half as strange as I bet you're finding it, brother. After years in the Anglican ministry you can expect anything. Churches where the incense is so thick you can hardly breathe and the decorations are not infrequently reminiscent of Italian art of the rather cheap and nasty kind. In other ones you cannot be sure whether you are in an Anglican church or a Baptist tabernacle. There are bishops who expect their clergy to kneel and kiss their rings; there are others whose British blood would boil at such a foreign outrage of English sensibility; there is at least one who claims not to believe in God! ...' By this time, my Catholic friend is usually ready with the next opening move. 'When you came into the church everything was so, well, so *certain*.' This is not infrequently accompanied by a look of nostalgia. It is important now to say nothing ... perhaps pout one's lips a little or non-committedly raise one's shoulders. One generally hasn't long to wait. The next bit goes something like this: 'Of course, I was born into it and brought up in it and just accepted it. But you made a deliberate choice and opted for something that just doesn't exist any more ...' What does my friend mean when he says that there has been so much change that the church which existed say in the mid-1950s is essentially different to the church that exists today?

This is the point I would like to develop, if for no other reason than to be in the fashion. So much has been said, and is being said, about changes, crises of faith, crises of authority, authoritarianism versus liberalism, conservative versus progressive, democracy in the church, etc., etc., etc., that we too ought to be in the fashion. No one could for one instant doubt that this is the fashion, even if ones' reading were limited to the daily press and the popular periodicals. The church is featured regularly in *The Bulletin*, *Reader's Digest* and American *Time*. A fairly recent issue of *Time*, with its jubilant message of instant dissolution of the church, pictured the pope on the front cover, and, as a background, the breaking of the Keys and the collapse of the whole edifice. Perhaps the author thought he was being original, but forecasts that the end of the Roman Church is at hand have been made with monotonous regularity since Peter was pope. Judging from what one reads in the evening papers and sees on television one might reasonably expect that before long the *Mirror*, ever sensitive to the newsworthy, will feature a shocking and dramatic series of sensational disclosures such as 'Nun in Happy Convent' or 'Parish Priest Remains Quietly at His Job for the Whole of His Ministry'.

First of all, let us dispose of the obvious. There has been change, much of it radical, and there will undoubtedly be more changes in the future. It is amusing to recall that there were not a few who thought that the inclusion of Saint Joseph's name in the Canon of the Mass would be about all the change wrought by Vatican II. Some of the most obvious changes have been made in the liturgical area, but there have been more significant changes in less obvious areas. Here I would draw particular attention to a change in attitudes. But many of these new attitudes can be accounted for by relating them to a more fundamental change, a change in emphasis, or rather a whole series of emphases in a number of important areas. I would like to return to these emphases later, as I think they are of vital importance, if we are to understand the Catholic Church after Vatican II.

But before doing so, I would like to draw your attention to the very fact of change. Whenever change occurs, or threatens to occur, there is invariably conflict between those who want no change, or as little as possible, and those who want radical change. This conflict between the naturally conservative and the naturally radical occurs in all areas of life. But the total intensity of conflict, in terms of both quantity and quality, depends on those areas of life that are touched upon. The more the *whole man* is involved the more intense or potentially intense the conflict. Most of us are less likely to devote time and energy to an issue involving new breakfast foods than to one concerning new methods of transport. But we would tend, most of us, to spend less time and effort becoming involved in the pros and cons of transport changes than in suggested new methods of education. It should not need to be spelt out that when religion is the area where change is concerned then the whole man is involved. Hence the total intensity of conflict can indeed be immense. Because the emotions are as involved as the intellect, there is the danger that more heat than light will be generated.

The same two extreme groups are as evident in the religious sphere as in any other: those who want as little change as possible and those whose aim seems to be to go further than anyone else has dared. It is members of this latter group who have news value. They are given an importance by the press, radio and television that seems to give them an influence and importance far out of proportion to what either their numbers or the maturity and consistency of their beliefs would warrant.

Who is going to receive the headlines, the nun who believes her order should be renewed in order to enable her, as a religious, to become a sister-in-Christ to all, or the nun who advocates that, in order to experience the full gamut of human emotions, and so identify more realistically with those with whom she works, she should have boy friends and that dating should be encouraged among our young nuns? This is *not* a hypothetical case.

We hear on all sides, not least of all in the newspaper editorials, that it is high time the Catholic Church became more *democratic*; and so it is argued backwards and forwards with neither side taking the trouble to define what they mean by 'democracy within the church'. If it is meant that bishops, pastors and religious superiors should sincerely seek advice—and take it—and discuss issues with those concerned, then this is certainly in tune with the teachings of Vatican II. Autocratic rule, 'Don't ask for reasons; your duty is to obey!' is out. But not only by virtue of the Council; it was condemned a long while ago. 'You know that among the pagans the rulers lord it over them, and the great men make their authority felt. This is not to happen among you. No; anyone who wants to be great among you must be your servant …' (Matthew 20:25-27). But another view of democracy—perfectly valid in the civil sphere—is that authority proceeds upwards from the governed to the government: a decision is valid when a majority votes for it. Whether they realised it or not this is the position adopted by those who criticised *Humanae vitae* on the grounds that Pope Paul rejected the majority decision of the commission he had established. Such a view of the Catholic Church cannot be supported by either scripture or tradition: it is overwhelmingly clear that Our Lord gave his authority to the apostles in general and to Saint Peter in particular. He did not give it to the Christian community who delegated it upwards to the bishops, who, if they proved unsatisfactory, could be removed at the next election.

One could continue almost indefinitely in quoting cases like this, cases which of their nature attract the attention of the mass media. Can we, perhaps, now try to view in perspective, in a historical context and without emotion, the changes that have taken place, are taking place, and which are likely to take place in the future? These, of course, could not possibly be enumerated here, but can we perhaps see the principles involved and some of the major underlying forces?

Both the ultra-conservatives and the radicals have an attribute in common; both share a profound ignorance of a sense of history. The former are petrified in their fear of change of any sort; the latter behave as though this is the first period of change the church has known. The church is a dynamic body, a living organism; if this implies anything it must imply change.

Of course, it must always have been so. But the changes over the past few years have been so far-reaching that we are inclined to regard the contemporary situation as unique. The well-known ecclesiastical historian, Philip Hughes, has given the title *The Church in Crisis* to his latest book. We could be forgiven if we assumed that this applied to the present situation.

The book is, however, an introductory history of the first 20 Great Councils of the church. The church moves from crisis to crisis, and no two ever seem to be the same. The church's inherent ability to reform herself is to me one of the greatest proofs of her divinity ... (that and some of the shocking, scandalous lives of men who have held high office). An interesting contrast with Protestant churches! It was a study of this function of the church that helped bring John Henry Newman into her fold.

The record of his heart-searching studies was published as An *Essay on the Development of Christian Doctrine* in 1845. Many have claimed that Newman was a man before his time (born in 1801, he died in 1890 at the age of 89) for so much that he believed and taught was verified by the Fathers at Vatican II. Central to his belief was the conviction that the faith once committed to the apostles needs to be interpreted anew to different generations. This does not mean that there is any denial of a belief once affirmed or affirmation of a belief earlier denied. This need to reinterpret the faith throughout the ages, to re-present the challenge of Christ to different cultures, brings us to the point I mentioned earlier, changes in *emphasis*. This can be examined in theory, but is more readily understood if one takes an example and sees it within its own historical context. It is interesting to take the view of the Catholic Church propounded very clearly at the Council of Trent, which met in the middle of the 16th century, and compare it with the concept of the church propounded with equal clarity by the Second Vatican Council. If we examine either of these concepts outside its own historical context it will appear to contradict the other.

The Council of Trent was called to counter and to contradict the excesses of the Protestant Reformers. Although each of the reformers fastened on to particular aspects of the church's teaching and practice, they shared a good deal of common antipathy. It is not the differences among the reformers that concern us here, but their common ground. Here we could include the view that the church was an *invisible* body of believers united by faith in Christ as saviour; that the pope was at best the successor to the Roman Emperor and at worst the anti-Christ; that the scriptures provided the only guide to salvation ... It is worth noting here that the reformers were sure that each believer, guided by the Holy Spirit, would arrive at the same conclusions drawn from holy scripture. Although the reformers differed in their attitudes to the eucharist, their followers in practice tended to see it merely as a memorial meal, hence there was no need for a sacrificing priesthood; the old scriptural notion of the priesthood of all believers was narrowed to a belief in the priesthood of every believer. It is understandable that the Council of Trent, in reaction to the reformers, stressed and emphasised particular aspects of the nature of the church. Against the Protestant thesis that the church was an invisible body of believers, Trent stressed the visible church; against Protestant concepts of the papacy and the episcopate, the church replied with an emphasis on the *hierarchical* structure of the visible church and also the *jurisdiction* granted to it by Christ; against heretical views of the eucharist which denied the element of sacrifice, the council emphasised the sacrificial nature of the mass and hence a sacrificing priesthood; in answer to the reformers' assertion that the Holy Spirit made clear the meaning of sacred scripture to the individual believer, the church asserted her right to interpret scripture in the light of tradition.

Of course, at earlier councils the church had condemned earlier teachings, but apart from their historical interest they do not concern us here. But Trent does, because it moulded the ethos in which all of us grew up. We should mention here the ecumenical council Vatican I, which met in 1869–70, between Trent and Vatican II. However, its main concern was to debate and prepare the way for the definition of papal infallibility; it was to have discussed the relationship between pope and bishop, but the meetings were broken up by soldiers. In a sense papal infallibility has existed in a vacuum until Vatican II when the council, after its discussions on the collegiality of the bishops, issued its *Decree on the Bishops' Pastoral Office in the Church* and the relationship between pope and bishop has been made clearer.

But to return to the period after the Council of Trent. Stress and emphasis has been placed on the juridical and hierarchical nature of the church … but this has led to under-emphasis of other equally important truths. For instance, that broad basis of the hierarchical pyramid, the layman, was hardly mentioned. He was defined in negative terms in Canon Law as someone who was neither a cleric nor a religious. Small wonder that the term 'entering the church' was frequently taken to mean, not baptism, but the reception of holy orders or religious profession.

Pope John was aware that conditions had changed, that many old religious animosities had died down, and particularly that the contemporary scene could not be presented in terms of Catholic versus Protestant. He could see that what the times required was the witness of all Christians and men of good will in a world which had become largely pagan, where Christian values had become irrelevant. So he called an ecumenical council. It is of supreme importance to realise that Vatican II denied nothing contained in Trent or any other council, but it *did* change certain emphases. For instance, to continue with our earlier example, the church is still a hierarchically-structured juridical body, but there is now an emphasis which would have been dangerous to press in the 16th century, because it would certainly have been misunderstood in the climate of those days.

The church is portrayed as the 'pilgrim people of God', with pope, bishops, clergy and laity all members, all striving for the same goal. There is a new emphasis on community of love and the worth of the individual, values which need stressing in a sophisticated technological society whose concomitants include dehumanisation and depersonalisation. Arising from these newly stressed areas is a new emphasis on the community meal aspect of the eucharist, but not for one moment denying the sacrificial nature of the mass. And so we could mention example after example of the church preserving the faith yet adapting it to new conditions and a new age.

To some of us, these adaptations are distasteful; to others, there is not sufficient change or it is too slow. To some, Pope John's 'winds of change' have reached some areas as the gentlest hint of a breeze. To others, they have assumed almost hurricane proportions. I am sure that every single one of us has some pet dislike in the new liturgy, but this is a test of our charity. (Personally, I intensely dislike the growing custom of standing for holy communion and I think some of the English translations are dreadful.) Some miss the old Latin mass; others are delighted with the vernacular and the almost universal practice of the presiding priest facing the people. Some are upset with the decline of sodalities and particular forms of individual piety; others regard these as outdated and as having encouraged a self-centred holiness. Of course there are issues of much greater moment than sodalities and folk-masses ... challenges to the church's *magisterium*, questioning of discipline, ecumenical implications, and so on. I am not attempting to minimise these, the pope himself is gravely concerned by them; but what I am trying to do is to get them into proportion. To me they are part of the inevitable ferment that always follows a council. This is not to underestimate their importance or to deny that they contain the seed of personal tragedy. After Vatican I, Archbishop Scherr of Munich had to excommunicate his close personal friend Dr Döllinger, who refused to accept papal infallibility. Please God that the present tensions may be resolved without resort to such drastic measures. I believe they can be resolved given time and a sense of history.

Some claim that an ability to adapt is primarily a matter of age; I disagree. I believe it is fundamentally a matter of temperament. I know an 86-year-old priest who has been praying for years that the present changes would come—in 1913 he was reproved by his bishop for suggesting that baptisms and burials should be in English. I know another priest, who is not yet 30, who believes Pope John and his council were disasters; when he uses the word 'council' he means Trent. As an ex-Anglican I suppose I tend to be attracted to the middle road; I am sorry for those who resist change and who confuse substance with accidents, who believe that the particular emphases they are accustomed to comprise the only presentation of faith.

But we have a lesson to learn from them; the advances of one generation have easily become the obstinately-held conservative positions of its successors. It is arrogant to believe that we hold the ultimate; and it's a salutary thought that our grandchildren will almost certainly smile at our splendid insights and regard them as 'old hat' or whatever the expression will be then. If I have little sympathy for the rigid conservative, I have less for those who want change for the sake of change; I have even less for those who claim to be anti-authoritarian, but who are in fact anti-authority. They are opposed in practice to any authority but their own and their spirit at best is Protestant; at worst it is anarchist.

I believe there is no essential difference between the church before and after the council. I believe that Vatican II is the means used by the Holy Spirit to speak to the church and the world today. Some may have seen 'The Council Man' on ABC television. This was an interview with Archbishop Young of Hobart. During the interview, when asked was he a 'conservative' or a 'progressive', he cast the tags aside with a characteristic wave of his hand and replied simply: 'Before the council I tried to feel and think with the church. Since the council I try to feel and think with the church'. How simple, and yet how true!

'With all these changes and all this turmoil don't you sometimes regret becoming a Catholic?' What a *silly* question!

ALAN K. JORDAN

The Moratorium March 8 May 1970

Although Alan K Jordan is not a Catholic, his article appeared in Nonviolent Power *(in August 1970), and is typical of the style of writing fostered there. Founded by Roger Pryke, the magazine became an organ for those Catholics troubled by Australia's investment in the Vietnam War. They belonged to such movements as Pax and Catholics for Peace. Apart from opposition to the Vietnam War, they were bonded by a quest for peaceful, i.e. non-violent, ways of behaviour. They searched the scriptures and Catholic tradition for guidelines to the future. They were in touch with similar movements elsewhere in the world and brought to Australia Dorothy Day, pacifist founder of the US Catholic Worker movement. In its openness to experience and simple clear prose, Jordan's article, like others in* Nonviolent Power, *is strongly reminiscent of Day's own writing in the (US)* Catholic Worker.

I had not intended to take part in the demonstration, but decided on the day that I would be in it. I have not felt much enthusiasm for the cause of 'peace', and have been saddened more than angered by the Vietnam war and Australia's involvement. Indeed, the whole drop-out, protest, confrontation, power-to-the-people, peace and friendship syndrome strikes me as dangerously simplistic, although valuable to the young as a means of self-identification and a place to stand. And I guess that I was a bit afraid of making myself ridiculous, as an oldie trying to get into the kids' thing.

The form of it put me off, too. It seemed to be another case of Australians aping Americans, a national habit that got us into Vietnam in the first place. Being pedantic, I was put off by the silly name, 'Moratorium'.

I was finally persuaded by the arguments of the opponents of the demonstration, not the organisers. The parliamentary Liberal Party and the conservative press not only misrepresented the campaign, but incited violence from the Right. If the choice was between genuine if muddled idealists, and frightened little people using contemptible tricks to defend a discredited status quo, then I would stand with the 'political bikies, pack-raping democracy'.

So at half-past-two I walked up Bourke Street towards the Treasury Gardens, past dozens of policemen standing quietly in little groups, wearing their summer helmets in case I hit them on the head, the mounted men with long batons slung from their saddles, to hit me on my head, the cars and brawler wagons. Traffic had already been diverted, the trams had stopped running, and the roadway was deserted. Hundreds of people, mostly very young, were hurrying in the same direction, towards the starting point. An expectation that something important was about to happen seemed to hang over the whole scene.

From the steps of the Treasury, on the fringe of the great crowd, I could hear no more than fragments of the speeches, enough to gather that I wasn't missing much. Rhetoric always sounds inflated and hollow, whether of Left or Right. Then they began to move off, along Spring Street and down into Bourke Street.

Untidy and rather disorganised, in the traditional manner of coalitions of the Left. Carrying NLF flags, red flags, black flags, the red-and-black flag symbolising the alliance of anarchism and socialism that first flew, I think, in Spain about the time of the Civil War. Banners identifying various groups. Monash University Labor Club, Theological Students for Peace, the Methodist Youth Fellowship, of all things. Slogans— 'If you were being raped would you demand negotiations or instant withdrawal?'—pictures of American atrocities, caricatures of Nixon, portraits of Mao.

But no Australian flags. I wondered why. I was here as an Australian, come to think of it, feeling that his pride in his country was at stake, standing up to be counted because he didn't need lessons in patriotism from Billie Snedden.

They asked Cairns that question on television afterwards. He said, yes, he regretted the absence of Australian flags, and suggested that the reason was that people felt, wrongly, that the Australian flag had become the private property of the Gorton government and the RSL. Which doubtless is true as far as it goes. Beyond that, I suppose, avoidance of superficial manifestations of patriotism, or of any emotion, is an Australian characteristic. We could carry our revolutionary flags for the very reason that we weren't entirely serious about them.

The marchers had been moving off for half an hour in a dense, continuous column, filling half of the broad Spring Street roadway, when I and a couple of people met in the crowd dropped in towards the end. From the top of the hill, Bourke Street was packed solid all the way along with slowly moving demonstrators. Very few people watching from the footpath, but the street packed. I tried to estimate the number, and could say only that there were tens of thousands. Eventually the figure of 70,000 was agreed on, more or less, but nobody knows. Many young and hairy, others young and shorn, and many not so young.

It was great fun, ambling down Bourke Street into Swanston Street behind the revolutionary flags, sitting down on the tram lines, going past the shops that had shut their doors this Friday afternoon, for fear of looting or who knows what, as though we really were in the process of taking over the city in the name of its people. And it was extremely impressive. In its way, deeply moving. Surely the largest political demonstration since the terrible depression of the nineties and the birth of the ALP, and possibly since the eight-hour movement a generation before that. Very Australian, perhaps, in its quietness and basic decency, as well as in the occasional lapses of taste. The police minded their own business, the demonstrators minded theirs.

Maybe we weren't just aping the Americans. Maybe we do have a style of our own. I remembered the tone of affectionate respect in which American reporters described student demonstrators in Canberra during one of LBJ's visits, 'drinking beer, singing protest songs and exchanging good-humored banter with the cops', while LBJ sheltered behind the bullet-proof windows of his limousine and the guns of his bodyguards.

Very Australian it was in its lack of passion. Somebody began a chant. It was taken up sporadically; most remained silent. Somebody began to sing, 'We Shall Overcome'. It quickly faded away. It seemed to me that the thing had only an accidental relationship with Vietnam and peace. It had no distinct ideological content. The expressed issues served for the moment as something to which we could attach feelings, rather than ideas, that we had in common. That much of the ugliness and brutality of this world can be banished if we so choose, that we and our children and our fellow men were somehow destined for something better than the particular reality that surrounds us. A feeling, too, of 'Blow them, who do they think they are?'

If so, then it was fitting that we should be walking down Bourke Street under the flag of that most likeable of revolutionary traditions, anarchism, which crystallises a vision of liberty and justice that we can never attain to as long as we are no more than human, but can never forget as long as we are no less.

We got opposite the Town Hall and stopped, while the orators orated some more from the city square and the young radicals climbed lamp-posts and hoisted NLF flags. Somebody fainted in the crowd, and they picked him up and carried him out. There were a couple of policemen standing on the footpath with their arms folded, ostentatiously non-involved. Looking around for a suitable resting place for the casualty, the people laid him at the policemen's feet. They looked down at him dispassionately but didn't move, whether for fear of exceeding their instructions or of being caught by a camera, bending over an unconscious body.

People began to drift away and I went off to the pub for a beer with a couple of friends.

The fashionable causes of the day will pass, important though they may be in themselves, and other fashions will take their place The great complexities will continue to be oversimplified. The young, the lazy, the tired, those lacking in imagination and compassion, will continue to reduce tragic dilemmas to issues of goodies against baddies, darkness against light. But maybe, three steps forward and two steps back, taking many a wrong turning on the way, we are approximating slowly to something better than we have known

Our people, down to and including the most ordinary of ordinary citizens, are having more and more invested in them by their society, and they are repaying that investment by taking their humanity more seriously, and exercising a more critical choice in how they spend themselves. Time is running out on the dealers in demagoguery and mystification, the self-appointed elites, the manufacturers of garbage. Personal freedom will increase. I hope that justice will increase with it.

I don't expect much to result directly from our big demonstration. I am sure, though, that we shall see more of that quiet defiance and assertion of personal dignity, those signs of inarticulate aspiration. Things will never be exactly the same. I am glad that I went.

CYRIL HALLY

Paulo Freire: Personal Impressions

Catholics in Australia have always been linked into an international network of ideas. Intellectual currents that flowed around the Catholic world made an impact here too: ideas about liturgy, sexuality, the lay apostolate, religious liberty and resurrection theology arrived in Australia from abroad and were given local expressions. That is to say, current thinking, however attractive, was not slavishly followed; rather, it was tested in the light of our own experience and put to work in Australian garb. Dialogue, a journal for educators, did this sort of work for a decade after Vatican II. It has become an archive of the reception of Vatican II initiatives in Australia. In this article, from Dialogue, April 1973, sociologist Cyril Hally (himself a key figure in the acculturation of Vatican II) reflects on his own exposure to the person and thinking of the famous Brazilian educator, Paulo Freire. In manner and content, Hally's writing is a rare example of the critical approach to the history of ideas in Australia.

When I began working in Belgium some six years ago I was surprised by the extent of the Belgian people's interest in Latin America, particularly in church circles. In my own office and in the various organisations I was associated with there was, for example, constant reference to Paulo Freire. I myself had found his classic work, *Pedagogy of the Oppressed*, difficult to comprehend. On the one hand it appeared to offer a solution to a number of problems I had been grappling with for many years, but at the same time it seemed to me to be based upon an unbalanced understanding of salvation. It seemed to rightly emphasise the goal of liberation but in doing so to prescind from that of reconciliation.

Late in 1970 I was invited to participate as a resource person in an education seminar for superiors general sponsored by Educ-International. Of the three keynote speakers, one was to be Paulo Freire, whose designated topic was 'Humanisation of Man: Its Educational Implications'. I was interested in a possible clarification of his views on salvation and also as to whether his method was universally applicable or could be applied only within the Latin American milieu.

My impressions after his address remained mixed. He was certainly a fine representative of Brazilian culture, warm, exuberant, subtle, idealistic, almost exaggeratedly optimistic, yet in some indefinable way marked by sorrow and tragedy—in a word, compassionate. The impact of the address on an audience of professional Christian educators was a mixture of something little short of awe accompanied by extreme exasperation.

The feeling of awe was evoked by the presence of an outstanding educational theorist, great humanitarian and humble Christian. Here was the end product that educationalists have in mind — a fully human, creative person. The exasperation was caused by the second most serious defect in the educational process — the failure of conceptual communication. Not only had Freire an inadequate command of English but he employed an exceptionally abstract terminology. However, the most serious flaw in the educational process was entirely lacking, namely, the failure in interpersonal non-conceptual communication. One experienced that exhilarating feeling which follows upon the first glass of a hitherto untasted vintage wine. One wanted more. A single lecture obviously was incapable of clarifying his method or of solving the problems in my mind.

Fortunately I was to meet him regularly over the next 12 months, for I had been asked by the Franciscan Missionaries of Mary in Paris to join a body of consultants, to be headed by Paulo Freire, to help in the formation of INODEP. I soon discovered that in normal conversation he demonstrated a more than adequate knowledge of English. Apart from the warmness due to his Brazilian culture, he demonstrated a remarkable capacity to make those he was working with feel his equal, indeed his friends.

As our discussions proceeded one soon came to realise that not only was Freire an intellectual of giant stature but that he had moved in a very sophisticated milieu in Brazil. I had laboured under the impression that Brazil was an intellectual backwater where Spanish and French thought and literature were accepted in a dilettante fashion. Freire constantly referred to Brazilian scholars and research. He seemed to genuinely believe that he was receiving credit due rightly to other intellectuals of his country. While it is true that Freire drew upon a range of ideas, theories and data circulating in Brazil, it does seem that he was the first to tackle the educational challenge of how to help the masses, as distinguished from the elites, to be self-consciously aware of their total situation. In this lies his originality. He realised that the illiterate is a proletarian in the strict sense of the word, i.e., his children are his only wealth. He is at the mercy of his employers who compete at exploiting him. His work is so stupefying that it does not give him an opportunity to be creative. His whole activity is polarised around satisfying the two basic instincts shared by animals, viz., subsistence and reproduction. He is a slave both of nature — droughts, crop failures, capricious fertility — and of his human masters. Freire succeeded in elaborating, and demonstrating in an adult literacy campaign, a method for extending to such people the critical self-awareness which had begun to dawn in the intellectual milieu.

Having myself spent a couple of years at university studying the phenomenon of development in Asia (where the vast majority of the world's poor live) I was aware of the inadequacies of any program based exclusively upon the assumptions of economists. Our tutors convinced us that the entire social and cultural background of a particular sub-cultural group had to be taken into account along with the international economic system. This eliminated either a capitalist or Marxist approach to the poor. No one, however, could point to a viable alternative.

I had previously for several years been chaplain to Asian students in Sydney. They too were critical of the Western approach to development in Asia but were unable to offer an alternative approach. We discovered that this was due to the fact that the students, a privileged group, did not understand the mentality of their own peasants or slum dwellers. Many were aware, and resentful, of being cultural hybrids as a consequence of their education. We spent hours discussing new types of education but failed to come up with any constructive proposals. I was myself at that time in danger of becoming educationally 'schizophrenic.' For example, as a seminarian at Werribee, I had spent much of my vacation time observing YCW groups employing their inductive formation system, while in the seminary I was being exposed to a deductive system. Later, while chaplain to Asian students, I was also a seminary professor, and was willy nilly trying to use two systems of formation which had opposite departure points. Now, bringing this sort of a background to our discussions, I was seeking to discover the essence of the Freire method.

It was becoming clear to me that he had elaborated a system of integral formation which eschewed both indoctrination and compulsory enrolment and which was aimed at helping people to become aware of themselves, as individuals, as members of a community, of nature, society and history. The cornerstone I found to be the recognition that in the teaching process there are two subjects, as he puts it, the educator and the educatee. Traditionally the educator imposes his understanding of reality (his cultural assumptions, values and goals) upon the educatee. This cultural domination by the educator leads to the alienation of the underprivileged educatee. To break this pattern of domination the educator must help the educatee to stand back and look critically at his familiar surroundings. In so doing he will gradually become aware of himself, as distinct from his surroundings, which he begins to realise are the object of his knowledge and a practical application of his action and that he himself is the subject of this knowledge and of this activity. He begins, firstly, to see nature not as uncontrollable but as something which by his work he can enrich, in the process enriching himself.

In this new understanding of nature and of the new meaning given to it by his work, he becomes aware of the other members of his local community as potential subjects, creators, also. This realisation has a double effect. A sharp distinction is made between natural objects over whom he has power, and other persons, like himself, who must never be treated as objects. Thus the new relationship with nature leads to a new relationship with other men, to a genuine community of free human beings responsible for their own common life. He begins to realise that just as man can create things, so men together can create social relationships. Thus the poor man becomes aware of history in the sense that the existing social relationships have been created by generations of bosses and that he and his friends are playing no active role in this historical process. He wants to become also a subject of history; he wants to participate in shaping the way of life, the culture of his people.

Finally, he looks anew at the religious aspect of culture. Is he an object or subject at this level also? The adoption of a critical stance leads to a demythologising of popular religion, to a rejection of fatalism and to an interiorisation of Christian experience. The institutional aspects of religion are not all immutable either, he realises.

It seemed to me that the genius of Freire lay precisely in enabling the poor to become aware of their potentialities with regard to themselves, other people, nature, society, culture and history. It is the internal coherence of the system that explains its efficiency, this combined with the employment, as the starting point of the process, of the emotionally-laden experiences of the poor themselves.

However, I could see difficulties. His method required on the part of educators an extraordinary degree of disinterestedness. Basically their sole objective was to use the psycho-social method to enable the poor to become aware of their potentialities at all levels. They were to divest themselves of all preconceived ideas as to what direction the people's future activity might take. If the movement was to reach large numbers of the poor, would a sufficient number of such disciplined educators be found? Freire told me that even in Brazil not a few educators either failed to understand the method or could not resist taking short cuts because they were action-orientated.

It should be kept in mind that the program was discontinued by the military government and so the long-term effect with ever-expanding numbers is unknown. In Chile the success was not so dramatic. Many of the Chilean peasants were already literate and the society on the whole politically sophisticated. Nevertheless the method proved capable of adaptation to the programs of adult education sponsored by the Chilean Institute for Agrarian Reform.

I took up with Freire the question of the relationship between liberation and reconciliation. He agreed that both are essential elements of the Good News. A condition for reconciliation in Brazil was that both the oppressing elites and the illiterate poor must be able to function as subjects. Not only will the elite be unwilling to give up their monopoly of power but they cannot give genuine freedom to the poor. The poor must first become aware of themselves as subjects and define their own situation. Once this conviction, that they are subjects, has dawned, they become self-motivated, a creative force in society.

Asked if this would inevitably lead to violence, he admitted that violence could not be ruled out, human nature being what it is. However, he distinguished between blind violence which is exclusively destructive and the violence caused by manipulators—in both cases the poor are the victims. If the poor become genuine subjects, the elites may learn to respect them. At present they despise them, thus providing no basis for dialogue. In fact, the elites fear them — the worst possible basis for dialogue. They fear them because the poor belong to the 'culture of silence', unable to articulate their aspirations, unable to contribute anything genuinely human to society.

My own confreres in Chile have been required to work within the pastoral plan laid down by the hierarchy of helping to build 'base communities'. This plan, as far as I could judge, incorporated many of the details, and certainly the spirit, of the Freire method. Whatever the effect this plan has had on the Santiago slum dwellers, it has been traumatic for most of the foreign priests. Once a basic community begins to function, i.e. take charge of its own destiny, a further problem arises, particularly for mission priests. They begin to wonder what is their role, qua foreigners. On the other hand if they leave Latin America they usually meet with blank incomprehension in pastoral circles back home. I do not know of a single one who has been able to employ the Freire method successfully in his own, Western, environment.

Though there is no doubt in my mind that the method is capable of transference to other milieux, nevertheless, there are formidable obstacles. Firstly, there is the question of terminology. Though most of the key words in Freire's book, based on Latin roots, can be easily translated into European languages, this by no means facilitates comprehension of the method. Secondly, Freire was able to draw both on the results of original research into the total cultural situation of Latin America and on the emotional commitment of many educators to help in the process of the release from alienation of their 'marginal' compatriots. Those two conditions do not exist everywhere. Probably they exist in Australia only in regard to the Aborigines and a very small number of educators. Knowledge of Latin America, whether secular or Christian, in Australian educated circles is conspicuous only by its absence.

Thirdly, the method has been designed specifically for adults in countries where 'universal education' is not a reality. The Christian education process has been essentially orientated in Australia towards children who are obliged by law to attend school. Lay apostolic movements and adult education programs have been peripheral and optional. The social structure does not permit adolescents to play an adult role in either society or the Christian community. Even so, it is my impression that the philosophy behind the Freire method underlies much of our 'progressive' education.

The final query concerns secular humanism. Freire is profoundly Christian. While it is true that he does not employ any theological rationalisation to justify the correctness of his method, its efficiency does depend upon a transcendental belief system. Any man by the use of his intelligence and will can transcend nature, but can he transcend human relationships? Whatever about the secular humanist's response, Paulo Freire has issued a challenge to all Christian educators. Let us not forget in our anguish at the growing gap between the rich and the poor that Christ entrusted the essentially Christian educational responsibility to a group which included the social outcasts of a despised minority people within the apparently insuperable Roman Empire.

JEROME CROWE CP
Eustace, my Nightmare Student

For 30 years Compass *has been a key Australian theological journal. Anyone doing theology in Australia has reason to be grateful for it; although he or she will not be surprised to find few of its articles in this anthology, for its usual fare is beyond the scope of this collection. The editors of* Compass *have always been aware of a world beyond the libraries and the lecture halls. So when they heard that participants in a seminar on seminary education had been asked to describe their dream and their nightmare students, they sent out search parties. This article, published anonymously, was a result. As to the identity of Eustace—make your own guesses about who he is and what became of him. The article appeared in the October 1975 issue of* Compass.

In preparing this anthology, we discovered that the writer of the article was Father Jerome Crowe CP. *He died suddenly, just as the book was going to press. His death deprives Australian Catholicism of one of its finest biblical scholars. His many friends remember him as an academic who could speak to all levels of scholarship, a human being in whom you saw the face of Christ, and, as this article attests, a wit who made you both smile and think at the same time.*

Eustace is intelligent. He knows it, he has read a lot of books and articles and got good marks in a lot of exams. He has studied obediently all the things his superiors and teachers told him he should and even read a lot of the suggested reading. This didn't leave him time for many other things and he has never shown any personal curiosity, but, then, he hasn't got into trouble with his teachers or superiors either. His studies were sometimes interesting but never exciting.

He is dogmatic, but he has good reason to be. He has spent years learning the church's teaching and attitudes. He knows Trent and Vatican I and is aware of Chalcedon and Nicaea but his long suit is Vatican II. So he knows what the modern church thinks about all the issues people talk about and can tell them.

Eustace argues very well and very logically and because he takes his position as an official minister of the church seriously he feels obliged to regularly defend the church's teaching against attack or misunderstanding. He knows that Vatican II spoke about dialogue so he can straighten everybody out on that too. He has learnt his Pastoral Psychology well and can make cases out of persons with great exactness. He is aware of the values and techniques of sensitivity training and is so sold on it that everybody avoids him like the plague, but then most others are not as sensitive as he is.

Eustace is not proud, just right. He has had advantages that others haven't. His training has helped him to understand the law of God and of the church, others who haven't had his advantages can't be expected to; one of the things he has been trained and ordained to offer to others is to tell them what is right and what is wrong.

He has never been violently angry, but pretty frequently impatient with incompetent teachers and students who didn't know much and especially when they didn't prepare. He would class himself as really a left wing type; but he has no time for the rosary or for anybody who says it, he simply avoids conservative colleagues and has never been able to make a friend or enjoy the company of anybody who thinks differently from him.

Eustace is well up in liturgy, he did a good seminary course and read a bit on the side. He composes excellent prayer services and literate sermons but isn't much good when circumstances don't turn out too well, when the children make too much noise or late arrivals break up the progress of a home mass. He has never been known to laugh during prayer or liturgy.

He has no close friends, though he doesn't seem to notice it, and he doesn't need them to help him with personal problems because he hasn't got any. He has never been much of a team man and it is getting more difficult to find a place for him in any joint venture. In fact, he is getting more and more inaccessible and unemployable, his area of interest and apostolate is narrowing all the time. He is impossible to retrain.

PATRICIA HINCE
A Garbage-oriented Society

Begun in 1936, the Catholic Worker *was a monthly paper which
was edited and written by lay people. Its focus was on Australian
society and the need for a middle way between capitalism and communism. After World War II it lost circulation because of its lack of
enthusiasm for B. A. Santamaria, who had been one of its early
editors. The paper offered a Catholic alternative to the hegemony of
the Santamaria movement. It drew inspiration from its American
namesake, founded by Dorothy Day and Peter Maurin in 1933,
although it copied neither the Americans' houses of hospitality nor
their personal journalism. For many years its articles were unsigned,
as expressions of communal discussions. The appearance of by-lines
and columnists in the 1960s marked a move away from such commu-
nalism. Patricia Hince's back page column was another landmark: a
female voice in what had been an all-male club. This one appeared in
May 1971. The* Catholic Worker *closed in 1976.*

I was shopping last week with my eight-year-old daughter when we
passed a boot and shoe repairer's shop—to me, an ordinary enough
part of the shopping scene. 'They wouldn't make much money in
there, Mummy, would they?' she said. 'Probably not', I replied absently, my
mind concentrating on cereals at eight cents off and the like. 'Because', she
went on after a while, 'when your shoes wear out you don't take them to
be mended. You throw them away and get a new pair.'

I was struck afterwards with the significance of this remark. For me,
boot repairers' shops are normal and ordinary, even necessary. They are
around everywhere, or at least they used to be. Have you had any shoes
mended lately? For her they are quaint survivals of the pre-throwaway age.
And, of course, she is right. Here is another trade that is passing away. The
shoe repairer will soon be as remote from life as the local dairyman who
used to deliver milk when I was eight myself, dipping it out into a billy
with a tin can on the end of a long hook. Progress made him redundant,
just as progress has made the shoe repairer redundant.

Members of the affluent society don't bother to have shoes repaired, or socks darned, or ladders in stockings mended. Besides, many of today's shoes are made from synthetic materials for which there is no repair technique, or else they are soled, like my husband's, with rippled rubber, on which no replacement sole could possibly be stuck. It is in a small way a case of planned obsolescence, and it is tied in with the large issue of pollution and the abuse of natural resources and raw materials.

We seem to be more and more engaged in processing our natural resources and turning them into a gigantic mass of garbage which we have no means of getting rid of. Consider for a moment the packaging industry. Virtually nothing these days comes naked and unadorned. Fish and chips may still come with a minimal protection of last month's newspaper. But what else can be bought these days which is not encased in cellophane envelopes, festoons of heat-sealed plastic, cubic yards of corrugated cardboard?

It is getting very hard to cope with the mass of rubbish that flows through any family home these days—vegetables in plastic, razor blades in metal dispensers in cardboard and plastic packets that break your fingernails and ruin your sewing scissors; shirts stuck together with 69 small pins, three pearl-headed pins, five pieces of plastic, all enclosed in a cardboard box, none of which needed to be manufactured in the first place, and all of which have to be got rid of. The logical place to unpack your shopping is right beside the incinerator—a quarter of what you've bought, and *paid* for, will end up in there.

In what my children call 'the olden days', that is, a generation ago, family houses often had a spare room, a small sewing-room, a storeroom, a boxroom in which were kept useful and reusable things like suitcases, gumboots, empty pickle jars. What the modern house needs is a rubbish room, somewhere to put the flood of uselessness that comes willy-nilly with the weekly shopping. Failing such a room, it's perhaps a little pointless for people to keep on warning us against rubbishing Australia. Even if we don't throw our cartons of poisonous plastic out of the car window on our next family picnic, we can't avoid rubbishing Australia. Under the guise of improved efficiency and hygiene, we have stimulated the growth of a great packaging industry designed to do nothing but produce rubbish.

The reckless abandon with which this rubbish is being multiplied may be even more dangerous than it looks on the surface. Many people are now alerted, and not before time, to the consequences of pollution of our natural resources. Articles on this subject are common in our newspapers and magazines. We know about mercury in tuna and oysters; we share Thor Heyerdahl's fears for the open oceans; we have seen pictures of the Elwood Canal and the Mordialloc Creek looking like murky mushroom soup. We have read about the death of New York, a city in which people cannot live any more.

But there may be implications for the human being that we have not thought about, implications such as those voiced recently by an English psychiatrist, Dr Richard Tredgold. He sees a type of personality emerging from this unsatisfying throw-away world that could endanger civilisation itself. He sees a sick society in which viciousness and destructiveness will become the chief motivating forces in the lives of too many people. His pessimistic vision is uncomfortably close to the philosophy of a garbage-oriented consumer society, the sort of thing my eight-year-old opened my eyes to with her innocent observation about boot repairers. If everything else is despoiled—all the hills for quarries; all the trees for corrugated card board; all the Lake Pedders; Westernport Bays for oil refineries; emus and kangaroos for pet food—then there may be only human beings to fall back on. That could be the last stage in the development of a factory culture which views all the world and its resources as material for processing into garbage. I hope that Dr Tredgold's view may prove to be unjustified— if it does not, this last stage may be closer than we think.

MARIE GRÜNKE
Preparing for prayer

One of the biggest changes of the Vatican II years was that Catholics learned to pray in their own way. I don't mean that before then they did not pray—that would be absurd. The pre-Vatican II church was an intensely prayerful church. Two things marked its style of prayer. It was mathematical, putting emphasis on the number of times one performed some ritual act, whether in the Nine First Fridays or the decades of the rosary. It was also formulaic, following words printed in a dizzying array of prayerbooks which survive as a rich archive of those times. What happened after Vatican II was that adepts of the spiritual life began to find audiences for what they had learnt of the wordless interchange between creature and Creator. Writing in Bread and Wine, March 1978, *Sister Marie Grünke sss gives a good example of such initiation. Significantly, she speaks always of prayer (in the singular), never of prayers (the plural). The distinction draws an exact line between two periods of spiritual history. Yet her story of the 19th century French peasant sitting before the tabernacle—a similar story is told of the scholarly Australian poet, Christopher Brennan—is a reminder that such an 'exact line' may have many waves in it.*

Each person needs to build some time into the day for *explicit* moments of prayer. If I do not take this time, I will lose touch with who I am; I will lose touch with my creativity that is the source of insight; I will lose touch with the faith dimension of life—that dimension through which God enters my world in the *Now* situation, as revelation, as meaning: yes, I will lose touch with the God in Christ who brought meaning into my life by loving me in death and sending me a Comforter. Finally, I will live isolated, not only from myself, but from other people, and drift in an alien world; then my loneliness will frighten and even terrify me and I will be tempted to enter into many superficial relationships seeking mostly physical intimacy as a substitute; or I will escape into the world of illusion because I cannot face a reality that has become devoid of the faith dimension.

But if I take time for prayer and meditation, I will, little by little, begin to feel at home with myself, in touch with who I am and radiate a quiet serenity; people I meet will find me approachable; gradually they will learn to trust me and risk coming to know themselves. As I learn to relax in mind and body, I will reveal a Presence, an 'attentive Presence'—to myself, to other people and to my world.

The amount of time spent in prayer will vary from one individual to another. Many factors come into play: vocation, profession, physical and mental health. But I believe firmly from what I have read, observed and experienced, that some time each day spent in prayer is essential, even if it is only ten or 15 minutes.

Perhaps our biggest problem is bad use of time. There are many moments of the day that are wasted on us. On your way to the bus or the letter-box, have you ever thought to look up and notice the sky, the clouds, the texture and pattern of bark on a tree or a butterfly in flight? If I build into my day a period of time for *explicit* prayer, I will find myself using other precious moments that come unexpectedly into my day; for instance riding on a tram or when I miss a bus and have to wait!

Some people prefer to pray first thing in the morning and some at night; others may prefer to take time in the middle of the day. Once you select a time slot, it is better to try to keep to it regularly for a period of time.

You may choose to pray outdoors; walking in the garden, or in a park or sitting on the river bank.

Perhaps you prefer a church or a chapel; maybe there is one to which you have access at a given time each day. Or you may prefer the privacy of your room, be it a study-room, bedroom or lounge room.

Physical posture is important and needs will vary from person to person. Some people pray better while walking slowly, reflectively; others prefer to sit or kneel; in any of these positions it is important to keep the small or lower part of your back straight and to breathe from the diaphragm; from time to time you may have to recall your original position.

An exercise to prepare for prayer

It is often very difficult to suddenly switch from one type of activity to another. The body and mind need a short adjustment period. If I am undergoing much stress, I may prefer to take it all to God just as it is and make it the basis of my prayer. But if I am vaguely distracted living in a world of illusion or lost in a useless cycle of thoughts, I may find the following exercise helpful.

The purpose of this exercise is to bring the thinking process to a halt; this will facilitate openness to God in prayer. Some people, and some religions, try to do this by force—by deliberately blocking off everything external and forcing the attention to the still-point within.

I am going to suggest another way, I am going to invite you to come home to yourself, to your still-point, through your body, through your senses.

Remember, this is not an intellectual process, not a thinking process; but I am going to ask you to use your imagination for the first part of the exercise.

> Take a few moments to be still
> and then close your eyes.
> Imagine yourself somewhat over-burdened
> by excess baggage.
> This baggage is attached to your head
> with pieces of string.
> You have been carrying this weight
> for quite some time now
> and you feel its heaviness.
> Allow yourself to feel its weight.
> Now take a pair of imaginary scissors
> and cut through each piece of string.
> As you cut the string
> feel the weight drop away.
> Keep cutting until it has all fallen away.
> Now experience the lightness.
> *Feel* the lightness.
>
> Freed of this weight,
> you can now notice your body
> and feel the areas of tension.
> Relax the shoulders and neck muscles,
> the palms of your hands.
> Relax the forehead,
> the eyes,

the corners of your mouth.
Breathe deeply
and feel the whole body relax.

With your eyes still closed
listen to the sounds of life.
Let them come to you
without analysing them—
the rustle of leaves in the breeze,
the splashing of water,
the crisp sound of the autumn leaves
crunching beneath your feet.
Hear the song of a bird,
the flutter of its wing,
the tapping of a branch on the window pane.
Listen to the sounds of a human voice
and the silence between the sounds.

When you feel you are ready,
gently open your eyes.
Notice a shape,
a curve, a line—
but again without analysing it.
Look at the colours in the carpet,
the light in the window pane.
Look at the candle;
notice its flame.
See its form,
its roundness.

Feel its smoothness,
its contour.
Feel the roughness of wood,
the bark on a tree,
the texture of a leaf—
but always without analysing it.
Feel the curve of the chair,
the texture of its surface,
the clothes on your skin.
Feel the breeze,

the cool air on your cheek.
Feel your foot in your shoe.

Smell the freshness of newly cut grass,
the scent of a flower,
the fragrance of a summer breeze,
the rain on the soil.

Let the stillness within arise
and touch the stillness without,
and wait.
Wait in silence,
in expectancy,
in relaxed attention.

Methods of Christian prayer

In the Christian tradition there are three basic types of prayer: vocal, mental and contemplative. They are not clearly defined areas of sharp distinction and progression; rather, they tend to intertwine and overlap; although I may tend towards either one of these methods of prayer for a given period of time.

Vocal prayer. This type of prayer needs little explanation; our religious tradition and upbringing will determine largely our experience of and attitude to this method of prayer. Some of us are familiar with the rosary and may still find it a very meaningful prayer; or the stations of the cross; or short aspirations. There are the psalms which address all our moods, personally and collectively; from praise to thanksgiving; from sorrow to appeal. If we were more familiar with the psalms, I am sure we would make greater use of them in our prayer to God. And there are the prayers composed by the saints down through the ages; and of course, our own creative prayers to God.

Mental prayer (*lectio divina*). Mental prayer grows out of 'spiritual reading'. I take a book, or the gospels, or whatever I respond to and need at the moment; I then select a small section, maybe a page or two, maybe a paragraph or even just a sentence.

I may like to use my imagination and place myself inside a gospel story; maybe I am walking with Jesus and the disciples on the road to Emmaus or standing with Mary at the foot of the cross.

Maybe I am captivated by a paradox: 'Anyone who loses his life will find it'; 'God is life in front and death behind'; 'He is the Dazzling Dark'.

The important thing here is to stay with what I am reading or meditating on, going over it again and again until it *touches* me; for prayer finally is a movement of the heart; of love. And it is at this point that I begin to pray either in my own words or the words he gives me in the Spirit.

Contemplative prayer. This method of prayer is often referred to as the 'prayer of quiet'. Essentially it consists of an attitude of deep listening, of quiet attention, an inner silence.

Perhaps I can make this clearer by quoting from Anthony Bloom in his book *Beginning to Pray*:

> In the life of a Catholic priest of France, the Cure of Ars, Jean Marie Vianney, there is a story of an old peasant who used to spend hours and hours sitting in the chapel motionless, doing nothing. The priest said to him, 'What are you doing all these hours?' The old peasant said, 'I look at him, he looks at me, and we are happy'.
>
> This can be reached only if we learn a certain amount of silence. Begin with the silence of the lips, with silence of the emotions, the silence of the mind, the silence of the body. But it would be a mistake to imagine that we can start at the highest end, with the silence of the heart and the mind. We must start by silencing our lips, by silencing our body in the sense of learning to keep still, to let tenseness go, not to fall into day dreaming and slackness, but to use the formula of one of our Russian saints, to be like a violin string, wound in such a way that it can give the right notes, neither wound too much to breaking point, nor too little so that it only buzzes. And from then onwards we must learn to listen to silence, to be absolutely quiet, and we may, more often than we imagine, discover that the words of the Book of Revelation come true: 'I stand at the door and knock'.

If my prayer is real and not an illusion, it will flow back into my life—into my moment-to-moment existence—informing it with Christian faith, hope and love.

VINCENT F. DILLEY
An All Hallows Man

This obituary appeared in the 1979-1981 edition of the All Hallows Annual, *the magazine of an Irish missionary college which has given many fine priests to Australia. Written by a priest of the Maitland diocese in NSW, it tells with loving detail the daily life of Monsignor Daniel Forde, former vicar-general of the diocese. He died in 1980 at the retired priests' home, aged 86. He had been 60 years a priest, for 44 of those years parish priest of Waratah where, as his obituarist notes, the church was named Corpus Christi. Some seventy priests came to the old man's funeral, among them his talented obituarist (who is himself now dead, RIP).*

There was once a saint who took a vow never to lose a minute in the service of God, but he did not recommend it to others. It was rather difficult. Daniel Forde may never have taken such a vow but some time in his seminary days he must have made some sort of resolution. His day was completely regulated. He had a pocket-watch, of considerable age, and he was frequently seen to consult it, as though he sensed it was near time for some duty or spiritual exercise. He rose at 5 am and was in the church for over an hour before his daily mass at 7 am. From then on it was a daily round of duties, with never a minute lost or wasted. At any function he was prompt to arrive and the first to leave; there were other duties to be done. At 4 pm, for example, you could depend on finding him in the church making the stations of the cross. There was a time slot for everything until, at 9 pm, his light went out and Dan Forde had gone to bed to rest against another day's work.

He was abstemious. He never touched alcoholic drink. His meals were simple. It was either jam or butter on his bread—never both. Half sheets of writing paper, not written on, he kept and used for baptismal certificates. He wrote with a pen he had kept from his college days. A real fountain pen which he filled by pouring ink into its barrel, and which formed letters with broad strokes—so worn was the nib. In his long career he had only two motor cars, the first one for over thirty years. A blacksmith kept it on the road for him, adjusting the rims to take modern-sized tyres. This is not to say that he was mean. It is rather that he was poor in spirit. Nobody came to him deserving of financial help who did not receive it; no tramp knocked at his door and went away empty-handed. He educated several students for the priesthood. He had a bank account called the 'New Altar Fund' into which he put most of his personal salary with a view to the extension of the church, when it became necessary. His special interest was always the St Vincent de Paul Society.

He did the visitation of his parish with machine-like precision. His calls were never social calls—always on his Master's business. He had never had a cup of tea in any home in the parish. His visits were of short duration. He asked about the spiritual welfare of every member of the family, gave advice if needed, and was gone. He divided the parish and its responsibilities fairly with his assistant priest and never interfered with the other's work, except that he reserved the right to visit every new family at least once to make them welcome, even outside of his own district. Once I told him about new parishioners in my own district. A few days later I called on them in the evening, only to find that he had been there already—in the morning!

He was a man of prayer: daily meditation, holy hour, stations of the cross, rosary and visit to the Blessed Sacrament, spread over the day between visits to the schools, public and Catholic, hospitals, and visitation of homes. Truly a life of work and prayer. He told me once that he had his eye on a small country parish where he could say his prayers, but instead he got a city parish with no parochial buildings in it, because it had been cut off from a larger one. Sunday mass was in the chapel of the Institute for the Deaf until he had built a new church—indeed two—then a Catholic school (later enlarged), a parish hall and a presbytery. He had an annual mission in his parish. A well-seasoned missioner once told me that he had never known a city parish with such a low proportion of mass-missers anywhere in Australia. Vocations were above the average from his parish; there are seven priests that I can think of, and numerous religious in various orders. He called his church 'Corpus Christi'. It was devotion to the Blessed Sacrament that urged him on.

He never sought the limelight. With reluctance he allowed the celebration of his diamond jubilee of priesthood. He remarked after the celebration that 'exaggerations are permitted preachers on such occasions'. The years of his retirement were spent in prayer. Call on him at St Joseph's Home and you would find him in the chapel before the Blessed Sacrament or in his room at prayer or spiritual reading.

He was humble enough to think that his approach might not win everybody to Christ. That is why he sometimes asked his assistant to visit persons in his own district, in the hope that he might succeed where he himself had apparently failed. I suspect, too, that that was why he had an annual mission. I never heard him speak unkindly of a fellow priest.

The one hobby, the one relaxation that he allowed himself was the filling of clerical vacancies—in the diocese especially, but also in his native Cork. It pleased him, as much as if he picked a winner at the races, when his guesses came true.

Truly one could say all his days, all his time, were for God.

MARIAN McCLELLAND sss
A journey begins

*This article is remarkable because it documents one religious sister's
path to a radical political position on a question which many prefer to
ignore. Hers is a very personal voice asking hard questions and ready
to look for answers in unlikely places. Readers who shy away from her
uncomfortable final choice may nevertheless find impressive the
honesty of this writing. She shows herself open to the truths she seeks,
wherever she may find them; but, as well, she seeks wisdom in its
traditional sources: the Bible, church teaching, her congregational
spirituality and, with a rush of gratitude, in a contemporary statement
by the Australian Catholic bishops. Her article appeared in* Bread
and Wine, *July 1982.*

'**T**he nuclear arms race? That can't possibly affect me…', and I
would turn away with a slight shudder, and begin to speak of
something more relevant—or so it seemed to me at the time.
That was only 18 months ago. To my shame, for less than 18 months
of my 34 years have I had any interest in, or knowledge of the single most
important issue confronting our world since 1945: the possibility of global
nuclear war. Amazingly, most of us here in Australia have been able to live
until now as if the whole question did not and would not affect us. Many
of us within the Christian churches also have felt the same thing: the
nuclear arms race is irrelevant to our Christian belief

Such was my stance till July last year, when I was asked to gather information concerning 'things nuclear' for a group of people interested. So I set
out, literally, to see what I could find in Sydney. It was difficult starting from
scratch, not really knowing where to turn for help. I thought of possible agencies: Action for World Development, Movement against Uranium Mining,
Catholic Commission for Justice and Peace and Australian Council of Churches,
which might act as starters. I began to collect small bits and pieces of information. None of these agencies was devoted full-time to working on the issue of
international peace, but all had some literature on the subject. Most of them

had someone who could spare a few moments to talk with me about it. Through them I presently was introduced to the Association for International Cooperation and Disarmament (AICD)— a politically non-aligned organisation working full-time for peace. After speaking with their staff, I joined this organisation, and have found its information and activities to be at the centre of much that peace groups are doing in Sydney. Its broad membership includes many Christians.

But what about myself as a committed Christian? What had I to answer to that increasingly horrific picture of possible destruction building up in my brain? Indeed, as I read, it was almost impossible to prevent a kind of empty despair taking hold of me—the picture seemed hopeless and frightening.

In all the literature I read of enormous stockpiles of nuclear weap-ons, I read of some 50,000 nuclear warheads, with a destructive power one million times that of the bombs dropped on Hiroshima; I read of the Trident submarine, whose multiple re-directional warheads are accurate to within a few metres over a distance of six thousand kilometres; I read of the change from the old tactic of Mutually Assured Destruction (MAD), to the more sinister tactic of counter-force or 'first strike'. This means that instead of each side (basically USA and USSR) keeping each other afraid of using nuclear weapons—with the threat that 'if you hit me I'll blast you off the face of the earth'—strategists are now thinking that a nuclear war is possible and winnable. The idea here is that, as weapons become more and more accurate, if I get in first I could possibly destroy the enemy's supply of nuclear weapons, and he'd have nothing to throw back at me. There also is talk of having a nuclear war, but only a small one—just Europe would be invited to have it at his house. Europe, of course, is suitably unimpressed by these suggestions of a 'limited theatre' of war. In fact, as I have read, the very earth could be destroyed many times over with the weapons already stockpiled. To all this add the various gruesome descriptions and predictions, and, as I found, the picture gets worse. Extra splashes of colour are added as one reads of expenditure on nuclear weapons and other armaments all the while increasing from the one million dollars a minute estimated in 1980. The picture is hung every so often as the superpowers flex their military muscles and shake their stockpiled fists. Many times have I asked myself what have I to balance this terror, this thought- and heart-numbing despair.

Soon after I had begun to discover this 'nuclear world', I met a girl who was very interested in the whole question. She had just returned from the USA where she had been following nuclear developments. She also had lived with Christian communities across USA and was aware of the reaction of many American Christians to the nuclear arms race. In Australia there had been so very little official or organised Christian reaction that nothing here on that level could possibly stem the tide of hopelessness I was feeling. I did know in my heart, in the place where I sense God's gift of resolute faith, that everything ultimately rests in God's hands: that this is God's world, and that God is involved in our destinies. But all that was like a last-ditch stand for me; I believed it, but found small comfort in it. From Jill I now learned that Christians in the US were awakening in large numbers to the challenge that the nuclear arms race is posing. Christians, indeed a number of our own Catholic bishops, were writing anti-nuclear material based on the gospels, based on God's call to life and not death. Surrounded by arsenals of nuclear weapons they were returning to the Good News of peace, to strong Old Testament themes of peace, to Jesus prophesied to be 'Mighty God, Prince of Peace'. They were finding their voices to preach that violence is not the way to have peace; that peace will not grow even from stockpiles of weapons used to deter an enemy. For them, as for me, it seems immoral to use nuclear weapons, or even to have them ready to use—an implicit willingness to use them. I had discovered that Vatican II had condemned 'any act of war aimed indiscriminately at the destruction of entire cities or of extensive areas along with their population' as 'a crime against God and man himself. It merits unequivocal and unhesitating condemnation' (*Gaudium et spes*, n. 80).

I began to take heart again, and to consciously adopt what we call Christian hope—and no mere blind optimism. I began to sense, also, that there was a battle going on inside me: a battle between what I now see as a part of me that wants to trust in 'protection' by weapons and worldly power—faith in a gun—and a part that wants to trust in God— faith in my creator and redeemer. Worldly wisdom was speaking strongly about the impracticality of doing without weapons. A certain type of politics spoke of the danger of the 'free world' being taken over by Communists (or whoever) if 'we' did not have a deterrent big enough to convince them that we meant business. There was also the voice of how right it was that Australia should have American bases on our soil, even if they were making

Australia a nuclear target; because we have to support the US in its fight for us and the 'free world'. Of course, the church has always supported the notion of a 'just war'. These and many other voices were strong in me. Gradually, though, I came to know these voices by different names: fear for my own skin; a fear of losing some illusion of control over my life; distrust in God. Scripture suggests that the fear of the Lord is the beginning of wisdom—not the fear of the bomb; and the person whose mind is fixed on the Lord is kept in perfect peace—not the one whose mind is fixed on protection by the bomb or the threat of violence.

My fears were in effect telling me that it was better to be dead than red, better that we should be prepared to kill hundreds of millions of people rather than be overtaken by, for example, the Russian Communists. In other words, the voices were saying, if we in Australia were overtaken by another, and perhaps totalitarian, government, God would somehow not be in that situation, we would be abandoned. Such a view, it seems to me, blasphemously limits the power of God. Persecution and suffering there well could be, but 'I am with you always, even to the end of time'. Worldly wisdom was counselling my utter moral demise: I would have to be willing to kill, or see killed, hundreds of millions of people, to save my own skin, or worse, to save my own lifestyle.

I sensed, though, that the voice of faith was telling me: if 'they' kill me they only kill my body. But if I entertain the idea of killing 'them' in some nuclear-nightmare, I remain or become a person of violence and not a person of faith: my soul, my spirit, my integrity as a Christian are lost; I am morally dead already. I cannot, and may not speak for others, but I can speak for myself and how I have come to view this question of nuclear warfare. I realise that my own journey along the path of peace has hardly begun; there is so far yet to go. The eucharist upon which I have, as a Blessed Sacrament Sister, focussed my life and my prayer is the sacrament of unity and peace. To be a person of the eucharist, indeed to become part of Jesus' eucharist, I must be a person of peace, and work for peace.

The Australian bishops have finally spoken, as a body, on the subject of nuclear war. It seems appropriate to end with a quotation from their statement of May 1982.

> We urge all Christians and people of good will to make their
> special concern the concern of peace. We urge all to recognise

and understand the dangers of our present situation for the sake of God's creation. The removal of the threat of war, and the establishment of peace are the most urgent tasks of our day.

The peace of the Lord Jesus Christ be with you.

PATRICK KENNA
Diary of a Country Priest

Some of the best writing in Australia goes out over the airwaves, particularly from ABC Radio. As a consequence it is usually lost to an anthology such as this one. St Mark's Review, the journal of an active Anglican cultural centre in Canberra, has always kept an ear close to the radio, so that it has been able to print some of these otherwise unknown treasures. Patrick Kenna's Diary of a Country Priest *was put to air in the ABC program* By the Way. *It was picked up by St Mark's and appeared in the December 1981 issue of the journal. The title reflects a famous novel by George Bernanos, which Kenna had quoted on a memorial card at his priestly ordination in 1954. The structure of this piece suits its original placement as a radio essay. Even cold on the page, it still carries enough of the author's speaking voice to make it a memorable evocation of parish experience along the rural coast of New South Wales.*

This is a series of random reflections and images based on my own experience in a particular country parish on the south coast of New South Wales. I am sure that, in many ways, it would be like its counterpart further down the coast and that it would have much in common with the local Anglican or Uniting Church parish. And yet, just as individual people are alike yet different from one another, so with the parish. This is a personal viewpoint based on almost eleven years with the community of Milton–Ulladulla and Sussex Inlet.

To begin with, three examples:

I am standing in a suburban presbytery. 'What's that?' I ask, pointing to a framed map on the office wall. 'It's the parish boundary map'. The parish, I could see, was equivalent to about two-thirds of a page of a suburban street directory. By contrast a country pastor in Australia will quickly come to experience the tyranny of distance.

My second is about a younger man supplying in this parish over a weekend while I was away. 'It was so quiet', he commented. 'Why, the phone rang only two or three times and I don't think there was a single caller at the front door'. While the city pastor will find plenty to occupy him within the presbytery, in the country he will normally go out to make contact.

The third example: a seminary lecturer holidaying at a local beach. 'There's a special sort of training needed for country-parish ministry'. It was the first time, indeed the only time, I have heard it put that way.

In the seminary the term of reference seems to have been the city where the seminary itself is located, and from *Going My Way* to *Menotti* popular imagination sees a priest at work in a suburban setting. In books like *Revolution in a City Parish*, *The People's Priest*, *Vessel of Clay*, the model is invariably suburban.

A word about the structure of the community where I live. There are the few local families who have been farming for several generations. There are the professional fishermen, a postwar phenomenon, mostly Italian. There are the retired couples who move here from the suburbs in search of retirement in a beach or lakeside surrounding. And, stimulated by their presence, there is a considerable building industry. Finally there are the visitors. Even in winter they come to their weekenders, towing caravans and boats all the way from Sydney, Canberra or Wollongong. And a holiday, beachside area such as ours will have more than its share of unemployed youth and single-parent families in search of cheaper rents.

In this kaleidoscope scattered in little groupings 50 miles or so along the coastal strip, where does a parish achieve its identity? What, in particular, is the parish priest's role? What model is he to follow? People sometimes ask, 'What do you do all day?' How many times I've been asked that question! And even after 27 years in the priesthood I'm unable to give a ready answer. Mostly, my hesitant reply will be 'I don't do anything … in particular'.

Three models for the country-town pastor

First, the **guru**. Imagine a small village where the people are going about their daily work. They are reasonably happy, and yet the more knowing villagers sense that something—or someone—is missing. They need a person to whom they can turn. Eventually a little fellow arrives on the scene, a quiet thoughtful man, a good listener, a man of depth. Someone, they sense, who might be the brother they have been searching for. So they lead him out to a hill overlooking the village. 'Here', they explain 'is where we'd like to build a little hut for you. We'll bring you whatever you need in the way of food or clothing. We want you to do nothing. Or at least not to be bound by having to work in the way we are. We just want you to stay near us. Sometimes we might call around and sit beside you in front of your fire to share one another's visions or for you to listen to our troubles. We'd be happy if you come down to the marketplace now and then and mingle with our people. You'll find them shy at first. But keep encouraging us. Show us how to celebrate.'

> When daylight came he left the house and made his way to
> a lonely place. The crowds went to look for him, and
> when they had caught up with him they wanted to prevent
> him leaving them (Luke 4:42).

A second model: the **boundary rider**. The children, the teenagers, the hitch-hikers, envy him his seemingly carefree lifestyle, not exactly John Wayne or the Man from Snowy River, just an easy-in-the-saddle horseman. You will see him squatting beside the railway line, yarning with the fettlers. Or he is on the outskirts of the town at the gaol or among the fringe-dwellers near the tip. If he is in the town itself, which does not seem to happen so often, you will find him in odd, unexpected places. At the end of a day sometimes he himself is surprised at the motley variety of faces he has been with.

The boundary rider model brings to mind this example:

A young Anglican priest, about to commence his first appointment, was given the following advice: 'Not long after you move there', he was told, 'take a large sheet of paper and write down the names of the people whose salvation is likely to depend on your *neglect*. Keep looking at that page and every now and then add to your list.'

> While he was at dinner in the house it happened that a
> number of tax collectors and sinners came to sit at the
> table with Jesus and his disciples. When the Pharisees saw
> this, they said to his disciples, 'Why does your master eat
> with tax collectors and sinners?' When he heard this he
> replied, 'It is not the healthy who need the doctor but
> the sick' (Matthew 9:10–12).

A third model: the **guest master**. Out near the monastery gates a bus load has just arrived. Nearby a couple of motor cycles are parked. The riders are combing their hair and moving their arms in and out to recover from the journey. All of a sudden they notice, coming out from the monastery entrance, a familiar figure—the guest master. He is smiling and waving. Soon he is shaking hands with them. Even after a whole year he remembers many of their names. The monastery does not seem to have changed much since their last visit. And the guest master is the same as ever. He is always there to welcome, to show them their rooms and make sure they have everything. Not only that, he seems to have just the right touch—the appropriate book or magazine article to put into each one's hand. Away from their regular setting they are more able to listen and confide.

> People tormented by unclean spirits were also cured, and
> everyone in the crowd was trying to touch him because
> power came out of him that cured them all (Luke 6:12).

I am suggesting that the country-town priest in Australia might be called to reveal three facets of the archetype, Jesus of Nazareth. An ever-present guide, the guru; the boundary rider, in touch with the powerless, the little ones, the outsiders; and the guest master, welcoming and strengthening the pilgrims who keep returning.

The local accent

In February last year, when I was re-entering Australia after several months overseas, I called at Mount Isa. One of the priests I met there was telling about a recent visit of Sydney Rugby League personality, Kevin Humphries, who had been guest speaker at one of Mount Isa's many clubs. Asked what advice he would give a football coach starting out with a new team, Humphries suggested that no coach can ever really train a team unless he first gets to know the local history: the fights, the struggles, the sufferings and tragedies that have left their mark on this community, the shifts in population in this place over the past 20 or 30 years ... and so on. When he knows a little about all of this then he can get started.

How often a new teacher will arrive, fresh and enthusiastic, at a school and begin writing on a nice, clean blackboard, full steam ahead. Some months—or years—later he may wonder what went wrong. And yet, if he stops for a moment and reflects, he will understand that, before he arrived on the scene with his particular contribution, that blackboard had had many layers of chalk on it; lots of life, laughter, suffering. It will pay us to move gently among these people and their ghosts. Maybe then we can begin to pick up the unspoken nuances, the particular quality of this community.

Firstly, I suggest that we need to be conscious that in every parish there is a local accent. Secondly, that we let the people know we are happily aware of it. And that we set about fostering and celebrating it together.

Incidentally, I am not about to suggest that the priest help the local people cut themselves off in some way from the world of the city or foreign countries, sealing themselves off in local activities and concerns. A parish need not become parochial.

We are to begin by being local before we become universal. When Peter was being accused by the servant-girl and others of being a follower of Jesus, they taunted his country accent: 'Why, he is a Galilean' (Luke 22:59). Presumably, Jesus himself spoke with the same country-town accent. Later he would be conscious of his *universal* mission and speak about 'Drawing all men to himself', but at the outset he was very local, Jesus of Nazareth, son of a carpenter. His apostle, Paul, who would go on to be the apostle to the nations and speak of himself as 'becoming all things to all men'—a universalist if ever there was one—was always conscious of his origins and is still spoken of as 'Paul of Tarsus'. This is interesting when we think of it: how many of the universal saints are linked in our memory with their particular township: Catherine of Siena, Teresa of Avila, Francis of Assisi. Or take the case of C. S. Lewis, so completely English, so totally 'of Oxford', and yet so universal. Here is another instance of the paradox that the more completely one is immersed in one's particular culture the more global one becomes.

In a television interview Malcolm Muggeridge was being asked what, in his view, was a person's first step towards God. He had no hesitation in answering that a person will inevitably move towards God when he or she begins to enter reality. I have often reflected on that wise answer: the reality of where I am living, my employment situation, my age, appearance, intelligence, education. To fly from these 'givens' is to fly from the ultimate reality.

In the parish there will be certain inescapable realities, no matter where. One of these will be its history. Another will be its geography. We may resent its isolation, its prevailing winds, its humidity or its frosts. We may contrast it bitterly with where we used to live, or long for a transfer, to be 'in the centre of things'. And yet, if we cannot believe that God is lurking in the depths of *this* terrain, in the lives of *these* people, in all their humanness, then we can never come to love or work with them as our very flesh and blood.

Here are a few simple ways of accepting the local reality that I have been exploring, or at least talking about, here in this parish:

1. Every place, no matter how dull and featureless, will have some landmark—a lake, or a hill, or a cliff-face. An annual hike to this landmark could be arranged. It could be drawn, as a nature-symbol of the community, on the parish newsletter cover.

2. We are becoming conscious of the reality that for some 20,000 years before white settlement in this country Aboriginal Australians journeyed where we are now farming or fishing. Quite probably there is, in your locality, an overhang or a midden they once used. A pilgrimage could be arranged to that place on Aboriginal Sunday.

3. Quiet and almost unnoticed in your community will be people who are carrying the local history in their hearts. They are in their fifties or their eighties or nineties. A series of interviews, one-to-one, could be arranged. These men and women could be coaxed to tell us about their childhood in this place, their memories of what it was like 30 or 60 years ago.

Some communities have compiled a Book of Wisdom. The older people are invited to contribute a certain saying or a prayer or poem or story that they have treasured. If this can be organised by the youth of the place, so much the better. It will put the old and the young in touch with one another. It will, above all, affirm the ageing and reveal what storehouses of wisdom lie locked away under those lined faces. A living stream of tradition is given a chance to bubble up to the surface.

The photograph album

Smile on them gently, these are the family ghosts,
Who once were persons: now they are stuck down flat.
They all were lovers of pies, puddings, and roasts.
Not one of them ever went out without a hat.

Rococco gardens dangling in blossomy loops
And canvas seats and improbable plants in pots
Incongruously surround these stony groups
Of maids and masters and patriarchs and tots.

What of this statuesque unbending wife?
This frigid frowning father? None will guess
That she was sprightly and lovable all her life,
And he had a name for fervour and friendliness.

What of this whiskered uncle, grave and grim?
This aunt, forbiddingly braced and booted and bodiced?
Gambling, drabbing, and drink were the ruin of him.
She, it is said, was scandalously immodest.

None of it shows, locked up in stillness, made
As blank as waxworks and as stiff as wood.
Their foxed and yellowing effigies, as they fade,
Betray no sparkle of laughter or lustihood.

A whirr and a click released them, years ago,
From the chill grip of momentary grimaces;
The photographer ceased his devilish to-do;
They sprang to life, resumed their ordinary faces.

And took their hats, and went about their tasks.
Until the tomb received them, six-foot deep.
All that the instant peephole caught was masks.
Fold them away, and leave them to their sleep.

John Thompson

Telling and re-telling our story is now seen to be a human imperative.
A parish can easily foster this—for example, keeping a parish album or
scrapbook; having someone relate how the present church building or school
or other organisation in the parish had its beginnings. Returning to the

birth or pre-birth is always uplifting because we are somehow recapturing the energy and vision of the pioneers.

One reason we need to keep affirming the local community is that, in a world of 'experts' and 'professionals', not to speak of streams of visitors flowing in and out of the place, the local parishioners can have a feeling of inferiority. Not only that, they will believe that the city is where it's all happening. This illusion is heightened by our national tendency to journey hundreds of miles or even interstate to a conference, a retreat or seminar. A manic-depressive syndrome to develop great excitement when heading off to yet another charismatic retreat or marriage encounter weekend but deep despondency upon re-entering Dullsville. And yet, 'The kingdom of God', we must never let ourselves forget, 'is among you' (Luke 17:21). 'The Word became flesh, he lived among us' (John 1:14). He pitched his tent among our tents.

Three images for the parish

The smorgasbord. A friend of mine who, for a number of years, worked in parishes around California, used to say to me, 'What programs is your parish offering this year?' I still find that a disturbing question.

> There is a variety of gifts but always the same Spirit
> (1 Corinthians 12:4).

The Spirit is one. But the people—the temples housing the Spirit— are infinitely varied. Each of us has the experience of our tastes and attitudes, changing as we grow older—not to speak of the difference between us and the person on either side of us in the Sunday pew. Culture, temperament, state of health, age, all kinds of factors enter in. Look at next Sunday's congregation in your small and seemingly static country town. Inevitably you will find a sampling of the human family.

Now if this widely divergent and constantly changing mixture of men, women and children is to be fed—that is to say, really nourished— the food on their table will need to be, to say the least, varied. Something approaching a smorgasbord is called for, so that each one's appetite can be stimulated, each one's taste catered for. I give two examples from my parish.

'Harvest Time' is a monthly session on the first Friday, for people in retirement. They come, some quite long distances, to take part in a devotion dear to Catholics of their age—Benediction sung in Latin. Afterwards they will meet one another over lunch in the parish house. This coming Friday it will be a little different because five of us will have taken part, the previous day, in a seminar called 'The Grief of Growing Old'. We begin by sharing that experience.

The second program we are calling 'A Wonder-full Day'. It is for children at the end of primary, preparing for confirmation. They will come in casuals, not school uniform, and the day will be mostly out-of-doors, down the paddocks that slope northwards from the church building. A hike, some non-competitive 'new games', songs for confirmation, a gospel meditation experience, a picnic lunch. One of the gifts of the Spirit is wonder; hence the title of their day.

A frequent image the gospels give us of the kingdom of heaven is the wedding feast, the banquet. Not the Oliver Twist soup kitchen. Not the germ-free Oslo lunch. Something else. Something resembling a smorgasbord.

The continental delicatessen. Even in a remote country parish the people can be made conscious in quite simple ways that, while they may seem to be 'far from the madding crowd', they are in fact part of the global village. Negatively, this will mean that even were we to try to turn away and be unconcerned, the events in distant cities must sooner or later make their impact. And on the positive side it will mean that we attune ourselves to the _zeitgeist_.

Take, for example, these five headings: World Development, Ecology, Racism, Ecumenism, Disability. In the 1950s the average parish would hardly have heard, much less cared in an active way, about such issues. But in the 1980s even an isolated rural parish is living as an ostrich with its head in the sand if it does not see these aspirations of the human family as their own concern.

> The joys and the hopes, the griefs and the anxieties of the
> men of this age, especially those who are poor or in any way
> afflicted, these too are the joys and hopes, the griefs and
> anxieties of the followers of Christ (_Gaudium et spes_).

Two local initiatives I can mention briefly in this context. The first is Milton Handloom Factory. This is a cottage industry in South India which our parishioners helped in its beginnings. Now, five years later, we still keep on sale a certain quantity of the cotton material woven at the factory, and in other ways keep in touch.

The second was last year, on Good Friday. Our open-air Way of the Cross was on the theme of prisoners. At every second station, a man or woman from the parish read about a Prisoner of Conscience, beginning with Jesus on trial. The list included St Peter and St Paul, Thomas More, Edith Stein, Dietrich Bonhoeffer and Maximilian Kolbe, and the contemporary South African Steve Biko. At the final station Amnesty International's work was referred to and their emblem, a large wax candle entwined with barbed wire, was carried into the church building where it was lit each month during 1980.

Home-made bread. Last Sunday morning, members of the Catholic Women's League were celebrating a birthday. Not only would they be serving the usual cup of tea after 9 o'clock mass, but they had arranged to do the readings, the prayers of the faithful, the offertory procession. Excitement, tension was high. Afterwards it was pointed out to me that, for these women, the whole exercise had been a daunting leap forward. I then realised that it had been an instance of 'home-made bread'.

A decade ago, when we were in the beginnings of learning vernacular songs for mass, we made use of a cassette player and even invited singers from other places. Now we can boast of a group of local guitarists. Shortly the group will be singing at a wedding and will be available for baptisms and funerals. Who knows? They may even start writing their own songs.

Once we used to import from interstate a weekly parish bulletin, with some space for our own announcements. Now, a seminary lecturer who lives in retirement here is supplying background notes for the scripture readings—admittedly an unusual circumstance for any parish.

If we believe that God's Spirit blows freely and mysteriously upon every forehead, then we may come little by little to encourage local initiatives, Home-made bread. There's nothing like it. It may take a lot longer and the initial efforts will be uneven, but it has a flavour all of its own.

Signs of hope

Small Town

Down here the starlings sit
on our television aerials (tall
for city reception) and yesterday
a woman drank Dettol.

Next door the forty-year-old
child is a collector of junk:
bits of old motorbikes, picture
frames, toilet seats, Singer

stands and old chains. His father
died last week and the son
lives now in a Home. Their old
house sinks further into

itself each day. There are three
 policemen, three hotels
and two schools. The woman who
drank Dettol died, and

Councillor P. might run
for Mayor again this year
and they're finally
building conveniences, for tourists.

Oh, and I forgot to put
the rubbish out last night.
Another visit to the Tip. I
always bring back something.

B. A. Breen

Driving through sawmill towns

You glide on through town,
your mudguards damp with cloud.
The houses there wear verandahs out of shyness,
all day in calendared kitchens, women listen
for cars on the road,
lost children in the bush,
a cry from the mill, a footstep—
nothing happens.

The half-heard radio sings
its songs of sidewalks.

Sometimes a woman, sweeping her front step,
or a plain young wife at a tankstand fetching water
in a metal bucket will turn round and gaze
at the mountains in wonderment
looking for a city.

Les A. Murray

Reading these two contemporary Australian poems one is reminded of Thoreau's fearful dictum: 'Most people lead lives of quiet desperation'. Is it possible for a country parish to lead these people—the ones Murray or Breen describe—out of their 'quiet desperation' into some kind of 'quiet hope'? I like to think of another dictum, from St John of the Cross: 'Where there is no love, put love, and you will find love'. To rephrase his words: 'Where there is no hope, put hope, and you will find hope'.

In what practical ways can a Christian parish become, for country town people, a sign of hope? Perhaps we could begin by returning to the drawing board to look at our models. Since the church has been often described in nautical imagery—'the barque of Peter', for example—let's think of the parish community in those terms.

1. In our immediate past—say the last 100 years—the response within a country parish has been to attempt to provide Total Care: a school for all-comers from infants to secondary; sodalities for every man, woman and child; even, at times, a hospital or an orphanage. An impressive effort which was quite unashamedly in competition with other denominations as well

as with government agencies. It was a world of **rival shipping lines**; but that era, for all practical purposes, has ended.

2. In contrast, many a parish today might be described as a **Liberian freighter**—a bulky vessel, fearful of revealing its identity, unaligned: so liberal that its school, its youth club, etc. have become almost indistinguishable from their secular counterparts.

3. Then there is that familiar, brightly painted and frequently photographed vessel, **the showboat.** It exists to take family groups out on the harbour for a pleasure cruise at weekends. They enjoy the bingo and take snapshots of the harbour views. Pleasant music is provided in air conditioned comfort. Then they return to the jetty and the harsh reality of their workaday world. It is an escape from drudgery for Mum and Dad and the kids, but hardly a sign of hope.

4. And then, there comes to mind a different image altogether. Not the prosperous shipping line. Not the fearful Liberian freighter. And certainly not the showboat, offering weekend escape. Something smaller, rather plain and insignificant. Nobody ever bothers to photograph it. It is so ordinary that hardly anyone even notices it. It is the **tug boat.** The dictionary definition says it all: 'Tug Boat. A powerful small boat designed for towing larger vessels.' The tug does not just point the way, it actually tows the larger vessels through safe channels. It is small but it is not inward-looking, self-serving, bobbing up and down like pleasure-craft. The tug is work-oriented. Its *raison d'être* is for others. It is in the business of leading. But it does not try to do everything.

Perhaps, at your next parish meeting, you could ask: 'Is this present project of ours a show boat activity or a tug boat activity?'

Groups in parishes can degenerate into the show boat world or they can become tug boats. How do you tell? Here are some pointers:

1. The tug boat will never be over-concerned about its image;

2. It will not be worried about its size: in fact, its smallness is an advantage; it means that it is manœuvrable;

3. It does not try to be omni-competent, omnipresent or omnipotent: it is happy to do one job at a time;

4. It never forgets that it exists for the bigger vessels, not for itself;

5. Far from being in hostile competition with the other ships, it has an

actual affection for all their passengers and crew. A love relationship begins to develop.

The Society of Friends (The Quakers) is a shining example of Tug Boat Christianity. The Catholic Worker movement begun in the depression years in New York is another. Both have had, through the years, an influence quite disproportionate to their numbers. Neither group has allowed itself to be cut off from the mainstream or to degenerate into an inward-looking, self-congratulatory sect. The compassionate love for the powerless, the vulnerable, the weakest and most oppressed, gives credibility to their anti-war stance. The Quakers and the Catholic Worker movement are tug boats because they have bravely kept on *doing* the truth in love: saying to the rest of us: No, not *that* direction, *this* way.

Could a small group in a country parish become a tug boat for the rest of the community? Here are some suggestions:

• Offering a sizeable portion of church property to Aboriginal people of the district as an alternative to continuing injustice.

• Welcoming one or two elderly people into the presbytery or convent or rectory as a sign of hope to the isolated and the institutionalised.

• Making the parish school classrooms available to low income families or ethnic groups during the holiday seasons or at weekends.

These gestures would be small, but not insignificant. They are certainly possible, manageable, and, in a world where most people will continue to live lives of 'quiet desperation', such gestures could be powerful *signs of hope*.

MARY KELEHER
Pedestals and power

Some time in the early 1970s, the spokesman for the Archdiocese of Sydney commented on the women's movement which was then emerging. He questioned their authenticity and their claims to be voicing real concerns. No woman he knew went on in this fashion, he said. The spokesman was gently ridiculed on the ABC's Coming Out Show; and his comments ended in the dustbin of history. Subsequent decades proved how wrong he had been. In convents, altar societies, sodalities and other parish bodies women were beginning to say aloud that they were sick of being treated as associate members of the church. They wanted to be full members. Mary Keleher's article, from the September/October 1985 Catholic Worker, expresses her frustration and resentment. This is not whingeing, it is righteous anger, coldly controlled and skilfully directed. Her article documents the price churchmen paid for not listening to the signs of the times.

If anyone had said to me three years ago that in three years time I would not want to go near a church, I would not have believed them, given my strong Catholic background. Now, I see no place in the church for me. In fact, efforts to work for social justice in the church have left me angry with men. The way women are seen and treated by the church is at the heart of my choice to work for social justice outside it, where women can participate comfortably. These are not the idle reflections of someone who has dabbled in church, with no feeling for gospel values or real effort to work within it. For ten years I taught natural family planning, including teaching the method with Mother Teresa's sisters in India.

A long-standing concern for the poor and social justice had come from my family. But I had seen this as separate to my connections with the church. The links between gospel values and my political beliefs were made a few years ago by a priest in the local parish. And indeed I had wanted these connections made, and felt I had to act on them. I became involved in Action for World Development, the local parish council, working within the parish and with other women to form a child care centre for women in the area, and studying scripture at a theological centre.

My experience has been that, in the church's words about women and its treatment of us, there is a fundamental and damaging contradiction.

The pre-Vatican II picture of Mary placed women on a pedestal. Yet women in the church are delegated to running the school canteen, arranging flowers for the altar, or mother's clubs. The real decisions, about finance, for example, are made by men. This picture of noble motherhood as an intrinsic good is not questioned or even allowed to be discussed. The injustice that a mother must work 24 hours a day at home, protecting the father from caring for a child in the middle of the night because *he has to work*, is not recognised. That a mother suffers the burden of guilt in believing that if she leaves her children they will be emotionally injured is ignored. Men rarely think *I've been a bad father*, while women would regularly think they have been *a bad mother*. As a mother of six, I don't want to be placed on a pedestal, out of sight of the real world and the real experiences of women as mothers.

The church reinforces the injustices which women experience. It puts down women who choose to work in the paid workforce. Children of women who work are seen as people in need of special care. The parish, while subscribing to the noble caricature, did not seem interested in women. I felt an overwhelming sense of oppression and powerlessness.

Sitting in mass, I'd resent the fact that a scripture reading which said something important about women's experiences, would be turned into 'gobbledygook' by the priest. This is to hold us in contempt. If the readings were about women, why couldn't a woman be asked to talk about them?

I felt the parish council on which I sat was a fraud, a rubber stamp. Attempts I made to stop things just going through were met with a hushed silence, as if I'd just said a four-letter word. To convince the parish to do anything, like set up a child care centre, the priest's values and language had to be used. He still had the power of veto.

Or again, after teaching family planning for ten years, I felt that we, as teachers, had a right to be consulted about the text books being written for us to use. I also objected to the way we were expected to toe the party line on moral teachings, such as about homosexuality and masturbation. Top theologians could not agree on these matters, I argued, so how could I go into a Catholic school and present a definitive position. My expertise, as a mother of six, was seen as in the physical side only. While I believe strongly that women's fertility should be controlled and understood, not altered, I couldn't buy the ideological rigidity that was expected. I was very hurt by my experiences when I made these views known. Although I had been loyal to the people involved in family planning for ten years, these people reacted rigidly to my concerns, and effectively wiped me. There was no loyalty in return.

I don't know what would need to change in the church to convince women like me to return. I am not optimistic, and think it will go on as it is. The crucial thing is that there would only be a place for me in the local church if the priest allowed it. It is not enough to be *let in*; it has to be on equal grounds. Changes in church language excluding women would have made me happy a few years ago. Now, it seems like just a token gesture to women, throwing us a bone. Married women at home are on the second-bottom rung of the church ladder. Single women are on the bottom.

Like many other disillusioned Catholics, I want to be part of a prayerful group where people care about each other. Along with my children, I meet with such a group for liturgy once a month.

The church does not seem relevant. At one stage, when youth home-lessness was a major issue in the local area, I went to mass hoping that the parish would do something. Instead I heard that the top priority for the sacrificial giving campaign for the next three years was to be paying off the church. I was angry about it, us worrying about a million dollars worth of real estate when there are kids with nowhere to live.

It was at that time that I responded by joining the parish council. Perhaps the most disturbing part of my experience as a woman in the local parish council was that incredible silence which greeted me when I raised these social justice issues. It was as if they were thinking *What is social justice; we just run the parish and the school.* It was as if we were on a different journey. To stay and fight now, again, would be impossible. There is too much to be done and too little support. There are other areas where I can work for social justice, and feel more comfortable doing it.

The journey I am on is a good journey — and I don't think I've gone astray — but I've finished part of it.

MIRIAM-ROSE UNGUNMERR-BAUMANN
Autobiographical reflections

Miriam-Rose Ungunmerr-Baumann's Stations of the Cross have become well known throughout Australia since their publication in a book in 1985. They marry a traditional Catholic form of prayer to Aboriginal art. Early in 1986 the Catholic Women's League, Darwin, invited her to speak at one of their meetings. A transcription of her talk, which preserves the personal cadences of her speech, was published in Nelen Yubu *for Spring 1986. The introductory sentences have been omitted here.* Nelen Yubu *(in the Nangikurrungurr language 'good way') explores ways of Christian commitment 'in continuity with ancestral traditions and in response to the conditions of living in modern technological Australia'.*

I was born in the bush in 1950 at Daly River, eight miles upstream from where the mission is now. My language is called Nangikurrungurr. I speak four other local languages.

I have been thinking over what I have learned from my parents and my group. It is summed up in the word 'culture'. I learned how to look out on my world, the country and the bush. I listened to the wonderful stories that told how everything came to be—hills, the waterholes, the river, the places of importance and the stories that went with them. My life was filled with beautiful stories. My people could not read. They did not write. They remembered and they told and they retold. Interest was always fresh, like new discovery. The countryside was somehow part of me and I was part of it; it was filled with named places and I came to learn so many of them. It was my home. It was me.

I watched my people preparing for ceremonies. We were deeply interested in all of them, even though we could not take part in all of them. Those we were involved in meant complete involvement of the whole group. I never felt alone in these ceremonies. Often now when I come to church I do feel alone. This worries me, because I know that as Christians we should never feel alone but wonderfully united.

I watched the men make our dugout canoes for fishing in the river and the billabongs. I watched them make their three-pronged wire-spears for spearing fish and their shovel spears for spearing kangaroos and wallabies, also at times for fighting. I watched them spearing fish at night with paperbark torches held high. I saw them diving to catch freshwater turtles in their bare hands.

I was shown how to follow tracks and challenge the cunning of the animals. Bush tucker was my natural food—bandicoots, blue-tongue lizards, rock pythons, porcupines. I waded into the billabongs with the women to gather waterlily stems and seeds. I watched the men catching duck and geese. I sat beside the women as they dug up yams, or went with them gathering the many kinds of berries and bush plums. I was taught to know what to look for at various times of the year. I learned to read the seasons.

I was shown how to tease out fibre from the 'marapan', palm tree, make string from it and from the string make dilly bags and fish nets.

Looking back I now realise how much influence my family and my group had in my early education, my cultural education. It also makes me realise how real and practical that education was. I learned by *doing*, and I *wanted* to do because I could see it was so important for my elders and for me. We were in the education process together. Education was naturally motivated. Education was part of life. Education was for living.

Looking back on these days of childhood I realise how independent we were. With very little difference, we lived as our people had lived for so many, many years before us. We had no house. We lived in a wurley. We had no money. Nature was our bank. We looked after its capital and drew on its interest. The new world that was beginning to invade us could fall to pieces about us, but we would go on. Our social ties were strong. The extended family was the human side of our world. It gave us support. We developed as people by interaction within that family.

I developed a love for the bush and especially for its quietness. I do believe that in quietness is man's very search for God. I began to experience in that quietness the great Spirit, the Father of us all. Today, often when I am out hunting, I am drawn to sit in the bush by myself, among the trees, on a hill or by a billabong or by the river and be simply in his Presence. To me this is the closest and dearest prayer.

The ceremonies brought us together on a religious group basis. They impressed on me the fact and the satisfaction of a communal worship, a worship in language and song and dance and action that is meaningful to all. I long for the day when our deep Aboriginal ceremonial instincts can find genuine expression in our Christian celebrations, when these celebrations will no longer be foreign but truly ours.

I was about five when I was taken under the care of my Uncle Joe Attawamba and my Auntie Nellie. The mission was just beginning at the Daly. Uncle Joe was police tracker at Daly River, working with Tas Fitzer. When Mrs Eileen Fitzer became seriously ill at the time of a big flood and there was no escape by road, Uncle Attawamba walked with record-breaking speed to Adelaide River township to ask for help. As a result, Fr Frank Flynn brought medical help up the river by boat and helped in the evacuation. Thanks to Uncle Attawamba, Mrs Eileen Fitzer is still with us today. After this incident Uncle Attawamba became the tracker at Adelaide River and, at various times, at Pine Creek and Mataranka. I went with him and attended school at each of these places.

When Auntie Nellie died, Uncle Attawamba retired and did light work for Mrs Fawcett at the Adelaide River Hotel. He sent me back to my mother at Daly River. I was about 14 years old. I continued my school work at the mission school under Sr Mary McGowan. At the age of 15 I was baptised by Fr Corry and made my First Communion five days later.

In 1968 I did a Teaching Assistants Course at Kormilda College. I was invited back again in 1971. At this time I became interested in art and painting. I began to develop my own particular form of symbolic art, as appears in my Stations of the Cross and other religious art expressions. Alan Marshall of *I Can Jump Puddles* asked me to illustrate his book *People of the Dreamtime* which I gladly did. I was also invited to a Christian artists conference in Bali. The theme of the conference was the 'Our Father'. As a basis for my contribution I used my Daly River pulpit design. The whole object of this symbolic drawing is to express the unity demanded by God, our common Father and Creator, and by his Son who brought about the new creation.

In 1972 and 1973 I taught as a teacher aid at the Daly River mission school. During these two years my interest in art developed further. It became an integral part of my teaching. I encouraged the children to express themselves—their inspirations, their perceptions, their aspirations, their joys, their ambitions, even their frustrations in colour and symbol. Symbols, true symbols, are such wonderful things. They draw on things deep down in you, expressing at times the almost inexpressible. They lend themselves to further and still further meaning. Aboriginal people are people of very deep feeling, and symbols are their deepest and favourite mode of expression.

In 1974, with a sponsorship from the commonwealth government, I joined the Primary Arts Branch of Victoria. This involved working with art teachers in primary schools throughout Victoria. At the same time I continued my prac. teaching in various schools throughout Victoria. After the completion of this year I was accredited as a fully qualified teacher, the first Aboriginal in the Northern Territory to be so.

In 1975 I returned to the Daly River school. During this year I met my future husband, Ken, who was contract building for Catholic missions. At the end of 1975 Ken was moving on. He told me he was 'looking for a wife' and 'would I be interested—three days to decide!' I decided in favour. At this time I accepted the job of art consultant with the Professional Services Branch of Northern Territory Education. It involved visiting all Territory schools as a consultant on Aboriginal art. In 1981 I taught at St John's College, Darwin. In 1982 I returned to the dearest place on earth, my country, the Daly.

After moving about among various schools I would make this observation: I found that non-Aboriginal children were deeply interested in and anxious to hear more about Aborigines and their way of life. I felt there was a great need far more Aboriginal teachers to work among non-Aboriginal school children.

Looking back over my comparatively short life, I am overcome by the suddenness of the deep changes that have come into our Aboriginal world from the time I was a child till now. Almost overnight there came citizenship, money, houses, supermarkets, transport, alcohol, missions, settlements, associations, councils, government interest and government policies, sometimes contradictory… etc. etc. etc. A new way of living came upon us. We had to make the unimaginable leap from being people 'of the beginning'— Aborigines—to people of these latest times. Europeans travelled a far, far slower road. They had hundreds of years to absorb change. I readily excuse them if they cannot understand what goes on inside us. However, I think, I beg that they should try to understand, be it ever so difficult, and be practically sympathetic. When outsiders do not show a spirit of understanding, do not try to understand, the position becomes, if it were possible, even worse.

In recent years the role of woman in Aboriginal society has become more and more prominent. Throughout Australia you will find it is the mother, very often the grandmother, who is struggling valiantly to hold the group together. The male, for the most part, has not found his role in the turmoil. The things that made him important, such as being leader of the ceremony, the protector, the supplier, the hunter, have gone or are fast disappearing. Sadly there has been no authentic replacement. The woman, the mother, continuing to hold the important role in the family, has lost less. The imbalance has been to the detriment of the family and the stability of the group.

Today I see my people caught in what I feel is a terrible whirlwind, tossed about and trapped in a circle of confusion, frustration, often despair, unable to escape. I myself have been thrown about by that whirlwind. I have felt the confusion, the fear, the helplessness. Yet, in some strange and wonderful way, God is, by degrees and ever so gently, lifting me out of the whirlwind. In addition, he has, through circumstances, asked me to assume a role not frequently taken on by an Aboriginal woman: as a teacher, as a spokeswoman, especially as president of an Aboriginal Council, I find myself trying to rescue my people from the whirlwind. Often I find in them a lack of response. They prefer the fear within the whirlwind to the fear of the unknown without. I have been accused by my own of not knowing my position as a woman. I have been told even of the danger I run of being 'sung' to death for decisions I make. Such threats affect me greatly. I am an Aboriginal. I have in me the deep, age-old fears of my people. Yet, thanks to God, in my Christian faith I have something that drives out fear. Such obstacles, fears, pains become a challenge to my faith and deepen it. They throw me closer to God, God who is love—love that drives out fear.

May my people find in God's love deepest confidence in their identity and the way to true development. May it support them in their struggles. May that same love produce among fellow Australians a spirit of understanding. Especially, may that love make us all one.

Let me conclude with a reference to my pulpit design. That design speaks about unity. The four fingers of the hand of Christ emerging from the wings of the Dove represent the four gospels going out to peoples of all cultures under the impulse of the Spirit to make all one in Christ, something

he so urgently wanted; a unity made rich by diversity. The ten command-
ments, under the wings of the Dove are fulfilled to perfection in the one
great unifying command to love God and God in neighbour. The cross at
the top and the circle for the nail wound represent the passion. We are all
redeemed and made one through the blood of Christ, bloodbrothers and
bloodsisters of him and children of a common Father. The circle in the
hand also represents the host, while the whole design is set within the
chalice. We are, in the words of St Paul, made one in one cup and one
bread. Let us pray for that unity. Let us do our best to live it.

BETTY BOND

A refugee story

Good writers are open to experience. Here the experience of Betty Bond, president of the St Vincent de Paul conference at the Medway migrant centre in Victoria, produces a fine piece of writing. Appearing in the March 1984 issue of The Holy Family Newsletter, *it scarcely needs any introduction. Betty Bond has also written a history of the St Vincent de Paul Society in Victoria.*

The couple did not want to leave their home. It wasn't a mansion, but it was clean and comfortable, with many little bits and pieces the man had made, or the woman had sewn. The worst thing of all, when the government ordered them out, was to leave behind the layette for the baby they were expecting.

They could only take absolute essentials, and hoped that it would not be too long before they returned. So the young mother packed linen for the birth, and prayed fervently that there would be some friend nearby to help her when the time came.

The man was angry, but quite helpless. he couldn't do a thing about it—they must go.

The journey was bad enough, but the worst thing was the coldness of people when they reached the end of the road. After travelling night and day, all they wanted was a place to sleep. Surely someone would take pity on a woman about to give birth.

But the people in the strange place didn't want to become involved. Some said, 'It's not *our* fault they're here. Let the government look after them!' Others complained, 'The town is full of their sort already, we must look after our own'. Still other townspeople muttered: 'How come they've got their own transport if they're so poor?'

The husband was becoming desperate, but at last the owner of a hotel took rough pity on them. Mind you, for a high price! He directed them to a run-down shelter at the back of his place, out of sight of his guests. Bad as it was, the couple were thankful to take it.

So the people in the town went about their business, eating and drinking and making money, and even saying their prayers, and because they lacked compassion, they missed out on a tremendous event. Because they begrudged a little of their plenty to the strangers, not one of them was present when Mary unpacked the swaddling clothes, and nobody saw Joseph cry with relief as he watered and fed the little donkey which had been his wife's transport. And later, when Jesus was born, it was shepherds from the fields, who knew what it was to be cold and hungry and powerless, who were summoned to share in the joy of the refugees.

ANNIE CANTWELL
Faces of suffering and joy

At the cutting edge of contemporary Catholicism, the Corpus Christi Community cares for homeless, often alcoholic men. Annie Cantwell's sentences are deliberately simple, so that they do not get in the way of the pain and concern. More than a mere description of a home for the homeless, her article takes a reader deep inside the life of one of the guests, Michael. This is honest, unsentimental writing without attitude. It becomes something out of the ordinary when Annie Cantwell goes on to explore the meaning of the life she shares with Michael. In its final paragraphs her article rises to a plateau from which she can observe universal meaning in the individual experience she has described. The article appeared in The Catholic Worker *for November/December 1985.*

It is easy for us to relate to joy and happiness because we long to rejoice. And yet suffering is so central to our lives. It is central to Christianity, central to a world of poverty, violence, injustice, it is central to our own human hearts. It is hard for us to see any meaning in suffering because suffering causes pain and it is natural for us to want to avoid it and to fear it. We use many ways of avoiding it, not only because it is painful, but because in a world that values power, control, and absence of suffering, suffering is regarded as failure. I work with homeless alcoholic men who teach me so much. They have known great suffering. Suffering which is cumulative.

Being with these men teaches me that what is deepest in the human heart is a desire to be loved and to love. It is through relationships where this can be expressed that I can learn to face the beauty and the suffering which is so much a part of me. They teach me that not only is it not helpful avoiding our inner suffering, but in facing who we are, our lives can be transformed—we can give our healing—we can be healed. It is in being who we are, that we can open ourselves to being loved and to love and find freedom.

The men who come to Corpus Christi Community have known great loss. They are men who are homeless, alcoholic, and frequently difficult to love. They are regarded, and regard themselves, as failures. They usually have no family ties, and find it difficult forming and maintaining intimate relationships. They are men who have done the rounds of institutions, and are physically handicapped by the effects of the alcohol.

They find it difficult accepting any sort of responsibility. Crushed by their life experiences they are passive and insecure. They are men who are frightened by their addiction and their power to be destructive.

Michael is 56 years of age. As a child he had a fragmented family life. His parents were poor and in response to multiple debt collectors moved from house to house. Friendships were severed in the moves. His father had a nervous disorder, and although intelligent and skilful found it difficult maintaining jobs. His mother was a gentle woman who was resilient, but also compliant. She worked hard at home trying to keep the family together but found it difficult coping with her husband's rages, particularly when things were bad. At these times Michael was often bashed by his father. His mother, feeling intimidated, would retreat, hoping peace would be restored. At various times the strain would become too much and Michael would be fostered out. In some of these families Michael felt stressed and misunderstood, other times he found the foster family joyful. But even at these times he felt some emotional reserve in preparation for the return home. Michael's stay within his own family varied, depending on the level of stress.

At 15 Michael was free to leave home and decided to go to the country. He longed for the fresh air, and the homeliness that country life promised. He settled in a small town in northern Victoria, working as a labourer on a farm. Although he enjoyed working with animals, he was soon restless. The other farm workers were much older and he felt lonely and isolated. There was no sense of family. The men lived in a small wooden dwelling together but kept to themselves. Usually on Saturday nights the men would go to the pub. Michael drank heavily to keep up with them and was often sick. Although he drifted on to other farms the pattern generally repeated itself. Finally at 20, feeling disillusioned, he returned to the city. He got another labouring job and would drink regularly with the other workers.

Two years after this he met Maree. She was a strong girl, who wanted to be a home-maker and have children. She seemed to provide the sort of stability that Michael craved. They fell in love and married. For a while things seemed to run smoothly. Michael maintained his job. Maree had three children, Tommy, David and Helen. It was some strain providing enough money but Michael took on an evening job to gain more money. However, stability was not to be maintained.

Life started to fall apart for Michael when one day at work he fell heavily and injured his back. He received some compensation and was retrenched. At the same time his beautiful baby daughter Helen was hospitalised and found to have a cerebral tumour. Although doctors performed several operations and battled to keep her alive, she died.

Michael still wasn't working. He felt inadequate, consumed by grief and unable to talk about it. Friends, feeling overwrought by the suffering, backed off. Michael felt consumed with hurt and loneliness. In compensation he drank heavily. Maree, herself grieving, and in need of love and support, felt enraged by Michael's behaviour and emotionally attacked him. This only increased Michael's drinking and depression and finally in desperation and despair he bashed Tommy. Maree packed up the children and left.

Michael drifted in and out of jobs. But he was full of grief, and felt no point in maintaining work. He had a succession of short-term relationships with women and one longer de facto relationship. However, he longed for family life, for Maree and the children. He continued to drink and relationships split up. He was hospitalised several times for his drinking and he tried rehabilitation centres, but any gain was short-term. He drifted into homeless men's shelters. He felt stripped of dignity, and overcome by the mess in his life, and he felt crushed by failure and pain. The release he found in a bottle was his main comfort. Often he would sleep out on the streets—several mates would join him, to laugh together and share their drink. Other times they would fight and he would end up alone. Michael saw several men die on the streets, including one mate who died after being bashed. Several times he was jailed for vagrancy, and for shop lifting. At 54 Michael agreed to try Corpus Christi Community.

Michael is encouraged to accept Corpus Christi Community as his home. We believe that what is most yearned for by the men, and what is most healing, is to give the men a sense of belonging, of dignity, a conviction that they are loved and able to love.

Hence Corpus Christi aims to build a community based on mutual respect and sharing in each other's lives. But this isn't achieved easily. So

often we fail. As in any place with people there are fights. There is a hierarchy of decision making. There is pettiness and jealousies. The men are not
always easy to be with. They have few social skills. They can be enormously
frustrating. And being with Michael is no exception. As well as these difficulties, there are the tensions and challenges that any sort of relationship of
intimacy involves. Let me explore this.

Sometimes I can delight in Michael. He has great sensitivity to nature. He can allow his spirit to dance. He rejoices at the flowers and the
birds. He loves telling me stories. He can be joyful. He expresses great
affection to animals. He yearns to be known and he tells me lurid stories
about his past and has me laughing at the freedom and the outrage of it. He
rejoices in being able to help and look after me.

Other times I can feel the destructiveness and the darkness inside
him. Sometimes he backs off from our relationship. He becomes jealous
and possessive. He does not want me to spend time with the other men
and is insensitive to the demands on me; he wants to control how often I'm
with him. He becomes crippled by fear and obsessive about small details.
Sometimes the hurt inside him becomes so intense that he goes out to
drink. Sometimes, quite unexpectedly and irrationally, he viciously attacks
me. At these times I become confused and hurt. On occasions I lash back at
him. Other times I can accept it as part of him.

And Michael calls me to feel what is inside my own heart. Even when
he is destructive, he helps me to know myself. He helps me to face how
dependent I am on being loved, how much I seek to control relationships
and rely on results. Also, how lost I feel when I am overcome by powerlessness and inadequacy. I need to be able to accept these, because when I fail
to recognise these feelings, then I become emotionally distant.

And feeling this bond, we can keep coming back to each other. I
come to know him and myself more deeply. There is quiet courage in the
way he comes back to me after a fight and says, 'I'm sorry Annie, let's start
again'. He helps me to feel my own weakness and failure and we grow
together. There is a mutual struggle against destructiveness, there is a mutual struggle to love. We can feel the richness between us and we can accept
each other. This means being able to let go of the barriers we place around
our hearts.

When I feel with him, I have to feel something that goes way beyond
the level of professional knowledge. I have to feel all the powerlessness, the

fragility, the weakness which is deep inside me. When I can, we can both let go. It releases in him a great gentleness. He can cry, he can express all the emotions that surround the loss. These feelings can swing backwards and forwards. There is guilt at the thought of not spending enough time with Helen, there is fear that she might have suffered, there is a terrible loneliness at the thought of her loss and there is anger that she wasn't able to live a full life. At another level too there seems to be an acceptance of her actual dying.

Homeless, alcoholic men can point to meaning in suffering. They show us the effects of cumulative loss. But they show us that what is central to the human heart is a desire to love and be loved. They help us to see that the barriers we place between ourselves and others are artificial, and that at any stage in our lives, regardless of the hurt we have experienced entering into relationships, where there is love there can be healing.

These men teach us that not only is the avoidance of suffering not constructive but that through its recognition our lives can be transformed. We can gain a sense of the Lord's great love for us. We can be ourselves. We can give ourselves to others and offer gentleness and compassion. We can love and be loved. In doing this we can feel hope and freedom for ourselves, for others and for our world.

KEVIN HART
God and Philosophy

Kevin Hart is Professor of English at Monash University, editor of
The Oxford Book of Australian Religious Verse *and a distinguished Australian poet. His interest in theological and philosophical
problems is long lasting. This short review of Eberhard Jüngel's* God
as the Mystery of the World *appeared in the September/October
1985 issue of the* Catholic Worker. *Its appearance here does duty
for the wealth of speculative writing which finds a home in journals
such as* Pacifica, *or* Australasian Catholic Record. *The lightness
and wit of Hart's opening paragraph make it feel at home in this
anthology. This is not some academic hack repeating a formula; this is
a person thinking.*

'**D**oes God exist?' and 'How do we talk of God so that we are
in fact talking of *God*?' These questions presume two ways
of conceiving God. In the first, God is seen as a mysterious
being, forever closed to our understanding by virtue of his absolute tran-
scendence of the world. This is the God of the Philosophers: a necessary,
perfect being summoned to prevent infinite regresses. And this is the God
of the Theologians: a creator conceived in the image of his creation. More
generally, this is the God in whom belief has become increasingly attenuated, first outside the church and then, just as surely, within. His demise is
well-known. Kant built a coffin, Feuerbach put on the lid, and Nietzsche
hammered in the nails. When we speak of God, Jüngel argues we do not in
fact speak of *God*, that is, of the God who reveals himself in the Word and
in the word. To do that, we need to conceive God otherwise: not as a
mystery above the world but as the mystery of the world.

For the Christian, the mystery of God is not first and foremost that
God's being is beyond human comprehension but rather that from the
cross he speaks to us of love. 'God is love' we are told in 1 John and Jüngel
tries to make sense of the tension between the confessions that God is love
and that this love speaks to us out of suffering. The book concerns two

deaths: the cultural death of the God of the Philosophers and the actual death of the Son of God. Atheism makes sense, Jüngel contends, as a response to the first death, but Christianity is a response to the second death. The question is, then, how can one talk of God so that one is talking of the God of Love and not a metaphysical entity?

The crucifixion of Jesus is regarded by Jüngel not only as the decisive event of his mission but also as the criterion for the proper understanding of his being the Christ. Without the humanity of God, as illuminated in Jesus, the very project of theology, of talking about God, would be impossible: theology must be grounded in the Christian's specific experience of faith in Jesus. Jüngel's approach is therefore diametrically opposed to the other main conception of theology at work within contemporary Protestantism, in which classical conceptions of God are removed from God in order to reveal the God in whom belief is possible. Whereas such an approach passes from a general theory of God to Christian faith, Jüngel works from specific faith in the crucified Jesus to a concept of God which claims universal validity.

Jüngel's most significant move in this direction, however, concerns the analogy between God and humanity. The classical solution to this problem acknowledges that all positive talk of God, whether scriptural or theological, necessarily frames God in human terms; and yet we know that such talk is a frame-up, for to represent God in language is at the same time to misrepresent him. Jüngel's theory is situated in this tradition of negative theology, but with an important difference.

Within classical negative theology the mystery of God is conceived in terms of his utterly transcendent mode of being. We can know God only by analogy, and 'mystery' is construed negatively. Jüngel, however, wishes to think God's mystery in a positive way, not in terms of how we *know* God but rather in terms of how we grasp God as love and respond to him in love. It is this relationship of love which, for Jüngel, gives content to the notion of God as the mystery of the world. We have, then, a mystery of love about which we can speak and indeed one of which we *must* speak; and it is this mystery which Jüngel privileges over the mystery of God's ineffable being.

While perhaps not drawing fully enough on the mystical tradition, and even overestimating the ease with which we can 'overcome metaphysics', *God as the Mystery of the World* makes a pointed contribution to contemporary theological debate. Whilst it does indeed illuminate the grounds of the dispute between theism and atheism, its argument in effect goes further. For Jüngel suggests that many Christians today believe more in a human conception of God than in the God who reveals himself in Jesus's death and resurrection, that when they experience a 'crisis of faith' they are only at the point of developing faith; and, if this is so, many of the faithful are closer to atheism than they might like to think.

JULIE MORRIS
ANDREA STRETTON

An Australian Creation according to Genesis

Each generation retells the old stories in its own way, often in pictures or music and sometimes in words. This retelling of the creation story from Genesis is a delight because of the accuracy of its details: macadamia nuts, black swans, flathead and wombats. When theologians talk at length about acculturation, this may be the sort of thing they have in mind. Certainly the example of Julie Morris and Andrea Stretton (not the same person as the SBS broadcaster) should encourage others to try their hand at this kind of retelling. The piece appeared in Compass *for Autumn/Winter 1988.*

In the beginning, when God created the land down under, the earth was formless and desolate. The ranging chaotic ocean that covered everything was engulfed in total darkness and the power of God was moving over the water. Then God commanded 'Let there be light' and light appeared. God was pleased with what he saw. Then he separated the light from the darkness and named the light 'Day' and the darkness 'Night'. Evening passed and morning came—that was the first day.

Then God commanded, 'Let there be a dome to divide the water and to keep it in two separate places', and it was done. So God made a dome and it separated the water under it from the water above it. He named the brilliant blue dome 'Sky'. Evening passed and morning came— that was the second day.

Then God commanded, 'Let the water below the sky come together in one place so that the land will appear', and it was done. He named the land Australia, and the water which had come together he named 'Sea' and formed the beaches, rocky coasts and the Barrier Reef. And God was pleased with what he saw. Then he commanded, 'Let Australia produce all kinds of plants, sugar cane and those that bear grain: hay, wheat, rice, and those that bear fruit: apples, strawberries, bananas, oranges, grapes and macadamia nuts'. So this land Australia produced all kinds of plants: the Wattle, Heath, Waratah, Cooktown Orchid, Sturt Pea, Kangaroo Paw, Banksia and Boab trees, the Blue Gum, Desert Rose and the Royal Bluebell. And God was pleased with what he saw. Evening passed and morning came—that was the third day.

Then God commanded, 'Let lights appear in the sky to separate day from night and show the time when days, years and religious festivals begin. The sun will shine, sometimes blaze, in the sky to give light to this lucky country'—and it was done. So God made the two larger lights, the sun to rule over the day and the moon to rule over the night; he also made the Milky Way and placed the Southern Cross in the sky to shine on the red earth and sandy beaches, to rule over the day and night and to separate light from darkness. And God was pleased with what he saw. Evening passed and morning came—that was the fourth day.

Then God commanded, 'Let the water be filled with many kinds of living beings and let the air be filled with birds: the kookaburra, cockatoos, galahs, magpies, emus, rosellas, jabiru, penguins and seagulls, the black swan and wedgetail eagle. God made the great sea creatures, the lobsters, crab, yabbies, blue jellyfish, trout, mackerel, snapper, flathead, shark, all kinds of creatures that live in the water and all kinds of birds. And God was pleased with what he saw. He blessed them all and told the creatures that live in the water to reproduce and to fill the sea and he told the birds to increase in number. Evening and morning came—that was the fifth day.

Then God commanded, 'Let the Australian earth produce all kinds of animal life, domestic and wild, large and small: kangaroo and platypus, wombat, koala, snakes, crocodiles, lizards, Tasmanian tiger, dingoes, witchetty grubs, brushtail possum, goanna'. So God made them all and he was pleased with what he saw. Then God said, 'And now we will make Aborigines, and they will be like us and resemble us. They will have power over the fish, the birds and all animals, domestic and wild, large and small. So God created these Australians, making them to be like himself. He created them male and female, blessed them and said, 'Have many children so that your descendants will live all over the country, in the desert regions, the bush, the coastal areas, and bring it under their control. I am putting you in charge of the fish, the birds and all the wild animals. I have provided all kinds of grain and all kinds of fruit for you to eat, but for all the wild animals and for all the birds I have provided grass, spinifex, saltbush and leafy plants like gum leaves'—and it was done. God looked at everything he had made and he was very pleased. Evening passed and morning came and it was the sixth day.

And so the whole of Australia was completed: the Nullarbor, Uluru, the Olgas, the Grampians, the deserts, the Blue Mountains and Flinders Ranges, Lake Pedder and the Kimberleys, tropical rainforests and snowy mountains.

By the seventh day God finished what he was doing and stopped working. He blessed the seventh day and set it apart as a special day because by that day he had completed his creation and stopped working. And that is how Australia came to be.

EUGENE D. STOCKTON
Coming home to our Land

Tjurunga is a journal of Benedictine history, theology and spirituality. In September 1988 the journal ran this article by a Sydney priest as a contribution to the Australian Bicentennial celebrations. It was different from the material usually found in Tjurunga. Father Stockton is a scripture scholar, archaeologist and a priest deeply involved in the Aboriginal ministry. In this article he describes his own personal journey along a way that brings all aspects of his life together. Intensely felt and deeply pondered, this article is a statement of belief by a remarkable man.

This is the story of one man's journey in search of his land. It is a journey shared with many other Australians for shorter or longer stretches of the road, a road along which may be seen travelling the spirit of our nation. Ours is a nation of boat people, who have crossed the sea at various times and landed on these shores, but who have yet to settle and find a home in this ancient continent—a people in search of a land.

I grew up in the Blue Mountains of New South Wales. Close to the village of Lawson there is a couple of square kilometres of mountains and valleys, gentle and unremarkable except to those attuned to the shy delights of the Central Blue Mountains. This I call *my country.* From the earliest years, while my mother was out working and my brothers at school, I found my playground in that bush. Every chance was taken to explore tracks, rock outcrops, caves, swamps and table tops, observing the ways of insects and birds, listening for sounds of animals which might fleetingly come into view, peering into clear pools to spot the motionless yabby. All these were my companions: I talked to them and felt their friendly response. The spirits of those who had lived here before also formed a friendly company, whose chatter was to be heard at times in falling waters, and they laid on me in turn to care for their country. Dreams are doomed to lift like mountain mists: one day my secret map of the area with its fanciful names came into the hands of my scornful brothers, and fantasy withered in acute mortification.

Curiosity awoke in the sunlight of a new day, with insatiable questionings into natural history. Books now told me about those rocks and plants and insects and animals, and the denizens of the bush lit up the words in books. Interest was stirred in the history of the Blue Mountains, the story of the road to the west opening up vast lands for grazing and farming, not to speak of the glamour of the gold rushes. I loved to hear stories of intrepid explorers, of pioneers settling lands beyond the reach of civilisation, of prospectors searching for hidden treasure. Australian art and literature, depicting man's battle with the bush, found a ready echo in the heart of a boy. Ours was a brave young nation coming to be in an old harsh continent. Pride was growing in Australia's endless stretches of pasture and crop land and in her unimaginable wealth of minerals. Long freight trains chugged past our home carrying the fruits of the land, much of it destined over long sea lanes to supply the needs of the world. Summer holidays brought the chance to work on farms—sheep, wheat, vegetables—playing a little part in the patriotic effort to make the land produce. Back in the mountains I set to clear scrub to make new pasture, feeling like a pioneer in modern times.

Closer contact with work in the bush also raised misgivings. The man on the land, or the company he managed for, did not always turn out to be so idealistic, rather greedy in fact. The country paid dearly for primary production in erosion, salination, forest reduction and in lost fertility—but it never occurred to me then that the original inhabitants had paid the greatest price of all. Later still I was to realise that we were not the benevolent providers to the world, but were competing with poorer countries to fill the same markets with primary products.

Still in my teens, I was to make first contact with Aborigines, though not yet in the flesh. I started to find stones in the Mountains which geology taught me did not belong there. So began a series of visits to the Australian Museum, where Fred McCarthy, then one of only two archaeologists in Australia, patiently taught me to identify Aboriginal stone artefacts. Fr Ernst Worms SAC, the German anthropologist, took me under his wing and guided me into archaeology, supervising amateur digs and insisting on reports for every site examined. Our first Cambridge archaeologists at Sydney University in the 1960s continued to direct me in serious excavation in the Blue Mountains. It was a thrill to romance that each worked stone I picked up had last been handled by black hands, and that it was as if we were shaking hands across the centuries.

By now a priest and lecturing in the Springwood seminary, I was sent in 1964 to study scripture in Jerusalem and Rome, later specialising in archaeology, with all the advantages the Middle East had to offer for field-work, for training in British excavation methods and for familiarisation with Old World prehistory and ancient history. I was to spend four years in the Holy Land and there, rather than amid the lush green of Europe, I felt at home in its stony arid hills, with their browns, reds and sunburnt greens, just as in my own country. One soon sensed the sacredness of the land, with hardly a square mile which did not possess a special memory in the Christian tradition.

Sadly that land too was in dispute. I found myself, as did many resident expatriates, siding with the Arabs. The Jews, a determined, modern people, whose claim lay in a shorter period of occupation in the distant past, and who were now more racially mixed than their Semitic forebears or opponents, had an advantage before the world in clever propaganda, widespread sympathy from wartime atrocities and in having as their sacred book one revered by Christian peoples. The world recognised the primacy of the land as sacred to its people over every other natural right, while ignoring that to the more religious Palestinians it was just as sacred. Standing on the border with a Palestinian companion one felt deeply the bitterness as he pointed out his father's orange grove another was picking, or his family's house and grounds where a Jewish woman was now pegging out the washing. All this was preparing me to understand Aboriginal feelings of being dispossessed of their land and sacred sites to make way for the more exploitative technology of a thrusting people.

After the bitter experience of the Six Day War I returned gratefully to a land of peace, where people could be seen walking about with relaxed carefree faces. It was good to be back among my own kind, my family and friends, in the security of my own home and in the welcome of my own country. It was to come back to the flurry of new academic activity, in the university and in the seminary, but also to a new and growing involvement as a priest with urban Aborigines, to whom I was appointed chaplain.

Miriam-Rose Ungunmerr-Baumann has succinctly caught the feel of being Aboriginal, to be

> overcome by the suddenness of the deep changes that have
> come into our Aboriginal world... Today I see my people

caught in what I feel is a terrible whirlwind, tossed about and trapped in a circle of confusion, frustration, often despair, unable to escape. I myself have been thrown about by that whirlwind. I have felt the confusion, the fear, the helplessness. Yet, in some strange and wonderful way, God is, by degrees, and ever so gently, lifting me out of the whirlwind (Address to Catholic Women's League, Darwin, 1986).

One day, walking a ridge top in the Blue Mountains, I had a strange experience. The westerly wind was blowing hard, and millions of gum leaves were rustling like the sound of countless people who had once lived there. Above this sound a voice seemed to say, 'Call my people', clearly meaning the original inhabitants. I replied, 'I cannot, I am a white man', but the voice persisted. 'You are neither black nor white. You are a voice in the desert and a voice has no colour.' It seemed sensible to check this message with an Aboriginal person, and my dear wise mentor, Eileen Lester, simply said: 'That is right'.

Archaeology seemed a useful tool to give a people pride in their past, so with this added incentive and fresh from the background of the Middle East I took up archaeology in earnest, with excavations in *my* Blue Mountains and in Central Australia, and with surveys in much of New South Wales, the Northern Territory and the Kimberleys.

Field work can never be purely academic. You wonder to yourself how you would feel camping at this site; how you might draw on the resources of its catchment area and how the local range would appear to hunter-gatherers. You learn to tell from different assemblages of stone tools the kind of activities carried out on each site. You begin to see the base camp as a kind of human focus for the surrounding country, and its hearth as the centering for all sorts of interactive human relations of the bands which camped there. You pick up a sense of what 'home' meant to these nomadic people. Sacred places begin to instil a primal awesomeness. The land becomes alive and peopled as you enter into the skin of its long-departed inhabitants.

Recent discoveries have shown Aboriginal presence near Perth and in outback NSW at around 40,000 years ago. Deep in the gravel quarries of the Nepean I found indisputable artefacts up to 47,000 years old. When people hear such figures can they image what that span of time really means? Can they realise that our race, Modern Man, was already in Australia before he was in Europe or Africa, and long before the Americas? Yet these figures are for certainly known human occupation in the *southern* half of the continent, so that the Aboriginal people must have arrived in the *north* long before then. The new science of molecular biology suggests that one component of the Aboriginal people branched off from the rest of the human family much earlier still. This means a race of people separated from the rest of mankind longer than any other, and so differing genetically and culturally from our own (or any other) far more than the differences between any two races on earth. It means that the Aboriginal race was in continuous occupation of their land, a continent at that, for a much longer time than any other people on earth, past or present.

By contrast to the Middle East, where you know the people whose site you are excavating had probably been overrun, exterminated, absorbed or dispersed by later arrivals, in Australia you have an eerie awareness that people represented by every level in your trench were ancestors to people still living in Australia, perhaps close by. Old World prehistory is the story of turbulent jostling between peoples, with conflict, advance and retreat, oppression and slavery, class struggle and exploitation, diffusion of new technologies and ideas, growing apparatus of power and social organisation—a story of development resulting from interaction, both violent and peaceful, between peoples. On present knowledge, during the extraordinary length of time that Aboriginal people were in Australia, they did not know war, subjection of one group by another or inequalities of wealth and power. The development of technologies, ideas, religion and social ordering were all, as far as we can tell, indigenous and internal, with few if any influences from outside. One is faced with a purity of race, culture and religion unparalleled in the rest of the world.

Yet neither was there stagnation. After the initial sea crossing from South East Asia—in itself an incredible feat and the earliest known for man—the new arrivals had to condition themselves to a whole new range of flora and fauna. Gradually the people multiplied and spread across the continent. My own excavations show their presence in the Blue Mountains at 22,000 years ago, about the same time as occupation in the desert of South Australia and in the bleak mountains of south-east Tasmania, so that by the height of the last Ice Age, Aborigines could be claimed to have occupied every ecological niche of Australia. The retreat of the Ice Age (hard enough in itself) raised sea levels by 150 metres, diminished the dry land mass by a fifth and brought on the most arid period in the human occupancy of Australia, at about 15,000 years ago. By 12,000 the Tasmanians were cut off by rising sea levels, never again to see another human being till European settlement, while New Guinea was separated from Australia by 8000 years ago.

After sea levels had settled at their present height 6000 years ago and the climate had greatly improved, the pace of developments quickened. Archaeological data show evidence of marked population growth, new technologies, improved methods of getting food, use of new resources and other cultural developments, including probably the elaborate religious and social structure which amazes anthropologists today. Interest in matters spiritual, however, is evidenced back to a great antiquity in the form of rock art, ochre painting, special burial practices and religiously significant ornamentation—some as old as or older than comparable finds elsewhere in the world. What the archaeological record cannot show, but can only be surmised from current ethnography, is that the long partnership between a land and its people had nurtured a spiritual attunedness of one to the other, to the point of becoming one.

Closer to European contact, constructional ingenuity was shown in planning and building large stone traps for fish and eel, permanent huts and even villages of stone houses. Aborigines were on the verge of sedentarisation, and the further technical developments which other societies at a similar stage had gone on to pursue, when Europeans sailed into Botany Bay.

What those Europeans met were a people who had never had durable contact or cultural exchange with any other people, the normal lot of other races, and, given the long isolation, a people more unlike them than any other race on earth. So began the severest and most unequal culture clash in the history of mankind. That story is too well known to need detailing here, and perhaps it is too soon to tell the story of how a people from the point of near extinction rallied in the 1950s and began to grow in numbers, in confidence, in leadership, in the ability to control their own lives and in the assertion of their spiritual ideals and practice. Certainly when I began to have sustained personal contact with Aborigines 20 years ago, I never dreamt of the vigour and growth that was to occur.

Central to that resurgence is the struggle for land rights. This has mystified Australians at large, who, aware of the many disadvantages besetting

Aborigines, supposed that the righting of these would surely take priority. Disturbing questions were raised in the minds of those who professed to be well-disposed to Aborigines. Why do they want so much land? Why should they thwart progress and development? Why do they not put the land they have to better use? The subject has been kept on the boil by government enquiries and legislation, by counter-propaganda of mining and agricultural interests and by successive claims before courts of law. The result is, in some quarters, a growing resentment to Aboriginal land claims, and in others a dawning awareness of what land means to Aborigines.

Australians are beginning to realise that for Aborigines it is not so much a case of land belonging to people as of people belonging to the land. Without being specific, they recognise an affinity and identity between land and people. With the chance of visiting many northern communities and of discussing the matter with friends in eastern states, I kept asking the question 'What does your land mean to you? How do you identify with your land?' The replies revealed a sense of identification very difficult to accommodate in European categories of thought. The western mind naturally and instinctively sees man as an entity separate from the land he walks on, superior to it in being an animate, sentient, intelligent, self-conscious person, and from there goes on to explore his links with the land. 'Identifying with the land' therefore becomes a metaphor for affection and emotional solidarity with the land, the only way two distinct concrete realities can be said to be identified.

The Aboriginal is speaking of real identity. He says simply and without qualification, 'I am the land'. For the Aboriginal, the land, together with its people, flora and fauna, and everything else it contains, is a corporate organic whole, at least as animate, sentient, intelligent and self-conscious as any of its organic parts. The best way I can find to understand how the Aboriginal relates to the land is as microcosm to macrocosm, for example, how a cell of my body relates to the whole of me. The cell is a living organism with the basic functions of life—breathing, feeding, growing, multiplying, moving, reacting to stimulus—and even with the characteristic individual stamp of my whole body in its DNA molecule. If asked who or what it was, a cell of my body could answer in my name.

To see a corroboree is not simply to see a performance in a bush setting, but, just as trees and all else spring from the earth, so the dance and song spring from the ground like the kicked-up dust, and the ground reverberates with its stamping. The man and the land are one in a single expression of song, and the man gives the land a voice to sing with. The overriding importance of the ceremony is that by it man is in communication with the whole and its respective components (of which he is one), by a land-rooted spirituality which celebrates and assures the well-being of all. While within the land the various orders of life enjoy a certain independence and autonomy in an egalitarian balance, each following its own law, man has a certain responsibility for the survival of the whole and of the respective species within it, both by rituals and management practices, so that for him the landscape is redolent with ethical values and dictates. Without being a hierarch, man serves the whole as a kind of priest. Land is the basis of his identity, life and spirituality.

The land is also the basis of his kinship, extending familial relationships beyond the family, the clan and the race to the whole and all its components. The land is his mother, in common with all other living beings, who are real brothers and sisters to him. Certainly he is born of a natural mother with a father's collaboration, but his origins are deeper still. He has pre-existed as a spirit child since the creative time of the Dreaming when his ancestral hero left both him and the spiritual seed of others who share his totem (human and *non*-human) in a certain place, which is the life-centre of his totem. Until such time as his natural mother passed by, allowed him to be incarnated in her womb.

The land is a sacred place, a spiritual entity. It is peopled not only by the spirit children and the spirits of the departed, but also by the ancestral spirits who gave form to the landscape and its denizens during the Dreaming and now rest at special places, the life-centres. It is not simply a landscape containing discreet locations known as sacred sites; the whole landscape is sacred, with varying degrees of sacredness throughout. As if they were superimposed on the physical contours of the land, those who know can perceive spiritual contours (like our weather maps). Each person has in his mind his own sacred map marking out not only places associated with personal and family memories, but also those of totemic interest to him, the travels and adventures of his Dreaming ancestor. So the spiritual map not only indicates spots where something happened during the creative time of the Dreaming, the resting place of the ancestor creator and the life-centres of the spirit children, but it is criss-crossed by lines marking the journeys of the totemic hero between camps and places of significant happenings. This is the map in stylised form which the old man will produce when he 'paints his Dreaming'. It is no wonder then that, as an Aboriginal travels through his country, it is alive to him with memories of events long ago and of recent happenings special to him, with awareness of spirits close at hand, both good and bad, and with the pulse of a living personality in the total landscape with which he is one.

The land is a sacrament, channelling the spiritual and conveying a message to those who are open to it. Sometimes I hear an Aboriginal describe his country as 'my Bible' or refer to developers as 'ripping a page out of my Bible'. For to an unlettered people, the land with all its special features associated with events of the Dreaming, kept alive by oral tradition in myths, ceremony and painting, is very concretely a record of creative events. As the Jew can designate his Bible as 'the Law', so too Aborigines have said to me 'the land is our Law', because the ancestral spirits in creating the existing form of the land and its inhabitants established a code of life and entrusted it to their descendants.

The land is home to the Aboriginal. The associations and feelings summed up in the English word 'home' loosely but fairly connote an Aboriginal's attitude to the range of territory he calls 'my country'. But the axiom that an Englishman's home is his castle suggests that for him home is a formidable defence structure within which to find comfort and security against others, while the surrounding estate further serves as a buffer to outsiders. On the contrary, for the Aboriginal, the whole estate without defences is the home, and, far from being formless, the sense of place and direction within it is created not by four walls but by focal points representing campsites occupied in turn throughout the year. So, in addition to a spiritual map the Aboriginal has in mind a domestic map. It tells him where to move to gather for his needs as the seasons turn. As home is pervaded by the sense of mother, so too the land is a bountiful mother offering variety in abundance, and the child of the land accepts unquestioningly what is offered. Not for him the single-minded persistence in pursuit of each resource which the European calls exploitation, but which he regards as rape. Further difference of mentality appears in the use of what the two peoples hold dear. While the European idolises his home-castle (and more recently his mobile defence unit, the car), he is dismayed by Aboriginal carelessness towards both. But the Aboriginal is equally dismayed by European carelessness for the land he calls home and mother.

The homelands (or out-station) movement is very instructive as to what land means to Aborigines. Over the last 15 years, hundreds of clans have quit the larger missions and reserves to resettle on their ancestral territories. The effort can only be described as sheer pioneering, with all the hardship which that entails, to establish an economically viable base with the minimal services that can be extended to isolated localities. But it is heartening to see the pride of these revitalised people. A man will proudly show you his crops and cattle, the house he has helped to build. Vegetables and poultry are mute testimony to discipline re-established over children. People speak of quiet, lack of alcohol, absence of pressures. Ceremonies have been revived. Here is a people with renewed control over their lives, a sense of direction and satisfaction, deriving strength for self-determination from their own land, where they camp once more in peace.

To describe the basic difference between the two views of land, one might say that whereas Europeans evaluate land by its resources or commercial potential, *Aborigines deem the land more important than any resource it contains.* If I were to analyse the chemical components of my body, and cost their value on the open market, it would amount to very little; yet those components, combined and infused with spirit to form the unique person I am, are together more valuable than their sum. When Shylock demanded, according to fair contract, his pound of flesh, it seemed a reasonable thing, except that he could not take the one without the life and integrity of the whole. In the face of rival demands for land, namely by developers and Aborigines, we see contrasted conflicting evaluations of land: the value of an exportable commodity it can yield or the value of a combination of components (including its people) which together make up a living entity imbued with Spirit and personality.

This growing awareness of how an Aboriginal stood to his country affected me profoundly and began to flow into a new and exciting spirituality, as I saw it also affecting others equally searching for the Spirit of the land. As a migrant people, we have yet to find our home. We do not have a song rising within us from the land, as other peoples closely linked to the soil have brought forth folk music which seems to be hewn from the forms of their land. All of us boat people, we have left other homelands and crossed the sea, but we stand on these shores as foreigners to this continent. To come home to Australia we have begun to feel the need of Aborigines: we need to share their feelings for this land, their traditions and their history, and (as far as our minds can grasp it) their spirituality for this country.

Before we have our own song to sing, we need a sense of sacred land and of sacred history, like the Jew and the Aboriginal. The history we often learned in school is hardly sacred: beginning with a British penal colony in 1788, it proceeds with the names of those who succeeded, with the conquest of nature (and man!) for monetary gain, with the development of primary and secondary industries, with the growth of commerce and trade and the interaction with worldwide trading blocs. This can read like the record of a business enterprise, 'Australia Incorporated'. It seems sterile and lifeless, laying bare the empty soul of a rootless people. It ignores the underside of our history, the story of most of our people, the 'little Australia' which has struggled, coped and survived.

Our nation is not simply the maturing of a British settlement, with a forgettable fringe of indigenous people and of exotic migrants. Around an Aboriginal core, we are fragments of peoples gathered from all around the globe, freed from some of the ancient hatreds which history has set between peoples in their ancestral lands. Perhaps on this sparse continent it is our destiny to make a new world. From a mix of traditions and out of the tragedies of history, both here and abroad, we might begin again with the ingredients of every human expression to rebuild in this land a new humankind. But as we set out to shape the dream of our future, let us remember our roots, which make us strong and lively.

I see our nation as a tree, a gum tree, tall, smooth-limbed and lightly leaved. Its roots reach out and draw goodness from soils throughout the earth, feeding through a single trunk to a rich canopy of branches, leaves, flowers and fruit. So, from many soils and climes we have come together, and as the living tips of the tree we are now spread out in the clean air and bright sunlight of a new world above. We own all our roots, not only those ancestral to each individual, but sincerely and warmly those which we share through our neighbours. One root, which is vital to the whole tree and all it bears, is the tap root which goes deep, deep down in the soil of Australia.

As we own our roots, we own the several stories that formed us, searching back our continuities into the past. As Christians we rightly see ourselves one with our spiritual forbears in the Bible. Even if our racial stock be different, the faith of ancestors has grafted us onto that of Abraham, and to us in him was the call first made:

> Go out from your country and your kindred and your
> father's house to the land I will show you.
> And I will make of you a great nation, and I will bless you
> and make your name great, so that you will be a blessing.
>
> Genesis 12:1–3

We have been travelling with Abraham ever since, setting out for the land God would show us. Our migrant fathers again heard that call. Again for them, what was foretold to the Jewish exiles has been repeated in our own sacred story with special fittingness:

> I will take you from the nations and gather you from all the countries
> and bring you into your own land.
> I will sprinkle clean water upon you and you shall be
> clean from all your uncleannesses…
> A new heart I will give you and a new spirit I will put within you;
> and I will take out of your flesh the heart of stone
> and give you a heart of flesh.
> And I will put my Spirit within you…
> And you shall dwell in the land I gave to your forerunners,
> and you shall be my people, and I will be your God.
>
> Ezekiel 36:2–28

Our Aboriginal forerunners too, though of different stock, are yet our spiritual forefathers, if we are willing to enter into and be grafted onto their spirit. Then we can read our story as the fuller history of human presence on this continent. We have been here 50,000 years or more. Over that immense span of time we have grown spiritually attuned to this land, so that in time the latecomer might learn from the first-born to revere her as mother. The sacred story of the firstcomer becomes the sacred story of the latecomer, awakening the sacred memory of the land so it becomes for both their Holy Land.

Let us learn from the first born what this land has to say to us. Let us learn like them to be alive to the creative Dreamtime that happened long ago and is happening still. Let us learn to celebrate creation, together, and to be tinglingly alert to all about us that is sacrament and ikon of our Father. Miriam-Rose Ungunmerr-Baumann spoke of the greatest gift her people have to offer their fellow Australians. It is *dadirri,* translated as 'inner, deep listening and quiet, still awareness'. It combines contemplation and patient waiting; it comes from deep inside and brings renewal, peace and wholeness.

Through Aboriginal spirituality I am led to a fresh understanding of God Three in-One. If land is seen as the sacrament of God the Father/Mother and Jesus is taken to be (as some Aboriginal Christians say) the great Dreamtime figure subsuming all others, another analogy for the Trinity can be found in the Land, Man and Song. The Land, stretching back to a timeless past, the principle of all else and the 'ground of our being', sustaining all, is the great parent, but expressing more the feminine traits of mother than other theological analogies allow. Man, the ultimate Dreamtime ancestor, susceptible to different forms both human and non-human, the one to whose likeness all are formed ('in him, through him and for him all things were created'), is distinct in person but one with the Land. With the Land he is timeless, but he has been drawn into time. The equally timeless Song of the Land-conjoint-with-Man, but breathed forth in time for us by Man, pervades the universe as a wind, renewing life and inspiration, drawing together all who hear in the dance of life.

Our Aboriginal forerunners teach us no more to battle and conquer nature, but to be one with her. Solidarity with natural creation, in joint yearning for fulfilment under the Spirit's impulse, was mysteriously described by St Paul (Romans 8:19-23):

> For the creation waits with eager longing for the revealing of
> the sons of God; for the creation was subjected to futility, not
> of its own will but by the will of him who subjected it in
> hope; because the creation itself will be set free from its
> bondage to decay and obtain the glorious liberty of the
> children of God. We know that the whole creation has been
> groaning in travail together until now; and not only the
> creation, but we ourselves, who have the first fruits of the
> Spirit, groan inwardly as we wait for adoption as sons, the
> redemption of our bodies.

St Paul, in a later vision, saw this fulfilment in the Body of Christ, which is growing to encompass creation under the headship of Christ (Ephesians 1:9–10, 22–23; Colossians 1:15–20):

> According to (God's) purpose which he set forth in Christ
> as a plan for the fullness of time,
> to bring to a head all things in him,
> things in heaven and things on earth.

The reign of God is close at hand as we begin to listen to the Spirit in the land and feel its inward groaning as our own.

Two years ago, Pope John Paul II came to us as God's messenger, and this he said to the Aboriginal people at Alice Springs:

> The church herself in Australia will not be fully the church that Jesus wants her to be until you have made your contribution to her life and until that contribution has been joyfully received by others.

In our capital he spoke to all Australians:

> Look, dear people of Australia, and behold this vast continent of yours! It is your home! The place of your joys and pains, your endeavours and your hopes! And for all of you, Australians, the Way to your Father's house passes through this land. Jesus Christ is this Way.

This land, through whom my Jesus-Way passes, is like Mary, a woman. I delight in her as a man delights in the woman he loves. She is also a mother, with whom I am one and in whom I have come to be, am formed and nurtured. If I was born in this land, by Aboriginal belief I have pre-existed here like them from the timeless Dreaming. So, on their reckoning, I have with them a common bond and common spiritual roots in this continent, although racial roots through my parents lie elsewhere. This land is a focus drawing me together with other Australians of diverse origins. We are becoming a single nation, not only by cohabiting one continent and sharing the economic, social and political opportunities she offers, but more deeply by sharing a spiritual link with the land, our mother, to whom we have at last come home.

So I return to my own country in the heart of the Blue Mountains. She receives me after many wanderings as she did in the innocence of my childhood. I speak to her and pick up her reply in the living things about me. For they and I, we are all alive with her life and infused with her Spirit, as her personality envelops us all. Perhaps it is true that, before I was incarnate in my mother's womb, I was already here as a spirit-child of the Mountains. So I sing our song, hers and mine.

ELAINE BRENNAN
The hills are alive

*In many different ways Catholicism works its way into peoples' lives
and links them together. Even those who have given up formal
commitment feel these connections and respond to them. Elaine
Brennan's charming vignette is thus about much more than a family
holiday picnic. Her light touches keep reminding the reader that the
holiday is Easter and the setting is Catholic. Though there have been
many changes since this series of Easter picnics began, the Brennan
family survives with its identity intact. The piece appeared in* The
Catholic Worker *for March 1985. Niall Brennan's 1961 memoirs,*
A Hoax Called Jones, *has more about his redoubtable wife, Elaine.*

Easter is always a crowded time for us. Years ago the church at
Warburton, which was tiny, used to be so crowded before the
Good Friday ceremonies that even the garden was full. People
from the whole wide world were building the Upper Yarra dam and all
decided to go to confession before 2.30 pm. And going up to kiss the cross
and to communion was a long, hot, sad struggle.

Our family comes home if they are within reach, and a lot of cleaning
up is done on Good Friday and Holy Saturday in readiness for Easter
Monday, which has drifted into being one of our traditions and seems to
have become part of some other families' traditions too. I think this because one year we didn't invite anybody and they all came just the same
time. That felt good.

It all started when our children were small—small and numerous—
and we hesitated to visit friends because they could well feel they were in
the middle of a swarm of bees. It seemed likely that other families had the
same problem. So we decided to invite all our friends with young families
to come to picnic on Easter Monday. We live in the hills, with plenty of
open space, so there was a hope parents might have time to talk to each
other while their shrieking young raced around like a flock of parrots.

The plan of the day hasn't changed much. First there is outdoor mass about midday. As the years went by small children made their First Communion, the child of one of the original small children was baptised. After mass the altar becomes a table again with the big barbecue behind it surrounded by people staking a claim of space for their sausages. Some people bring chairs and tables, some cups: it's the easiest way to entertain people I've come across. They do their own cooking, set up their own meals, cope with the children. Niall offers Land-Rover rides up the bush and round the top of the creek, someone leads a pony round with grinning children on it.

Now the parents of the original Easter Mondays are a lot greyer and their children bring children of their own. A lot of young people who have given up going to mass stay around and I remember their delight over the baptism and what Father Maguire had to say about it and about them.

Somehow a lot of things seem to go wrong or be particularly tiresome in Lent, and Easter Monday seems a trial to come. But the day itself is always great and after Easter things go well again—or feel as if they do.

A. J. HILL
Ruffy Church

Anthony Hill, a priest of the Sandhurst diocese, wrote this when he was a theological student. It appeared in the 1983 issue of Catholic Theological Review, *journal of Corpus Christi College, Clayton (Vic). This threnody for the past is a sharp reminder that change, in the church as elsewhere, comes at a cost. Hill quotes the work of early 20th century Irish historians, who saw devotion to the mass as the centrepiece of Irish Catholic resistance to oppression. He thus gives historical dimension to the intense experience of his family's church. Our Lady Help of Christians, Ruffy, was an 'Irish' church. This essay explains what that means. Throughout the essay the poet quoted is the bard of the Irish Australian Catholics, 'John O'Brien', parish priest of Narrandera (NSW), Monsignor Patrick Hartigan.*

Where do you begin to speak of the ritual and the symbol of something you've been brought up in? It would seem to me to be difficult to be objective in describing the rituals and symbols we lived out at Our Lady Help of Christians Church at Ruffy. As we lived, our rituals operated, and as we worshipped, our symbols tipped us into many different, other realities. We were rarely aware of them as such. We were not conscious of these things which were so rooted into our beings that every week they played upon us as we went to church in Ruffy.

It seems too technical to say that we were conditioned by our heritage, but we were. We, the church in Ruffy were, almost to a man, descendants of Irishmen who had brought their Irish faith and deposited it in a tiny corner of Australia, saw it flourish and adapt, and who passed it on to the next generation, who passed it on again until it came to mine and ended.

Our tiny corner of Australia has the laughable name of Ruffy, pronounced as it looks. To us it was never laughable. Much Australian literature uses a river or mountain or other geographical feature to situate its tale, such as the Murray, the Castlereagh, the Blue Mountains. For me it is the Ruffy Tablelands, and the names of some of the original selections such as 'Tarcombe', 'Strathearn', 'Habby's Howe' or 'Dropmore', which conjure up the vision of Ruffy for me. Our selection was named 'Innisfail', an ancient name for Ireland meaning 'Island of Destiny'. Innisfail is still standing, in fact it is still lived in by my cousins. It is still the brand name emblazoned on our wool bales.

Six miles from Innisfail is the township of Ruffy. Here, there are the Ruffy Public Hall, the burnt remains of the Ruffy Pub, Ruffy State School No. 2785, three houses, the Ruffy Fire Station, two street lights, and Our Lady Help of Christians Catholic Church which has been added to, converted, renovated and painted brown and which is now a weekend holiday house. I drive past the church quickly when I go that way. The memories of my last day there are bitter. A rusty key is all I have as a symbol of something very precious to me which has so much to do with that building the way it was.

One of my earliest memories of Sunday mass at the Ruffy church was a particularly cold day in July. The fog clung to the valleys but up in Highlands there had been enough snow to settle the night before, and, driving up to the church, (we didn't go to mass, we 'went to church') you could see the hills of Yarck, Gobur and Terip Terip blanketed in white. I remember being disappointed that the snow never seemed to settle for long in Ruffy. All we ever seemed to get were frosts, and while now I appreciate their beauty, then I hated the intense cold they brought with them. No cement paths to process upon to the church door, only frosty, wet grass, but that was a relief as you left the car and walked through the mud to get to the gate.

'Father' was clever; he drove his car into the churchyard and up to the door of the sacristy. I doubt that it ever occurred to us to do that; mud and wet grass were nothing. No one had a cemented backyard, just a 'good load of sand from Hughes's Creek'.

'Father' would be inside 'hearing confessions' in the fifteen minutes or so before mass, so the ladies would gather at the front door, the men under a great cypress tree and one or two Polish families would form a cluster away from the others. The children would play around the churchyard. The ladies spoke of the cold, of their families, of someone's new coat, and of everyone in the district. The men spoke of football when Euroa was the team to beat in the Warangah North-East League, of straying sheep and cattle, of the weather, of the summer to come. A season never really came in these conversations, in the sense that the men always spoke of the next one. In summer they spoke of autumn, in autumn they spoke of winter and so on.

> 'It's dry all right', said young O'Neill
> With which astute remark
> He squatted down upon his heel
> And chewed a piece of bark.
> And so around the chorus ran
> 'It's keepin' dry, no doubt'.
> 'We'll all be rooned', said Hanrahan,
> 'Before this year is out ...'
> In God's good time down came the rain
> 'There'll be bushfires for sure, me man,
> There will without a doubt;
> We'll all be rooned', said Hanrahan,
> 'Before this year is out'.

We weren't 'rooned' at all. Certainly droughts and bushfires and too much rain, cattle bloat, plagues of grass-hoppers and pea-mite, footrot and tetanus among our sheep set us back, but we weren't 'rooned'. No farmer ever left Ruffy because of hardship. The only reason to leave was in old age when some would retire to the town.

Just as I could get carried away reminiscing, and be called back to the present, so was the Ruffy folk's conversation stopped by the altar boy ringing the bell to summon them into mass.

Inside, the change of scene was dramatic. The chattering would stop at the door and silence became the order of this next hour. It used to strike me that simply entry into the church was also an entry into a different mood altogether. Now, when I think back it was a moment of withdrawal from one place to another. It was an entry into something very serious. In the days of the Tridentine mass this was especially so. We went from our casual conversations into a deeper reality. No one in Ruffy would have explained it that way, but the ringing of the bell took us from everyday life into something other.

In the porch the older men removed their hats and hung them on brass hat hooks. All reached for the brass holy water font and moved reverently toward *their* seats. And here again a symbol could be seen to operate. The women had entered first and taken their positions in the family's seat—

nearest the wall, then children, then men—nearest the aisle. But whereas the women, children and men came in as groups, inside there was a dispersal back into families.

Once again, no one would have been consciously aware of this. It seemed to happen as a matter of course. In some churches youths sit up the back, but no one sat in the back at Ruffy. This seems to be one of many things which gave Ruffy away as being an Irish church with Irish customs embedded into it.

Looking back into the history of the Irish church, we see an oppressed group unable to worship publicly, and, for fear of their oppressors, a group which had to worship silently. Cardinal Moran in 'The Catholics of Ireland Under the Penal Laws in the Eighteenth Century', speaks vividly of various priests and bishops who moved among their people in disguise for fear of the British. In those penal days the faithful who could not worship publicly turned to private worship in one another's homes. All of the community of a village would assemble at a designated home for eucharist.

> In some places opportunities for assisting at Mass were re-
> stricted, and the Holy See, in consequence, granted permission
> to have the holy sacrifice offered, with due reverence and
> solemnity in suitable places outside the churches. The rude
> altars that are still pointed out in the glens and lonely valleys
> of the diocese are memorials of those far off times when our
> fathers heard the Mass at the peril of their lives (J. Begley, *The
> Diocese of Limerick in the 16th and 17th Centuries*, London,
> 1927.).

> Mass is celebrated generally in a ditch, sheltered with a few
> bushes and sods, and sometimes in a cabin (Augustine OFM
> Cap, *Ireland's Loyalty to the Mass*, London, 1938.).

These designated places came to be known as the 'stations'.

None of the many volumes of Irish history available to me refers to the name 'stations', but Irish folk in Australia speak of them. The *New Catholic Encyclopaedia* gives three meanings to the term. Firstly, the Latin *statio* means a gathering at a fixed place for any fixed purpose; secondly, that 'to maintain a fast' and 'to maintain a station' came to be synonymous in the early church and, thirdly, that it was a military term referring to an outpost and the sentinels assigned to it. Each of these suggests some sense of liturgical gathering. In the fourth century, Ambrose seemed quite sure that the church had deliberately applied the military term to liturgical assemblies because Christians were the militia of Christ who gathered for prayerful vigil. In the early church with the increase in the number of churches in their jurisdiction bishops found reasons for celebrating the solemn liturgy now at one or other of these churches. As early as 386 AD there is an account of stational liturgies in the Holy Land.

Later, in establishing a cycle of stational visits, the bishops of Rome, like other bishops, saw in it an apt symbol of the unity of the shepherd with his flock. For although the whole diocesan community could not be present at the stational mass, this mass would still be the official diocesan liturgy and delegations would be on hand to represent the various city districts with their own clergy to minister to them.

In the following there can be seen a link with the above and the Irish situation in the eighteenth century:

> Not uncommonly one would come across men and women
> with their hands joined in prayer—having got the signal that
> Mass was begun and thus they united themselves in spirit with
> those who, afar off, were praying on bended knee …
> (Augustine, op. cit.).

I have gone into a fair bit of detail on this point as it seems that much of the ritual and symbol of the Ruffy church draws from the fact of it being Irish. Just as the illegal masses during penal days in Ireland were called the stational masses, the Ruffy church and other country churches were called 'stations'. The link seems too strong to dismiss. (I mention two below, Tangambalanga and Avenel, which were not Irish, but which were still designated 'stational'; this would reflect the predominance of Irish clergy during their beginnings.)

The situation of the Irish stations explains the dispersal into family units on entry into the Ruffy church. It had always been the done thing among our Irish fathers. In Ireland families would arrive at the stations together and would sit together for safety's sake during mass. Their fear of being discovered by traitors was strong.

Dad and Mum remember going to mass at Avenel 20 years ago and having to separate inside; men on one side and women on the other. The Avenel church was founded by German Catholics, and in this simple ritual, the difference of one church from another can be seen plainly. Just as the return to family seats spoke deeply to the Ruffy folk, so would the separation speak to the Avenel folk. It would not be evident on the surface but when in the different situation at Avenel, Mum recalls that she and Dad laughed nervously. This was an alien symbol which spoke only of separation to them.

I mentioned above that we did not 'go to mass', we 'went to church'. The entry into the church marked the beginning of mass. The arrival at the church was the beginning of the ritual of 'going to church'. It seemed as if mass was only a part of that broader ritual. It was as if mass was the liturgical action separate from 'going to church'. When I worked in Melbourne I went to mass every Sunday; I did not 'go to church'. If I had known the people with whom I worshipped in Melbourne, I would have felt as if I was 'going to church'. But 'going to church' could only be something I could do where I felt part of a community. No one would have described it that way in Ruffy but it was there. No one ever said 'church is starting, the bell's gone', it was 'mass is starting ...' Church began in those conversations outside, but at the same time those fifteen minutes or so before mass were not named. They just happened. I'm sure that people intentionally arrived early for that time together. It was part of the overall ritual of 'going to church'. Mass was therefore a kind of 'sub-ritual' as was the time beforehand. (I cannot remember ever arriving late for mass at Ruffy because we always got there early to talk.)

In many ways, 'going to church' was the central thing in our lives. During October, which was shearing time, we would have to watch the weather intensely, especially on Saturday. If it looked like rain, the sheep would have to be put in the shearing shed (and under it) on Saturday so we could have the time free to go to church. Some folk would 'pen-up' their sheep on Sunday morning, but most would rather be ruled by a kind of fate which said that if it was raining on Sunday morning the sheep would *have* to get wet because we couldn't miss mass. (I remember that we 'went to church' but at the same time, probably because of the simile, you couldn't 'miss mass'. This is a language notion, though the root of the fear of 'missing mass' was that of mortal sin.)

Before going on, I might mention the third stage, or the third 'sub-ritual'. For up to an hour after mass the people would stand outside and resume the conversations which had started before. Very rarely would the topic turn to mass. It seems now, looking back, that mass interrupted life. But it didn't interrupt rudely. The three sections of going to church flowed into each other. Silence fell as we walked through the door and remained until it was broken as we moved outside. No one spoke inside. The only noise was shoes on the bare boards as we stood, knelt and sat, and in summer, an occasional blowfly might have come in on someone's back and its buzz might rudely remind me of outside. But for the most part it was silent.

> Refuge it gave the weary heart,
> Beyond the sordid din
> And conflict of the crowded mart,
> One sweet, sequestered nook apart,
> Where all might enter in.

There was no reservation of the Blessed Sacrament, but no one would dare enter his seat or leave the church without a reverent genuflection. Until the latter days no man would go in without a tie and no woman or girl without a hat.

My family and a couple of others always sat on the right hand of the church. In front of us, blocking our view of the altar a little, was the plaster statue of Our Lady. It was this which determined on which side we would sit in any church. Those on the left sat looking at the Sacred Heart statue. (No matter what church we were in, we would always sit on 'Our Lady's side'. If her statue was on the left, in another church, after an initial disorientation, a seat would be found on her side.) And God help anyone who chose to sit in another family's seat! Nothing would be said (nothing ever was, inside) but disapproving looks in there spoke much more than mere words. That family could well have sat there every Sunday for 50 years.

The interior decor of the Ruffy church was almost unbelievable. The nave had a floor of unstained, smooth, knotted pine. The walls and ceiling were stained, knotted pine. Four brass bars stretched across the nave up near the ceiling from which hung kerosene lanterns for the few night masses. (How well I remember the hiss of Tilley lamps during night mission masses.) The sanctuary was the brightest pink. A window behind the altar was painted sky blue (panes and all). The altar was lighter pink. It must have seemed garish to outsiders, but it was our church and no one among the community ever thought to change the colours. There were possums in the ceiling and an enormous rabbit warren under the floor. But warts and all, it was our church and, though we saw rich splendid furnishings at other churches, it was Our Lady Help of Christians, Ruffy, that was ours.

Another element of Catholic faith in Ireland is pointed to by Fr Augustine, which seems to explain a little the simplicity of ornamentation in the Ruffy church resulting from the hard times of the penal days.

> Protestantism had at last discovered that the vigour of Catholicism did not depend on an appeal to the senses, and that it was not the stately church, the artistic altar, the beautiful flowers, nor yet the numerous lights that explained the fervour of Irish devotion. These things, at one time, were supposed to explain the fascination of the Catholic religion and the magic of the mass. But the enemies of our Faith saw now that the harassed Catholics flocked to the mud cabins as they had flocked to the churches, and bent as low before the rough altar as they had done before the work of art.

This is further emphasised by going to the nearest Catholic church to Ruffy, and that is eight miles away at Caveat. The Caveat church (Our Lady of Sorrows) is a station of the parish of Yea. But in sharp contrast to Ruffy's Irish simplicity, Caveat flaunts a certain Polish flare for embellishment. This little church was built by the Polish community of Terip Terip, Highlands, Gobur and Caveat, about the same time as Ruffy's. What strikes you first is the Crucifixion scene outside, complete with a circular picket fence. Further in is a stone grotto with Our Lady of Lourdes and St Bernadette. Then on a brick bell-tower is a giant mural of a Polish saint kneeling in a ploughed field. Inside above the altar is another mural of Our Lady of Sorrows.

When I first served mass at Ruffy, it was in English, and that was just as well because Latin was not on the syllabus of Ruffy State School. I learned to be an altar boy by being 'apprenticed' to someone growing too tall. He had learned from his brother who had learned from my father! For years after he was married, Dad was Ruffy's altar boy. He was the only one who knew the Latin responses. I can remember, when very young, watching from my seat as Dad knelt on the sanctuary, serving mass. It never occurred to me to be odd or out of place—there was no one else to do it.

The change to the vernacular and the new liturgy in the 1960s seemed to me to be accepted surprisingly well in the community. Everyone had a copy of the missal and was ready to join in, and the mass responses were quickly part and parcel of it all. Only one thing never really seemed to catch on: the Sign of Peace. It was embarrassing somehow and any priest who omitted it went up a notch in everyone's eyes. It seemed that mass and prayer were private. Anything which broke the inner silence of the people seemed to be a nuisance. It seemed to be one thing to join in the responses and pray together to God, but quite another to speak to each other, much less to shake hands during this solemn proceeding which began upon entry into the church. I wonder if it is stretching things too far when I take into account the fact that the people of Ruffy never sang during mass to suggest that, inside, faith was a very individual thing.

This seems to be a sweeping indictment, but I think that the uneasiness expressed in our attitude towards the Sign of Peace showed strongly that the mass was a place and time for individuals to pray. A sense of a community offering *with* the priest was not strong. There was no doubt that there was a sense of community but that belonged outside.

Only once in the last 15 or so years have I seen a stational church 'enjoy' the Sign of Peace. This was at St Francis' Church, Bethanga, high up in the Upper Murray. What first struck me as odd was that conversation did not end at the door. Then during the homily the priest asked a rhetorical question and got an answer from the congregation! 'I wouldn't reckon!' That would never have happened at Ruffy. Then the Sign of Peace came and I almost thought it wouldn't stop. The clue to this is once again in the backgrounds of the two churches. Tangambalanga is, once again, a Germanic establishment. There was no oppression, so no fear of expression whilst in mass.

There were three highlights in the liturgical year at the Ruffy church. There were Christmas, Easter, and an Episcopal Visitation. Often I feel that 'city people' look upon us as backward in some areas. I suggest here however that, while our lives may have lacked some of the sophistication of city people, they also lacked the complication that seemed to go with that. I remember being at a parish council meeting of a large parish a few years ago where discussion centred for a couple of hours on who would mow the lawns around the church for Christmas. In Ruffy the men would have decided in two minutes after mass whose sheep would be used! Ten head of sheep would cut the grass perfectly in a week before Christmas or Easter more thoroughly than any motor-mower and probably trim the lower branches of the trees as well.

The ladies were meticulous and constant in supplying flowers for the altar and the statues. Each took her turn to do this and to wash the altar linen, the alb, sweep out the church, dust the seats, lay out the vestments, and, in all seasons, find a few flowers for Sunday. I do remember one sore point, however. We gave generously to the Parish Planned Giving but when it came time to replace the raffia matting which ran up the aisle, we had to buy it ourselves. Euroa, with everything it had, always needed money. Out of this and many similar examples, the possessiveness we felt for our church grew very strong. Anything we had, we had done ourselves. When the church needed painting, the community painted it. When the cross fell off the roof, the community replaced it. When holy water ran out, the next one going to Euroa refilled the old whisky bottle that looked as if the original builder had left it behind.

A visit by the bishop was a great occasion. Bishop Stewart seemed to love Ruffy and when Ruffy folk see that in someone, they think a lot of him. I could never believe that on one episcopal visit he had gone swimming in the 'Boat Hole'. I often taunted my Methodist schoolmates with the jibe that my bishop had swum there when we went swimming from school.

During mass, the presence of the bishop did indeed 'galvanise' (in the sense of electrify) the Ruffy church.

> The bishop sat in Lordly state and purple cap sublime,
> And galvanised the old bush church at Confirmation time ...

It is hard to resist telling a story my father told me of just such an occasion. The bell had rung and the men were moving into the church. A certain gentleman, who was less than popular in the district, led the way, a mean man with a reputation for being hard. When he got to the door he saw the bishop sitting on the sanctuary giving that '... scornful look, as bishops sometimes do'. Before the rest of the farmers from Ruffy, he reached for the holy water font, on both knees, bowed low to the floor and blessed himself. Dad, following with one of Ruffy's more saintly men, had to contain himself as he heard in a whisper meant to be heard, 'Couldn't you just kick him, Jim?' I thought at first that this tale might reflect a little the uneasiness of the people with such a dignified visitor as Dr Stewart, but I rather think that it reflects the easy-going nature of the community. The

Ruffy folk were delighted with Bishop Stewart who preferred to shake hands rather than have his flock kiss his ring.

We were far enough away from the centre of the diocese not to be awed by its power. We knew we belonged to Sandhurst, but never thought much about it. The bishop was made as welcome as any 'strange' priest. (A priest on supply was always called a 'strange' priest; just a practical term.)

Most of our encounters with the Shepherds of Sandhurst had a comic twist to them. If I may digress for a moment, I wonder sometimes how seriously we took them. When Bishop Keville was once on a visit to Ruffy, he was driven out from Euroa by the parish priest. On the way they called at Innisfail. My grandfather noticed that the pane of glass in the priest's car on the passenger's side was missing, and because it was such a cold and wet day, he suggested to the priest that he might repair it then and there. My father told me that the reply of this secular priest who had no love of Augustinian bishops was in terms of: 'Leave it alone, Bill, and let his red face get a lot redder' (Expletives deleted).

One of the saddest days of my life was the day they auctioned the Ruffy church. I hadn't been inside it for three or four years, and it was hard for me to go to the auction. Inside, the people waited to begin. I had been the last altar boy in Ruffy and therefore one of the last to know where the key to the sacristy was hidden. So I went and retrieved it and pocketed it. I still have it, nearly ten years later. No one could really appreciate how much of a symbol that key is to me. If I may borrow the expression, 'a symbol tips you over into another reality'; just holding the Ruffy church key as if to unlock the door, sends me into enormous chasms of memories, and recalls to my mind so much. (It was the only key which could open the church. The front doors were bolted from the inside and the side door was nailed shut in latter years because the steps were rotting.) In a way, on that day the Ruffy church closed forever. I remember thinking how ironic it was that an outsider, the auctioneer, had to break a window to get into our church.

And inside it was dreadful. Our little, pink, wooden altar had been hacked to pieces to remove the tabernacle. The pedestals for Our Lady and the Sacred Heart, made lovingly a hundred years before out of kerosene crates, had been upended. The Stations of the Cross, the crucifix, the gleaming brass candlesticks, our chalice and tiny ciborium, the cruets, the linen and the vestments were all gone. Nothing much remained to say that the Lord had ever been present in any way in this little Church. (I use a capital 'C' here on purpose.)

The auction was insulting. The bidding opened at $8000 and someone cracked a joke about being given $8000 to pull it down and cart it away. There were very few Catholics there. The Methodists were out in full force, sitting in our seats and seeming to think to themselves many thoughts. Three miles away in Terip Terip, the brand new Uniting Church of St David exclaimed something that could not be heard because the Catholics chose not to attend this humiliation.

I sat for the last time ever in my family's seat. My father, his father and his father, had come from Innisfail every Sunday to sit here as a family and pray. I had sat here with my family every Sunday for nearly 20 years. From here I had gone to the altar rails to be crossed with ashes. From here I had gone to the altar rails to receive blessed palm. From here I had gone to the altar rails to make my First Communion. From here I had gone to kneel on the sanctuary to be confirmed. And from the sanctuary later I remember watching my family proudly watching me serve the mass for my community as they sat in the seat the Hills always sat in.

Perhaps the Catholic people of Ruffy can identify well with the Jews after the destruction of the temple. We can go to mass, and we do, at Longwood, but we can never 'go to church' in quite the same way again. We have no church to call our own. No one would really understand this, I doubt that anyone ever will.

I cannot capture the Ruffy church in an essay such as this, fully, it is/was a lived experience. Longwood has accepted us well, but we don't clean it or paint it. The church in Longwood is not ours, it belongs to the people of Longwood. The statues are different, there has always been electricity there. We will never hear the hiss of Tilley lamps or the smell of kerosene there at a night mission mass. There is no long grass to walk through, no brass hat hooks, no pink sanctuary, no sky-blue windows, no possums or rabbits, not even a fence to contain ten head of sheep. There is no snow to see in that low country and the frost doesn't settle there.

Under the auctioneer's hammer, a Church and a church ceased to be.

> Though high and grand cathedrals shine,
> To my mind grander still
> Is that wee church of knotted pine,
> That rampart on the outer line
> That stood upon the hill.

MORAG FRASER
A funeral in Mooroopna

*I have great personal affection for this piece. In the middle 1980s
some Melbourne Catholics got together to revive the old* Catholic
Worker. *They were a new generation, whereas the old CW people
had been through the great Depression and their paper showed it,
these Catholics had been through the highs and lows of Vatican II and
their paper showed it. The new* Catholic Worker *lasted for four or
five years. The last issue, in January 1989, reprinted some of the best
of past crops, including Morag Fraser's* A Funeral in Mooroopna. *I
had no idea who she was but I'd been reading her with pleasure in the
paper and recognised her as a fresh new talent in Australian Catholic
writing. I especially remembered this piece. So when they reprinted it,
I wrote to her to say how much I had liked her work and how I
hoped that she would go on writing. After posting the letter, I began to
worry: would I sound intrusive or like a condescending old goat? Such
are the disabilities of our postmodern times, when we have learnt to
stifle the candid responses of our hearts. But history proved that I was
right to chance making a fool of myself. For Morag Fraser went on to
become the editor of* Eureka Street. *Her early work was a warm-up
for her stellar performance on the most significant Catholic magazine
of our times.*

Eleven years of teaching accustom you to hearing the vocabulary of
racism. It's not as commonly used as are sexual expletives but it is,
amongst the Catholic school kids I've taught, more familiar and
frequent than blasphemy. At my first school (boys' Catholic secondary)
'wog' and 'Jew' were the 'preferred' epithets. There was little malice in their
abuse. Often it was part of friendly banter. A 'Jew' meant your mate who
wouldn't shout you a Wagon Wheel at the canteen or donate one of his
smokes to your nurtured addiction. And as a popular teacher or two sometimes used the term too, it was like a password into camaraderie, a cosy
private language which had lost touch with its reference source. But it
nonetheless reflected the insensitivity that enclaves can breed, and the

offensiveness of 'you Jew' came sharply into focus when a Jewish teacher joined our staff.

'Wog' was more frequently and less naively employed. Often it did refer directly and aggressively to the strangers 'out there', the people who were different, who filled a bus or a fruitshop (these were their typical stereotypes) with language you couldn't understand. 'Wog' didn't really mean Paul or Chris or Frank or Nick with whom you played footy. And Paul, Chris, Nick and Frank would themselves often claim immunity from inclusion.

I remember passing around a blank sheet of paper in one of my first classes (neophytes do foolish things) and asking the boys to list their names. There were earnest sons who printed Daniel Connell or Peter Dugan and a number of wits who became Alex Jesaulenko, Cecil B. de Mille or Maxwell Smart. But the one which struck me most was an emphatically texta'd *Chris—I am not a wog—di Pietro*. Chris was resolutely one of the boys and very popular. He was also an imaginative, lovable individual, bursting with exuberance. He should have been popular anywhere. But the price, at that stage of his life (he was 16) was public, almost exhibitionist repudiation of his Italian origin.

I now teach Catholic girls and quite a few are Greek, Italian or Lebanese, many second generation in Australia. Acceptance for them is often signified by phrases like *But you're blond. You can't be Italian—you* look *Australian*. They are received because they don't threaten group identity or solidarity.

There are very complex and subtle social mechanisms at work here, I know, and there are exceptions and variations. But nonetheless, amongst the students I've taught, it takes a brave girl or boy to assert cultural difference, to maintain individual identity.

Their reluctance is particularly striking in working classes. All kids write well about their families and about ritual occasions. It's familiar and rich territory. But I find that only after much prodding and encouragement will my Italian or Greek or Lebanese girls write with any telling detail about their families and rituals. And not because they are unhappy or ashamed or deprived. They simply assume that I, and their fellow students, will not be interested. When they do open up, and describe the specific traditions, the family structures, with their interplay and conflict, how they celebrate, what they eat, what presents they exchange, which uncles they like or dislike and why, their writing can be marvellous and often wryly perceptive about what happens to traditions and cultures wrenched into new contexts. But they will rarely initiate the revelation. And one can understand why there are pressing reasons for their diffidence: they want to be 'normal', accepted.

One can understand what is happening on both sides, in fact. Fear, insecurity, ignorance, inherited prejudice and the strong desire to be a member of the group underpin the racist behaviour I've seen from Australian students in Catholic schools. One 16-year-old girl who was *disgusted and outraged* that most of the people on the city bus she took during her work experience were Greek was not moved by unemployment statistics or economic considerations. She was angry because she felt suddenly and unexpectedly isolated.

And it is also fear, insecurity, sometimes prejudice, and the strong desire to merge into the group that inhibit and impoverish the expression of individuality, legitimate racial pride and cultural identity in young people whose origins lie beyond Australia and Britain. That identity may well be in transition. But you need to know who you are before you can grow into new roles.

The kids I've taught parrot the prevailing economic and political arguments about migration, multiculturalism, integration, as a flourish or a gloss over their deeper fears. Few of them are threatened seriously by the prospect of poverty or unemployment, so they adduce unemployment figures as a way of making respectable their resentment of difference.

What to do? You can't lecture kids into tolerance, let alone love. Shame is a treacherous springboard. But I think you can effectively value, acknowledge and nurture courage and confidence in individuals. I've known much timidity—some of it my own—but I've also come across, from time to time, brave people—students and teachers—who risked being themselves, being outsiders. And they are potent models. What follows is a brief account of one of them.

In April this year I went to a funeral in Mooroopna, a country town about 200 km north-east of Melbourne. It was the funeral of a young Indian Australian.

His name was Mark Patrao. He was 18 when he died.

Mark finished his HSC at Notre Dame College in Shepparton in 1984. This year he was studying nuclear medicine technology in Melbourne.

(Mark's father Renu, is a general practitioner in Mooroopna and Mark's grandfather, Stanley Patrao, has been a well-known medical figure in Bombay for most of his long life.) Just before Easter Mark was coming back from the Bruce Springsteen concert with the rest of the fifty thousand. Getting out of the tram he tripped and fell. He suffered extensive head injuries and consequent brain damage. He died just over a fortnight later.

Mark's funeral was held in St Mary's, Mooroopna, on a warm autumn Wednesday. St Mary's is a rather stark red brick church but for this occasion it was busily articulated with rows of metal chairs set outside to take the overflow. There were people everywhere. One of them was Mark's uncle who dispelled gloom by smiling his welcome and giving us practical parking instructions. Beethoven's Fifth was blaring through the loudspeaker system. It seemed more celebratory than solemn. And oddly appropriate at the funeral of a boy who first played the organ in his church at the age of seven. Not that Mark went in as an obtrusive prodigy. It happened that Father Maurice Duffy, who was then parish priest, heard Mark picking out a hymn tune by ear one night when he was sharing a meal with the Patraos. (The priests, lacking a housekeeper, often ate there and Father Duffy liked Indian food). He persuaded Mark to repeat his performance at mass on Sunday. Mark did so. And continued to play, for mass, at his school with his friends, in their bands for the next 11 years of his life. No one makes fun of such long-established skill.

Inside, St Mary's was white, sunlit and inviting. Mark's coffin was surrounded by his family (extended by relations who had flown out from India); there were school friends, his old HSC classmates, people from the town, friends of all ages, nationalities and religions, from Melbourne, from the country, from Shepparton, from interstate. I sat with my Australian Catholic mother and my Scots Presbyterian father, all three of us gradually realising that we were with Indian Catholics, Hindus, with atheists, with Italians, Irish, Australians, with women wearing saris, schoolgirls in short summer uniforms and young men in jackets and carefully pressed slacks. The differences between us all were visually expressed, remarkable and completely irrelevant.

What we were all there together to do was to celebrate and to commemorate the life of a young man who had been unobtrusive but extraordinary. I don't know where Mark Patrao found the courage to be himself and live out that self here in Australia, but clearly he did. The people who spoke about him were not conventionally eulogising. They spoke with the conviction that comes from experience. Father Duffy flew down from Queensland to concelebrate and to speak about Mark, whom he had known for ten years. Maurice Duffy is a huge man and he takes risks. He spoke about Jesus Christ and about Mark Patrao and about the way these two young men had challenged him and had altered his life.

Afterwards, in the Patrao's kitchen, we were talking to three of Mark's schoolmates. One of them said to my mother, *You know, what Duff said about Mark—it was true. He got him right. He was like that.* Australian boys don't go in much for hyperbole. And these three were neither envious nor sentimental. Mark had challenged and enabled them too.

Mooroopna is a friendly town. After the funeral, tea and cakes were laid on by the local Mother's Club. Earlier someone had just appeared to mow the lawns. As we pulled up onto the nature strip outside the Patrao's house a vivacious Italian lady called Bruna Ryan greeted my mother and father with an invitation to stay at her place. She'd put clean sheets on the double bed the night before in expectation. In the Patrao's backyard people talked, about Mark, about the children playing round the laden trestle tables, about Indian politics, about Father Duffy's words, about the way this big Australian priest had been able to cherish and proclaim the integrity and determination of an Indian boy he loved.

Mark Patrao was a good scholar and something of a businessman. He paid his own way around the world at 14 and his savings have now endowed a memorial scholarship at St Mary's School. He was also a fine golfer (no mean achievement for a boy who lost one eye when he was 12 months old.) The Mooroopna Golf Club now boasts the Mark Patrao Memorial Trophy, a testimony to Mark's sportsmanship and his generous nature.

Mark is buried in Mooroopna's cemetery, a large, open Australian bush space fringed by arching gums and, oddly, but fittingly, great, exotic, wholly naturalised palms.

KARIN DONALDSON

The first letter of Rebecca of Bethany to the Western Church

When I first read this article I mistakenly thought that Karin Donaldson might be Aboriginal. I made this mistake because the end of the piece carries a note, 'I first heard that Bethany was probably a shanty town via Ted Kennedy', and Father Kennedy is the pastor of Redfern, where Sydney Aborigines live. Donaldson's Letter retells the Martha/Mary/Lazarus in Bethany story from the gospel in terms of modern Australian Aborigines. Told in simple language, it can catch the reader off guard. There are more 'letters of Rebecca to the Western Church', which may soon be appearing as a book. This article was in the December 1986 issue of Bread and Wine, *a devotional magazine produced by the Blessed Sacrament Fathers.*

reetings and Peace to you.

Since you have asked for an account of how we women
came to be involved with Jesus, I have decided to write
something of my own memories and impressions of him;
and also to tell you of some of the thoughts us women who
knew him came up with when we talked about him
together. In order to do this as clearly as I can, I have decided
to write you a series of letters, and in each of these to
recall one impression.

I should explain to you, from the start,
that ours is a shanty town,
and we are the people-of-no-account who live there,
enough removed from Jerusalem not to offend
the eyes and nostrils of the religious.

We live close together here,
little dusty tracks between our humpies,
kids and dogs everywhere, old people sitting in the sun,
smoke rising from fires.
Not much privacy, inside or out.
But Jesus seems to like us, and to like our shanty town.
Bethany, we call it.

It might surprise you that Jesus took up residence
among the likes of us; in fact, built himself a lean-to
behind the shack where Martha, Lazarus and Mary lived,
so he could come back here to rest
after his long trips around on foot.
And there was a little hill nearby where he used to go
when he wanted to be alone to pray.
We got used to him. He became like one of us.

You must know that among our sort of people
life is hard-lived. We can't afford to be religious.
I mean in the sense of being scrupulous.
Because we are the people who are lucky to get *any* food,
we can't afford to be fussy about how 'clean' it is.
And we are the people who get irreligious diseases:
things the priests at the Temple say make us unclean
and unacceptable to God.

Well—so be it; we are ' unclean'
… or if we are not, then our relations or neighbours are,
and how could we turn away from those
who have been with us all our lives?
So we are all unclean and irreligious together,
and we live by a kind of sharing and caring
… and to the religious we are a stink and a scandal.

Jesus is like us: he takes no notice
of who is supposed to be 'clean' or 'unclean'.
We are all sisters and brothers; everyone knows everyone
and that's all there is to it.

I can't honestly say that I was a real disciple
at the time of that week of Jesus's passion;
but I was curious, amazed, and very drawn to him.
He spoke of another way
—a way to live in freedom and justice and peace and love—
and it sounded too wonderful to be true
and it sounded scary.

I say it sounded wonderful because his way
eliminated all oppression.
He spoke seriously, solemnly and gladly
about the last being first
—once I heard him pray out loud in a public place
moved almost to tears of joy, as if the words
were torn from him: 'Thank you, Father,
for hiding things from the educated religious toffs
and revealing them to the little ones'.

It was good news to the likes of us.
We knew who 'the last' were! And it blew our minds
that our type should be first in the eyes of God.
We knew by experience how great
the people-of-least-account can be, the poorest of us poor.
Well, Jesus kind of confirmed and underlined
what we really knew was true, but what the Status Quo religious
thought was sacrilegious and beyond redemption.
Jesus and the Status Quo didn't see eye to eye on much.
I often noticed that.
And whereas the Status Quo left us to rot,
Jesus invited us towards fuller life.

And what Jesus said was wonderful for us women
—he took it for granted that we had *minds*,
he *conversed* with us; he invited us to be disciples
on equal terms with men.
All this is unheard of in the history of our people.
And, again, it blew our minds and made us realise
how deep was our thirst to know God
and how deep was our thirst to know our full humanity.

But what Jesus said was scary, too.
Because it was easy to see he was on a collision course
with the Powers That Be.
He wasn't naive; he was quite clear-sighted about it.
He once said 'people who want to be my disciples
must live in a way that will probably result in
their public execution'.
Stark, blunt words. He meant it.
So a serious commitment as a disciple of Jesus
was really a step towards becoming an outlaw.

Not just any kind of outlaw:
an Enemy of The State and of Respectable Religion.
Well, us-fellas in Bethany are already outlaws in a way.
Outlaws-for-no-fault-of-our-own.
But a step towards Jesus would be a step
towards a more active kind of lawlessness.
Outlaws by choice-and-belief.
Strewth. As if we didn't have enough burdening us already.
But Jesus kept inviting us to try his 'burden' for size,
and see if it wasn't the lightest thing we'd ever shouldered.
He himself carried the looming threat
of his own probable execution with extraordinary sanity.
He lived as if he had been caught up
in a truth and a reality that left everything else for dead,
and he was inviting us to get caught in it too.

And that's what I say—it was wonderful and it was scary
and when I tried to think it out,
I couldn't really decide what to do—
but the events of Passion week
took the decision out of my head and into my heart.
Those Galilean fishermen used to joke
that they'd fallen for Jesus 'hook, line and sinker'.
Well, that's what happened to me and my old man—
our defences went down and we found ourselves in free fall.

ROSEMARY CRUMLIN
Spirit in story

One of the marks of being Catholic, especially in these times, is that you tell your faith in story. So when Rosemary Crumlin wrote about an exhibition of Aboriginal Christian art she had co-curated at the High Court of Australia, it was natural that she should do it as story. Her article, in the first number of Eureka Street, *in March 1991, tells how she was asked to take responsibility for the exhibition and how she set about finding possible exhibits. The article shifts pace when she finds herself in the Central Desert in 49-degree heat and ready to give up the search for more. A nun at Turkey Creek persuades her to come for a visit; and there she discovers what she calls knockout works of art, which she judges to be the equal of the greatest works of Western religious art. Rosemary Crumlin is the historian of the Blake Prize for Religious Art. In 1988 she curated the epochal* Images of Religion in Australian Art *show at the National Gallery of Victoria. The catalogue of this exhibition has become the standard text.*

Would you be interested in curating an exhibition of Aboriginal Christian art at the High Court? The question came from Frank Brennan, director of Uniya (the Jesuit research and social action agency). Frank was keen that Aboriginal people should have a presence at the World Council of Churches Assembly, and he believed that the best way for this to be achieved was through Aboriginal art.

My first instinct was to say, 'Hmm, no, I don't think so', because all the Aboriginal Christian art I had seen was kitsch—very bad—and I didn't want to be involved in that. So I delayed, talked to friends, including directors of Aboriginal art galleries. One, Gabrielle Pizzi, offered the crucial encouragement: 'I think you should do it, and do it really tightly. That could be a great service to Aboriginal people'. By 'tightly' she meant 'professionally', not accepting anything that wasn't first rate.

So I negotiated with Frank. My co-curator for the exhibition was Anthony Waldegrave-Knight, a friend and a long-time collector of Aboriginal art. Anthony and I proposed that the exhibition should comprise traditional spiritual works. If we found anything good enough that was also Christian—re-thought Christianity rather than cloned—we would include that as well. As curators we agreed on three criteria. First, we said that the works should be able to stand alongside the best in world art. That was a very controversial criterion to set up in this context. The second thing we insisted on was that the pieces would have to communicate an immediacy of spirituality, touching something deep. Finally, we would omit paintings that had already been shown frequently. That wasn't a severe restriction because there is just so much work available, mostly dating from the 1970s, and we had access to the best collections throughout the country, including the Holmes à Court collection of recent urban works.

Our first journey into the outback was full of adventure, incredible 49-degree heat, and quite a lot of disillusion. You see, part of the process involved visiting remote Aboriginal communities to see whether we could discover any art that gave evidence that people were re-thinking Christianity in their own symbolic system. And what Christian art we did find was often as bad as I'd expected.

But at Balgo, in the Central Desert, we came across some huge wall-hangings and panels rolled up in the church the people there use for liturgies. I knew we were at the edge of something. But the heat was terrible and Anthony and I and even Frank (who looks like God, walking around in his hat) thought we'd had enough. It wouldn't have taken much to persuade us to omit Turkey Creek from our itinerary.

I rang Sister Clare Ahern at Turkey Creek, admitting to some hesitation. Her reaction was unambiguous: 'I think you should have come here first'. So we caught the little mail plane to Turkey Creek and arrived at the Merilingki Centre.

There, on the walls, was what we had been looking for. Startling! It was just like being bombed right out of your mind—absolutely knockout works from the people of the Warmun Community. But particularly astonishing were those of Hector Sundaloo, George Mung and Paddy Williams. These three had been Christians from way back, and now, in their late fifties or early sixties, which is quite old for Aboriginal people, they are the unmistakable community leaders. Hector is regarded as a *ngapuny* man, a man of God.

There were many paintings we might have taken from Turkey Creek, all of them done not as an artist would paint in a studio but as part of liturgy, done for use.

George Mung had carved a statue out of a piece of tree, a work of extraordinary beauty. Here it was, sitting on top of a hot-water system. About a metre high, it is an Aboriginal woman, a Madonna, pregnant with a man-child who stands in a shield just below her heart, his feet extended and his hands tipping the edges of the shield. It's almost like the image you get in the Leonardo drawing, but also like a Russian icon (which George Mung could never have seen). The woman's body is painted with the paint reserved to young Aboriginal women before they have children. Accompanying her is a carved wooden bird, because Aboriginal people in this area believed in the holy spirit long before Christianity came. They believe that each person is accompanied through life by a holy spirit, male for male and female for female.

This work of George's would take its place, I believe, beside the great sculptures in the history of art. It is as moving as the carvings at Chartres, as great as the Germaine Richier crucifix in the church at Assy or the great Lipschitz sculpture at Iona. It is incredibly moving.

This image alone raises major questions, as did the whole Turkey Creek experience. The art would be worth millions of dollars to a collector. It is not well-known as yet. I wondered, what if we take a sculpture like George's and show it to the world? What happens to the community? We spoke of this together with the people, backwards and forwards. Our argument was that this work of theirs no longer belonged just in that little group. The world is entitled to its greatness. Not that the people expressed it like that themselves. George Mung said simply (of his sculpture), 'You take it. You take it. I'll do another one'. Never was it so clear how different was his sense of time, value and ego from that of European Australians.

So that is how the exhibition got started. I think it will be one of the most important exhibitions of Aboriginal art ever. It will break stereotypes. A lot of people think Aboriginal art is about dots and circles on canvas. In that they are really just thinking of the Central Desert and what has happened with Central Desert art. In fact, Aboriginal art differs in each part of the country and has its own local tradition.

What you have are people with a highly developed sense of vision, and because their languages have not been written down until now, their eyesight and sense of story—their visual and oral traditions—are enormously well-developed. That will change, of course; the young people's eyesight will not be as finely tuned as the elders', nor their psyche as captivated by story.

Two of the Turkey Creek paintings exemplify that outer and inner vision. When I asked Hector, the painter, about one, he explained in a softish voice (he's a big, tall man): 'This is the young Joseph and the young Mary before they came together'. Since, in the tradition of that area, they would not be able to speak to each other, each is seen to have a holy spirit, and so their spirits can commune. It is a marvellous image.

On my return to Turkey Creek to collect the paintings, the people invited me to an adult baptism. Though a priest spoke the words, it was in fact Hector, regarded by the community as their own *ngapuny* man, together with the elders and the community itself, who performed the ceremony. We discovered something from that: the second criterion Anthony and I had set ourselves—a sense of immediate spirituality—meant that the paintings in the exhibition have all been done by an older man or an older woman, since it is they who have the law. For Aboriginal people, art is valid and good if it truthfully tells a story, and if the story is told by someone with the required authority.

I was struck by something Salman Rushdie said in an interview shown last November. Rushdie claimed that he couldn't imagine a world without story. I feel that very strongly myself. It reminded me that those who do not understand story or its importance will never understand Aboriginal art. Nor can anyone who undervalues symbol find a way into the art.

This exhibition presents connections rather than depictions—which is appropriate since art's role is not to describe or define but to explore and communicate. Because the work is symbolic, each person viewing it will see differently. Nor does the exhibition provide a definitive understanding of Aboriginal spirituality. Spiritualities vary among Aboriginal people of different areas and the diversity and complexity will be quickly apparent.

The exhibition will not be uncontroversial. There are many who argue that we shouldn't bring in Christian imagery. But the reality is that it is there. We haven't forced it. We have used art which is Christian because the historical reality is that many Aboriginal people are Christian and manage to live comfortably in both worlds. It is also true that many live in discomfort and that the churches have been very oppressive. They are more enlightened now. The other reality is that this is great art and that is our reason for showing it.

I hope people will go out from the exhibition thinking how wonderful Aboriginal art is, that it can speak across boundaries. But I would also hope that people who see this art in Canberra or in another capital city will return after a first visit to sit in front of one or other particular work and see what happens to them in the face of it. The exhibition is too rich for one situation. For visitors, as for the curators, it could be the beginning of a journey of discovery.

There has been so much uncertainty on the way through. So much work. But I think it has all been worthwhile. Time will tell.

FRANK FLETCHER MSC
No exit

Father Frank Fletcher is a Missionary of the Sacred Heart who teaches theology at St Paul's Seminary, Kensington (NSW). He is also a key player in the Sydney Aboriginal Catholic ministry. Theology and life come together in this ministry. You can see that happening in this personal reflection on the death of Alice Dixon, founder of the Watch Committee for Aborigines in Custody. It appeared in the monthly National Outlook, *April 1993.*

In years of ministering among Aboriginal people, I have come to know a number of committed women, pillars of strength for their sisters and brothers. In Alice Dixon, I sense the plight of these women I know. She is a symbol.

But I mourn Alice for herself. My meeting her (only once) was a tangible grace. We talked, shared, prayed. I felt the flow of pain inside her. We embraced in farewell with moist eyes.

Like the Nungas of South Australia, I was shattered at her death by her own hand.

We met at the World Council of Churches' Assembly in Canberra in 1991. I was assigned by the Aboriginal Office to assist 40 Aboriginal persons from around the country who had been invited to represent their people, organisations, churches. Alice was a devout Lutheran.

She told me the story of her son, Kingsley, who died in gaol, January 1988. As I recall it, he was a religious young man, had the scriptures with him, was to be freed in a comparatively short time, was in good spirits when visited by his family. To them his suicide made no sense.

He was the first of the 99 deaths in custody investigated by the Royal Commission. The Commission judged the police inquiry into his death defective. Indeed, this judgement brought the only charge that arose from the whole Deaths in Custody commission —a $50 fine for one policeman.

However the Commission confirmed the finding that Kingsley had died by his own hand. Yet it stuck bitterly with Alice that an expert testified the rope knot had to have been tied by a right-handed person. Kingsley was left-handed.

After Kingsley's death, Alice threw herself into visiting prisoners (white and black) three or four times a week and comforting their families. From that work arose the nationwide Aboriginal Watch Committee which became a voice demanding investigations of these doubtful deaths.

Alice hanged herself in precisely the manner that Kingsley was supposed to have done. Why?

Her family says that she was deeply upset by the lack of any worthwhile change coming out of the Royal Commission and by the slowness of governments, correctional services and police to respond to those recommendations that were made.

The stress and frustration of the nationwide struggle gnawed at her sensitive spirit. Shortly beforehand, Alice was picked up for a traffic offence and had a confrontation with police.

But these considerations don't get to the meaning of Alice's death. As her husband said: *Alice did not take her own life, she made a statement.*

I can begin to get the meaning only from my white and priestly side. I keep thinking of a priest I knew who worked courageously for Aboriginal people. After some time he announced: 'I have given what I can to Aborigines. It is time for me now to pull back to more regular church work'.

I could feel his tiredness and need to get respite. But whatever the continuing struggle, he (like myself) could exit back to the regular white middle-class world. Our capacity to exist contrasts with the fate of 'Mum Shirl' Smith, Alice Dixon and the less famous but similarly confined Aborigines who carry the struggle of their people.

Alice was nailed to the cause of Kingsley and all her children in custody. The pain of it kept devouring her. Her statement may have carried despair, but was also a statement of solidarity with those who suffered as Kingsley did.

Her statement is akin to that of Gertrude Stein, the Carmelite nun, who freely chose to tell the Nazis that she was Jewish. Stein's death was not forced on her. It, too, was a statement of solidarity.

I think of the Buddhist monks in Vietnam who immolated themselves protesting the immolation of their people and land. And there is a Christ dimension. Incarnation is a complete confinement in that struggle. Incarnation and the cross are fused.

BISHOP HILTON DEAKIN
On anniversaries

*When David Kehoe was a university student, he thought he might
have a vocation to the priesthood. Because of the strong Jesuit presence
at Melbourne University he was attracted to the Society of Jesus. But
a very short acquaintance with the Society proved him wrong. As he
expressed it later, he found that he wanted to be a priest, not a
member of a religious order who happened to be a priest. So Kehoe
went off to the diocesan seminary and in due course was ordained. He
was a good priest; but when he died the waters of history closed over
his head and he began to be forgotten. This fine essay revives the
memory of David Kehoe. Written by Melbourne's Bishop Hilton
Deakin as one of his regular columns in the diocesan fortnightly*
Kairos, *it appeared there in the issue for 22–29 August 1993. The
bishop's column in* Kairos *is always worth reading.*

Last week saw the anniversary of the death of a member of my year
of ordination. 'My year' are those men who were ordained
together, although not at the same place. The memory of his death
is a sobering time for all of us, I am sure. It encourages us to recall times
past, fond memories of things achieved, of people helped through priestly
ministry, work done, shared times of prayer, what might have been, God's
ways not being our ways.

But somehow I am urged to remember something else as well. I
remember another death, of a young man, about the same time of year. I
saw him only twice.

On the first occasion, I was walking along the iron-laced verandah
that skirted part of the old blue-stone pile close to St Patrick's Cathedral,
called the Bishop's Palace. The night was cold, and the fresh, biting air was
just what we needed after a night of 'instruction' for marriage, and also
conversions, as was the lot of priests on many week nights in those days.

It was close to midnight, but suddenly a young man appeared at the
gate that used to open out onto Albert Street, and made his way below

towards the front door. He was dressed in a tuxedo and bowtie, and appeared to be Malaysian. He noticed my priest companion and I walking along, and asked if he could see a priest. One of us advised him to ring the bell, as a priest was 'on duty.' It was my classmate who received the visitor.

After about half an hour or so, the young man re-appeared and walked down towards the city centre past the front of the cathedral. Over a cuppa before bed, we spoke with the duty priest, and heard the story. He was a Malaysian illegal immigrant. He had been out seeking work as a waiter in restaurants—and there were not so many of them in those days, and very few Asian-food ones at that. He had been out of work for months, had no money, and, as it turned out, was also starving. Fr Dave Kehoe, the priest, took him to the kitchen and gave him a good, hot meal and talked away to him. As he told us and as I recall, he said he detected in the young man what he called the 'dead calm of a man who has no more hope'. The man had a room in Carlton, so Dave gave him a few pounds, as the currency was called in those far-off days, and off went the midnight visitor.

The next time I saw the young man was two days later. I was on duty at the presbytery. That meant I was on call from 9 am to 9 pm answering the door, the phone, and responding to any other miscellaneous requests that public fancy might express. The phone rang. It was a call from the city morgue. This rather unpleasant end-of-the-road establishment was down along the Flinders Street extension past Spencer Street, behind the railway offices, and opposite the site of Melbourne's other founder's farm site, John Batman's cottage.

The custom in those days was for the attendants to call the priest on duty to any deceased found about the city and brought to the morgue who had any sign on their person that they might be Catholic. The priest would administer conditionally the last rites of the church. It was the young Malaysian. He had been fished out of the river not far from the morgue. On his person was found a calling card of one Rev Fr David Kehoe, priest of St Patrick's Cathedral. I gave a blessing and said a prayer and went out into the cold daylight. Dave was right. 'The dead calm' had taken over.

He had no known relatives or friends, no information about where his family was back home, just nothing. David had his address in Carlton, but there was nothing there. So we buried him from the cathedral. The St Vincent de Paul people met the cost of the funeral. It was a lonely funeral, all the same. Two priests, two men from the St Vincent de Paul Society, and three men from the funeral directors.

This mention of that young man of so many years ago is most likely just the second time that the last several days of his short life have been made public. I recall that Fr Dave used the story once in a sermon at the cathedral to make a point about hope.

And I guess that one will never know any more about him at least this side of eternity.

The sparse story of the midnight visitor comes to mind for me each year. But for some reason or other, I have come up against similar stories this past several months. Not so much of young Asians out of work, or, once seen, then buried. But they are stories of people dying—four to be exact—two of them quite young, one by her own hand, the other from terrible illness, and two older people, each of them all alone in our busy city of three and a half million. In each instance, a priest appeared on the scene, somehow, somewhere. And in each instance they died and the priest had to muster forces to help with the burial. I will never know how often this sort of thing occurs, but I hazard the guess that it is tad more often than we might realise. Without a doubt, many welfare groups, church and non-church organisations, assist in similar cases. But it is comforting to know that such firm and dedicated witness is being given by priests, as by others, at a time when the image of priests is suffering from severe batterings. It also gives me cause to thank Almighty God for priests and the priesthood at this time of year when so many of them celebrate the anniversaries of the grace-filled day of their priestly ordination. Remember them in your prayers.

MASLYN WILLIAMS
My friend Parer

*Many of the great 19th century essays were disguised as book reviews.
I thought of that when I read this long article in* Eureka Street,
*November 1994. At first glance it is a review of two biographies of
Damien Parer, the World War II cameraman. In fact, the review allows
Maslyn Williams to revisit one of the sacred sites in his own life, his
great friendship with Parer. Thus he reflects on the nature of friendship,
the craft of film, love of country, Parer's religion, and their youth
together. I review books; when I read this essay I knew it was no mere
book review. Maslyn Williams, who has himself produced prize-
winning films and beautiful books, here marries poised literary skills
to a lifetime's wisdom and produces an elegant, memorable essay. It is
a meditation on the meaning of one man's life.*

Peleliu Island, in that emptiness between the western fringe of the
Carolines and the northern part of the Philippines, is a measly
island about five miles long and 250 feet at its peak. Fifty years ago
Peleliu was a Japanese outpost, and on 15 September 1944 it was invaded
by US Marines. Within three days they had taken the island at a cost of
5274 wounded and 1251 dead, and among the latter was my friend, the
cameraman Damien Parer. The fact that many high-ranking Americans
considered the operation unnecessary is now irrelevant. Years have passed,
and events that then seemed momentous have become attenuated memories. Yet there is still an emptiness.

This year the memories have suddenly become more real, even vivid,
because I have been reading two new biographies of Parer. *War Cameraman:
the Story of Damien Parer,* by a lecturer in communications at Charles Sturt
University, Neil McDonald, has Parer's war work as its primary focus. *Damien
Parer: Cameraman,* by the Catholic writer Niall Brennan, portrays him as a
unique kind of Christian crusader who used his camera as a tool if not a
weapon. An inset quote on the cover makes this plain: ' ... part–child, part–
poet, part–genius, part–saint ...'

These are good books, both for the general reader and for the film historian. The authors have evidently spent much time and effort on research, some of it with doubtful informants. Their different approaches combine to produce a wholeness that has been missing from previous efforts in print or via radio and television, though it is necessary to read both books if the reader wishes to get a three-dimensional impression of a man who was an artist-craftsman with an interesting personal history and a unique spiritual motivation.

The latter facet of Parer's character is underlined by an opinion Brennan obtained from the senior Catholic chaplain to the AIF in the Middle East: 'He was the most completely spiritual layman I have ever known'. Coming from a man who, without the military trimmings, could fairly be described as a level-headed rural parish priest, this is an acceptable assessment. Coming from Brennan, who seems to me to row the 'Holy, Holy' boat with too much vigour, there is a danger of making Parer seem too much of a prig, even as a schoolboy; Brennan writes of him running away from boarding school because of the 'conversation and behaviour of evil schoolmates'—a phrase which, I suspect, originated with Parer's wonderfully loving and deeply religious mother.

A few pages later comes the story of Parer attempting to induce an expression of heartfelt reverence on the face of a young model by speaking to her earnestly about the Passion; and further on comes a suspect story in which he warns a famous imported film star of the danger into which he was placing his immortal soul by his shameless, predatory behaviour. I do not suggest that these are apocryphal concoctions, but I doubt if they are true enough to be useful.

McDonald is more reticent about the religious aspects of Parer's character, and this is sensible of him because when he does venture into Catholic territory he tends to fall into error. He refers, for instance, to one of his most unreliable informants as a 'former priest' when the person concerned had been briefly a seminarian before becoming a semi-official photographer of ceremonies and activities connected with the church.

And he tells of a 'pilgrimage' that Parer made, walking about 20 miles to attend Midnight Mass at a monastery and reciting the rosary as he went. It seems that I was invited to take part in this exercise and declined because of other commitments, but was 'deeply moved' by the invitation, which was a 'decisive moment' in cementing our friendship.

It is a moving little anecdote but pure gobbledygook. The reason for the pilgrimage was Parer's wish to visit his brother, who was a Franciscan friar studying for ordination. Another friend, also invited, considered Parer to be 'some sort of nut' and probably still does. Brennan also goes astray on the subject of this Franciscan, whom he has celebrating the mass at his brother's wedding; the actual celebrant was a Jesuit, Richard Murphy.

It could be said that minor errors of this kind are not important and may reasonably be ignored, but it seems to me that Parer has a place in the panorama of Australian history, and anything written about him in future will in part be abstracted from these two books: therefore they should be accurate.

So it is careless then of McDonald to have Parer's father discussing his son's future with the film-maker Charles Chauvel when travelling in the *Spirit of Progress* in 1934, three years before the *Spirit* made its first trip; and the anecdote that has R. G. Menzies informing me of Parer's death is just thoroughly muddled.

Even more bemusing is McDonald's thumbnail account of my own early years of 'deprived childhood' and being forced to subsist 'on various forms of charity for most of (my) life', a sadness that has left emotional scars. I have been ignorant of such scars all these years, though I wish I had known about them earlier. It would have allowed me to give a Dickensian twist to the autobiographical book that I have been working on recently, replacing those cherished dreams of joyful schooldays, magic holidays with relatives in Devonshire, the Golden Valley of Cashel in Ireland and the mountains of North Wales, to say nothing of visits to an aunt who had an old farmhouse in the south of France.

But for McDonald, I would not have known that when arriving in Australia as a youth I 'was placed with a wealthy doctor in Bowral'. I have always believed that within days of arriving in Sydney I boarded a train that took me to New England, where I learned to be a jackeroo and, in fact, wrote a book about it that gained me a handsome award.

But it is a well-known cliché that memory plays tricks, and in any case it is probably improper to introduce personal interpolations into what is, I suppose, meant to be no more than a commentary on two books. But as I have already said, I am making use of this opportunity to evoke memories and thoughts that have lain dormant for 50 years and more; memories of my friendship with a man who for a decade was closer to me than a brother.

For this reason I want to make it plain that although McDonald and Brennan have done an honest and excellent job I have doubts about the memories of some of their informants. So when Brennan tells of an occasion when Parer and the often surly and curmudgeonly Frank Hurley shared a tent in the desert, and that Parer by example shamed Hurley into getting out of bed and kneeling to say his prayers, I find that, however hard I try, my imagination is not sufficiently elastic to accept anything quite so unlikely.

Putting these quibbles aside, however, it is obviously more important to consider the treatment that the authors give to the middle years of Parer's development both professionally and in a religious or spiritual sense, because in the end these two aspects of his character became fused into the unity that Thomist theology describes as piety or religious motivation (put it as you will), becoming an integral part of day-by-day behaviour.

Parer's lifespan was 32 years. After leaving school at 17, he spent the next few years training as a still photographer and picking up odd bits of film studio work whenever he could, for that was where his heart was. We met in 1935, working as juniors in a new film studio in Sydney, myself in the script-and-editorial and Parer in the camera department. These were the middle years of his transition from being a professional photographer to becoming a film cameraman.

It was a learning period for both of us; a period when things were coming together in the personal search for a sense of direction and purpose and, for Parer especially, the achievement of technical perfection. Together with a group of other youthful film enthusiasts we began to discover what was going on among the most advanced European filmmakers and theorists, yet McDonald and, more especially, Brennan both seem content with references to the influence that the Russian cameraman Vladimir Nilsen and the British documentary pioneer, John Grierson, had on Parer's thinking.

It is true that he studied Nilsen's *Cinema as a Graphic Art* thoroughly, with much underlining and note-taking, and for a while was fascinated by aphorisms such as 'Fluent simplicity is the secret of visual literacy' (neat but simplistic, and ultimately meaningless). He was also much taken by Grierson's theory of 'mobile and fluent composition' until discovering that the phrase was borrowed from *The Poetry of Film*, an essay written 20 years earlier by the Hungarian, Gyorgy Lukacs. This essay included another phrase which ultimately became Parer's driving maxim—'to catch the absolute reality of the moment'. That was what he was trying to do on Peleliu Island, when a Japanese machine-gunner cut him down.

This is not to say that Nilsen and Grierson were not important in shifting Parer's thinking away from the merely poetical and pictorial and towards the day-to-day realities of human behaviour in a continuously changing world. Both were men of cultured integrity, but both were ardent propagandists—Nilsen as part of the machinery of the socialist revolution, and Grierson as the prime mover in Britain's documentary movement, which sought to use film to meet modern sociological, political and educational requirements, a statement underlined in Parer's copy of Paul Rotha's book *Documentary Film*.

The idea that film could and should be used for such purposes was not new. In 1896 Maxim Gorky had been worried that the exaggerations and fantasies of the popular cinema would make people less willing to accept the realities of ordinary life. In 1915 a Benedictine monk, Cecil Bognar, had written 'film itself is merely an instrument, a raw material like paint or type, that may be used for all forms of communication and even perception'. The last word was the key: film would become a means of making people perceive reality from a number of different angles or view-points chosen by others.

It would be tedious as well as unproductive to list the books and specialist magazines that Parer read in his quest to equip himself as a first-class cameraman. Books not read because they had not then been trans-lated from the languages in which they were written (mostly Russian, German or Hungarian) were discussed with others who had read them, but books and their theorising, however enlightening, did not give him a particular goal apart from being able, one day, to be involved in the making of good films with first-class camera work and a gentle moralistic quality.

As one of the group who shared these hopes and enthusiasms, I con-sider that this period of four or five years was by far the most important for the would-be filmmakers of that age. The books and the on-and-off employment in studios were a splendid apprenticeship, but they lit no fires in the mind. For this reason I find it strange that neither McDonald nor Brennan give more than a few haphazard paragraphs to this period. McDonald apparently sees it simply as a link between Parer's early years and the war period, which is his main interest and which he covers better than anyone else has yet done.

As for Brennan, he does his subject no service whatever by beating the Nilsen-Grierson drum so lustily that one is not able to hear the rest of the orchestra. It is quite wrong to suggest that Parer's eventual method of operating was 'the pay-off for the years of quiet and intensive study of Nilsen's diagrams and Grierson's theories'. Both had their place in his professional development, but in terms of actual film-making neither would have claimed to match the genius of Dziga Vertov to whom both were indebted, or of Alexander Dovzhenko, whom the film historian Basil Wright refers to as 'probably the greatest poet of cinema the world had ever seen' Nor did any of the theorists have the inspirational effect of the sometimes lush and sometimes stark imagery of Robert Flaherty's *Moana*, shot on a Pacific Island, *Nanook*, about Eskimo life, and *Man of Aran*, about the people of a bleak island off the Atlantic coast of Ireland.

One could go on with a catalogue of such films, citing those of Cavalcanti, the Dutchman Joris Ivens and Pare Lorentiz in America, among others. It was a time of ferment in the 'realist' film world, and in spite of Brennan's religious fulminating about the 'shabby products of Hollywood; wasteful scoriae filling the coffers of uninterested millionaires' there were many great films turned out by Hollywood studios which kept the enthusiasts going back, three and even four times, to squeeze that last nuance of structure, lighting, directing or camera work from a beautifully conceived sequence or episode.

Again, one could reel off the titles of films and the names of those who made them year after year, not only in Hollywood but in England, France, Germany, Hungary and Russia. Films that were great entertainment but which could sensibly be classed as examples of a genuine art form. From France came Julien Duvivier's *Carnet de Bal* and *Pépé le Moko*, René Claire's *The Paris that Sleeps* and *The Italian Straw Hat*, and Marcel Pagnol's *The Baker's Wife*—a story about the village priest and the Communist mayor joining forces to avoid a community calamity. Parer's guffaws at the shot of the mayor carrying the priest across a river made people in the audience turn in their seats. From Germany came *The Love of Jeanne Ney*, directed by G. W. Pabst and brilliantly edited. And from America? Frank Capra's *Lost Horizon*, with Ronald Colman; Hitchcock's *The Lady Vanishes*. Lists as long as your arm.

To be sure, there were also cartloads of tinsel and tawdry stuff that Brennan would call prurient; that has always been the case, in every field of visual and literary yield. But in filmmaking, from the earliest days there were great films and splendidly creative filmmakers who provided the inspiration and incentive for people like Parer. We saw Garbo, directed by Rouben Mamoulian in *Queen Christina*, and sat as if magnetised at the almost unbearably desolate shot of Garbo standing at the bow of the ship that was taking her away. And again, in *Ninotchka*, directed by Ernst Lubitsch, she sits alone in her hotel room looking at a photograph of Lenin who almost imperceptibly seems to smile at her. But the film shots and sequences that still stick in my mind, as they did in Parer's, were in John Ford's *The Informer*, made in 1935.

First, the full close-up of Gypo Nolan being interrogated by a leader of the Irish Revolutionary Movement: the tortured face, whisky-sodden, torn between self-preservation and shame as he teeters on the brink of betraying his mate. (Years later I used the shot myself, when making a film in Germany about the interrogation of refugees.) Then Gypo staggering through dark streets towards the church to ask forgiveness for what he has done. The off-scene voice of a woman in a pub singing *Mother Machree* (sob stuff, for sure, but wonderfully done). In the church he stumbles down the aisle towards a crucifix hanging above the altar. The only other person in the dimly lit church is Mrs McPhillip, praying for the repose of the soul of her son, the victim of Gypo's betrayal. He swallows the blood and mucus dribbling around his lips and whispers drunkenly, 'Twas me was the informer, Mrs McPhillips, can you forgive me?' She is weeping, empty of everything, even the capacity to hate her son's murderer: 'I forgive you, Gypo, you didn't know what you were doing'. Parer and I walked home in silence that night, knowing that if we were to be filmmakers we had a long way to go; and I had the feeling that in his mind, along with Gypo and Mrs McPhillips, were these deeper things, sin and forgiveness; forgiveness even of that most heinous sin, the betrayal of a mate. Things that great films, like great literature, should be about. The mystery of human nature.

I wish Brennan had seen this. If he had he might not have filled this period of Parer's development with pages and pages of his activities with the Campion Society, bushwalking or making little films about religious occasions and the doings of the Grail ladies, even though these, too, were relevant to his development. Thinking about it now, I believe that Brennan should have called his book *Damien Parer: Crusader*, or something of that sort. It would have given the thematic cohesion that it needs while at the same time making plain that Parer became the legendary wartime camera-man because of the inescapable nature of his vocation.

The story of Parer's war years begins several months before war was declared, by which time I had become director, editor and scriptwriter of the Commonwealth Government Film Unit in Melbourne, producing films about eggs, butter, sultanas, wool and other such exportable commodities; an occupation to which I brought as much of the technique of Eisenstein, and as many of the theories of Grierson, as the subjects and the authorities could assimilate. Meanwhile Parer, with two workmates from the studio days, had set out to make two short films under the general heading *This Place Australia*, based on the Henry Lawson poems *The Waratah and the Wattle*, and *The Storm to Come*. They were shot mainly in the Blue Mountains and when released were highly praised, with one critic saying 'The star of the production is cameraman Damien Parer, whose work is as breathtakingly lovely as anything that ever came out of Hollywood'.

Though living in different cities we had kept in close touch, and as one of my own two cameramen was retiring I asked Parer to send me clippings from these films. On the strength of their quality and his back-ground of studio work he was hired to take the retiring man's place. I dreamed then, for a little while, that working together at last we would show them the way films should and could be made in Australia, but within weeks he had been conscripted into the government's War Film Unit and in January 1940 was on his way to the Middle East.

I followed him a few months later, as 'scriptwriter, producer and as-sistant cameraman' under the veteran Frank Hurley. We worked together in North Africa, Greece, Crete and Syria. We grew up, made discoveries of all sorts, and became so much closer to each other that a British major with whom we had frequent dealings used to say, 'Here come Damon and Pythias'. When Australia's interests switched to the Pacific and a completely differ-ent kind of fighting we became separated, Parer moving to New Guinea and onwards with the frontline fighters, while I became a minor pawn on the propaganda chess board moving back and forth between Canberra and MacArthur's headquarters in Melbourne.

McDonald and Brennan are on firmer ground when dealing with this period, with access to genuine records and firsthand stories provided by trustworthy informants who saw Parer in action, and shared the same daily experiences. McDonald's professional bent becomes evident here and his coverage is more methodical and complete in detail, so that it adds up to the best available assessment of Parer's war work yet published.

Brennan deals with the various campaigns less extensively—though treating them with respect and at times in a most moving manner—while pursuing his interest in the effect of Parer's deeply-held beliefs on both his war work and personal relationships. This insistence on underlining Parer's evident, though at times almost eccentric, spirituality makes Brennan's book important for a complete understanding of this many-faceted man. At times Parer's behaviour and Brennan's language may seem extravagant, yet there is no gainsaying that, to many who knew and worked with him, this was a essential part of his captivating good nature and of his willingness to take frightening risks to get the shots he wanted.

For example, after the battle of Guam the respected correspondent Denis Warner wrote: '... the marines think of him as a sort of legendary figure the bullets cannot touch because four of their corps of cameramen have been killed in the fighting here and none of them took the same risks as he did ...'

An American correspondent who knew what it was to have close calls adopted the motto, 'My paper pays for live news, not dead correspondents'. When I mentioned this to Parer, during one of his brief leaves, he just grinned as if he knew something that I didn't.

Coming closer to the centre of this question, Brennan quotes the chaplain, Father McCarthy, on Parer's attitude towards the mass, to which he went daily whenever possible: 'He knelt straight up, without kneeling on anything, his hands clasped together, as if enraptured. He remained like this for the whole of the mass and for some time after'.

It was this 'otherness' that made him, at times, seem strangely and even comically separate. I can remember that when in Cairo on leave we often went to Groppi's for dinner and he would ask a girl to dance, then trundle her back and forth across the floor like a farmer ploughing a furrow, his eyes fixed on some invisible object above her head and a look of ecstatic reverence on his face. He would bring her to our table for a drink and say, 'Thank you, that was lovely'. On one such evening he asked the dance band leader to play Gounod's *Ave Maria*. The girls wondered what was wrong with this handsome odd-bod.

This could all be seen as some peculiar kind of affectation, but there is evidence in plenty to put against such an interpretation. More than 20 years after Parer's death, Bernard Hosie, a Marist, wrote a pamphlet for the Australian Catholic Truth Society with the heading *A Unique Australian*. It follows the well-worn track that others have carved in trying to identify what made Parer different; the difference that made him an enigma to many. But then Hosie quotes a conversation which Parer had with his oldest brother, Stan, before going back to the war-front once more: ' … this can't last, Stan. On the law of averages I've got to stop a bullet. I don't mind much; it's in the Father's hands'.

Reading that brought back several memories. We were in Queensland, at Maleny, visiting his mother and others of the Parer clan when I said, 'There'll be so much to be done when this is all finished. So much and so many to be mended. So many big subjects to be covered where the right kind of film will be useful'. He was squatting under a bank on the edge of a paddock, because he always had troubles with constipation. And standing there, looking at the scenery, I was thinking of films about refugees, rehabilitation problems and the two of us working together.

Then he said, 'That would be bloody wonderful', but I knew that he wasn't altogether sure; I waited for him to pull up his pants and speak again. 'God allots the jobs. He gives us the skills we have and he can take them away when he wishes. Let's go and have a drink.'

Now, sitting at an old typewriter working at this piece, I remember driving with him across a desert and Parer reciting Chesterton's *Lepanto* with a kind of breathless urgency heightened by some kind of excitement, tripping over its exhilarating rhythms.

> Gun upon gun, ha! ha!
> Gun upon gun, hurrah!
> Don John of Austria
> Has loosed the cannonade …

Then he said, 'Did you know that the feast of Our Lady of the Rosary was proclaimed to celebrate that battle?'

The memories run together. There is a hawk of some sort high in the sky, hovering with rippling wing-tips. Parer's expression changes into an enraptured ecstasy and we have Gerard Manley Hopkins:

> I caught this morning morning's minion, king-
> dom of daylight's dauphin, dapple-dawn-drawn

> Falcon in his riding
> ... the achieve of, the mastery of the thing!

Silence for a while and we turn to St Winifred's well and the *Golden Echo*.

> When the thing we freely forfeit is kept with fonder a care,
> ... do but tell us where kept, where .—
> ... We follow, now we follow.—
> Yonder, yes yonder, yonder,
> Yonder.

His voice had sunk to a whisper. He already knew where he was going. There were people who spoke of his death wish, which was silly because nobody enjoyed being alive more than he did, forever conscious that God was close by. He loved his wife and was excited by the idea of fathering a child. He no more wanted to die than his namesake, Father Damien, had wished to die of leprosy on Molokai. But he had once quoted to me a line or two from something by Jacques Maritain, to the effect that death to 'self' leaves one free to die for ideals and beliefs.

I am grateful to McDonald and Brennan for bringing back these memories.

CHRIS McGILLION
Image breaker

*The beatification of Mary Mackillop got Australian Catholics talking
about the question of sainthood. What were the differences between
being a saint and being a hero? What demands did Australians make
on those whom they turned into icons? The death of Fred Hollows
raised these questions too. The ex-Communist Party, humanist, rebel
eye-doctor, who delighted in stirring the possum, was given a send-off
in Sydney's St Mary's Cathedral. Which got people talking. There
was even a bishop there. In this letter to* Eureka Street *for March
1993, Chris McGillion reflects on the discussion. Editor of the*
Sydney Morning Herald's *opinion page, McGillion occasionally
writes there about Australian spirituality. He also contributes to* The
Tablet *(London).*

Fred Hollows was an iconoclast, not a saint, and it is his iconoclasm
that we shall miss most about him. Other people (either
encouraged or empowered by him) will carry on Fred's work against
blindness born of poverty. But who will shake us out of our complacency,
challenge our prejudices, confront us with uncomfortable truths, and in
the process inspire us to imagine and accomplish new things?

And yet Fred has been eulogised in saintly terms. This strikes me as
ironic, but also as a possible insight into the Australian psyche. Ironic because Fred was no saint. Anyone who sat, and drank, and argued into the
night with him knew that. Saintliness, of course, is a Christian concept. But
as Fred wrote in his autobiography: 'Sex, alcohol and secular goodness are
pretty keen instruments, and they surgically removed my Christianity, leaving
no scars.'

Fred was raised in the Church of Christ and studied to become a
minister before becoming an agnostic and dying an atheist. But the fact
that he sent his kids to a Catholic school, and that his funeral was held in
Saint Mary's Cathedral, Sydney, will give the church apologists great heart.
He never strayed too far from the gospel message, some will say. But that is

not the point. Fred was always quoting the Bible but I suspect he believed that the church, not he, had done the straying. Others will argue that Christianity was the original source of his thirst for justice. But the first few pages of his autobiography show that this argument is completely false.

Fred loathed the 'odour of sanctity' that surrounded many people in the church as well as in the professions. But he had faith in ordinary people. In one of the last interviews he gave before his death he said; 'My definition of God is that within humans which causes them to strive for liberation—liberation from poverty, fire, drought, oppression of any kind'.

Could it be that Australians view Fred Hollows as a 'saint' because he understood their struggle, identified their particular demons, and, in his own inimitable style, gave expression to their quality of endurance in ways that institutionalised Christianity in this country has never done? Could it be that the popular appeal of this brusque, knockabout humanitarian tells us something very profound about Australian spirituality?

TRISH HINDMARSH
You are a priest forever

Some questions will not go away, despite any number of official answers. Trish Hindmarsh's reflections on the ordination of a Uniting Church minister are an example of this. Written the morning after the ordination, her article begins with a loving remembrance of the connections between their two families. Her three-year-old son interrupts her writing, just as the ordinand's child had interrupted last night's ceremony. She sees these, not as distractions, but as pointers to the way life is: 'That is how much of the reflection and prayer is done in family households'. This leads her to consider her own family's pain—for her husband is himself an ordained Catholic priest. The developing structure of Trish Hindmarsh's article is worth noting. Even more remarkable is the absence of bitterness or recrimination in her essay. It appeared in the theological journal, Women-Church *in Spring 1990.*

Last night, together with my husband and two children, I had the occasion (unique in our church experience so far) of being present at the ordination of Michael Barnes of Strathfield Parish into the Uniting Church. His wife, Mhairi, had worked closely with my husband in community development programs, and so we had shared vicariously in some of the preparation the couple had been making as the time of ordination approached, including their marriage and the birth of their first child. I doubt if any minor and major seminarian could have been given a more appropriate pastoral or theological preparation! Mhairi's first-hand involvement in all the issues related to social work—multiculturalism, an option for the marginalised, political lobbying on their behalf, and community-building—were discussed over many a meal Michael and Mhairi shared in their Marrickville unit, prior to ordination.

Michael's studies at Sydney University and his pre-ordination study have been integrated as well into the couple's daily lives as they share the nappy changes, house cleaning and cups of coffee. Such concerns, together with the commitment to the scriptures and to prayer that the ceremony of ordination spoke of, are as central to their lives as are their forays to Franklins to get the groceries. (How many of our pastors have the chance to chat with their parishioners in Franklins?)

A formative influence in Michael's vocation was in many ways his father, ex-Moderator of the Uniting Church and noted church historian, a man who must have meditated many a time while walking the floorboards with his own babies. Michael's induction into the church at baptism was by his grandfather, also a Congregational minister. This morning it is possible that the family, so much in the public eye of the Christian community last night, are carrying out the domestic basics most of humanity are called to. In fact, as I sit here trying to reflect a little on what God is saying to ourselves in all this and to the church, Tom—our three-year-old—is assisting the theologising process by reading his own signs of the times, pretending to be a baby like one-year-old Janika Barnes. Great mileage in being one of these, he found out last night! No personal space, wrapped in tranquillity, or mellow lights of an oratory here to aid the processes of reflection. However, God *is* here, and is determined to intervene: 'Mummy, I'll help you', Tom says, tapping odd keys on my typewriter.

But what a level of reality and community the presence of the children added to the ordination ceremony! Just as a Greek tragedy can have its chorus to amplify the theme, so the ceremony had its own chorus. I don't refer to the choral offerings of the magnificent parish choir which contributed so much richness and atmosphere. I refer to that small voice, totally unrehearsed, as timeless and as insistent as humanity itself, that called out 'Daddy, Daddy!' within the flow of the ritual.

> 'Will you exercise pastoral care of the family of God in the congregation of this parish?'
> 'Daddy, Daddy!'
> 'Do you commit yourself to the service of all people, especially the defenceless and oppressed?'
> 'That's Daddy!'

I have a constant *chorus interruptus* of my own going on here. It wants to know at this point whether 'yachts are faster than boats'. Important question. It extracts me from the aura of the moment into the world of real people, and that is how much of the reflection and prayer is done in family households. I suspect Michael and Mhairi's will not be so different either. These little anecdotal snippets may not seem to have great bearing on the teachings of Vatican II, where reading the signs of the times received its mandate to become state of the art discernment in our recent history. However, I feel that ordained ministry constantly interrupted (or is it constantly inspired?) by the needs of kids in intimate family life and the needs of people in parish houses like its own, with all their 'joys and hopes, fears and anxieties', must have something to say to the Catholic decision-making hierarchy, far removed as they often are from concerns such as these.

Our family and a number of other couples experienced an embarrassing moment during the Christmas mass in my home town when the celibate leader of the liturgy, speaking about the Christ Child who came to rescue humanity, paused midstream in his homily and asked in quite an irritated tone that whoever owned 'that child' (wandering onto the sanctuary to visit the baby Jesus in the crib before the altar) come and 'rescue' it. 'Let the little children come to me' seemed very distant to the embarrassed mother.

The exhilaration of being part of the ceremony of induction into the Christian community, and sharing that sense of seriousness when a young man takes his place among the ordained women and men of his faith community, was mingled with tears for me when I glanced at my ordained priest-husband beside me. The call to discipleship and all its implications is a hot topic of conversation at our own table, and we often spend time together trying to discern where God could be calling a church like ours which still imposes the yoke of celibacy on all its candidates for priesthood. Some carry that yoke joyfully and with dignity; for many it has been a means of hampering the call to be a person 'fully human and fully alive', witnessing to all that is humanly blessed and reflective of the love-life of God. Many have regretfully left the church's public ministry and have gone underground to express their call to ministry in employment or voluntary service not directly related to the church's work, expressing the same call to discipleship with their families, but rejected as 'unfaithful', unemployable and sometimes unwelcome by their own church. If the Catholic community had the opportunity to share as the Uniting Church does in the preparation, selection and induction of their ministers into the parishes or communities, would our Catholic families and laity in general see marriage as an *impediment* to priesthood as the celibate hierarchy do? I wonder how many of our own bishops and priests would have been surprised by last night's ceremony if they had had the experience of being there. Or whether their celibacy allows them the capacity to be so surprised. There is no need felt for the Uniting Church community of Strathfield to defend the married status of its priest; it is accepted as given, holy, natural. I also wonder whether many ministers feel the need to abandon their calling in such a church. How many Catholic priests have not been able to sustain the expectations of celibacy is well documented. Surely a church losing as many as 50–70 per cent of its ordained ministers in pockets of missionary involvement, for reasons seeming in most cases to be connected to celibacy, is a church which needs to ask some questions. This demands a response of discernment of this sign of the times, rather than a stubborn insistence on traditional practices.

Even if our Church could *try* a different model. While we talk and theorise, there are too many psychological barriers. How many of us will remember in the 1960s the huge emotional leap it was (can you believe it?) for the church to entertain the idea of women religious showing some hair, or leg, after all those centuries? Once the deed was done, it became as natural as air. It was as natural as air for married people (women and men— Dorothy McMahon gave the homily and another woman concelebrated with the secretary of the Presbytery) to be priests, and we sat there and saw it, knowing that the experience is denied to the decision-makers of our own church who could stumble along for another century denying priest-hood rights to *most* of the believing faithful. Last night, lest we all become too heady with the wonderful spiritual nature of the occasion, Michael's father, in an extremely moving piece of father-son sharing, told Michael not to forget his humanness. 'You have a right to be human. Mhairi has a right to be human. Janika has a right to be human. The Christian commu-nity you serve will be denied your service if you pretend to be other than forgiven or human.'

Which brings me to the final question running round in my mind last night after Mhairi had said to me, 'I wondered how a Catholic ex-priest might feel during that ceremony?' Our own church has seldom wondered how someone like my husband might be feeling about his non-acceptance as a married priest and the denial of his right to exercise the call to ministry. The question is inevitable in a highly ecumenical context where one could sense the spirit of the Acts in an experience of Christian community where those present were remaining faithful to the teaching of the apostles, the community, the breaking of bread and prayer. The question is: Which is the true church? Surely verbal and theological protestations do not make an authentic church. The true church must surely be that church community, wherever it is found, regardless of denomination, which is most truly reflective of the Spirit of Jesus and most reminds us of that community of faith at the beginning of Acts.

The challenge is to discover and be part of such a community or, I suppose, if one is hard to find, to set about trying to form one!

JOHN O'HEHIR
An open letter to the Pope

The stories of those who left the priestly ministry remain, for the most part, untold. Some retellings of such stories have been spoilt by point-making or score-settling; others show all too painfully that some priests took a long time to grow up. Yet every story, told or untold, was about a process of decision more dramatic than merely changing one job for another. In each person—and often in those who loved him or whom he loved—there was a seismic shift which went deep below the surface. So deep, perhaps, that only a genius could bring it to the surface and tell it truthfully. Something of that seismic shift is caught in this piece, which appeared in Eureka Street, December 1992– January 1993. *It is no surprise to find that the writer had been a Columban father—they have always had a wealth of writing talent.*

This letter is addressed to Pope John Paul II. I am writing it to apply for reinstatement in the ministry of the priesthood, from which I resigned a decade ago. I am now married, with three young children, and live as a member of the Catholic parish of the Resurrection, in Keysborough, Victoria, Australia.

I was ordained to the priesthood within the Missionary Society of St Columban in 1959, and spent 30 years as a Columban and 23 years as a priest. I was a missionary in the Philippines for ten years and in Chile for five years. Now I am almost 60 years old. Why, then, do I apply to return to the priestly ministry at this time?

The operative words are 'at this time'. At this time of crisis, we hear of the formation of 'cluster parishes'. We hear that many parishes will have to invite priests to celebrate an occasional eucharist with them, and that fewer and fewer priests will be available for pastoral work. My parish priest frequently reminds us to prepare for priestless parishes in the near future. The future appears bleak; but have all options been considered?

In Brazil a few years ago the Catholic Church made an impassioned plea for missionary priests to come to that country, since the Christian communities there had only a few priests. And you, the present pope, have stated that no Christian community is complete or can survive unless it is a eucharistic community. However, there is a viable option! There are more than 3000 married priests living in Brazil, as shoemakers, tradesmen, social workers, etc.

I firmly believe that I have grown as a person in my role as husband and father. My understanding of love and service has deepened. My awareness of truly belonging to others has heightened my understanding of my relationship with my Lord. I can bring that understanding and awareness to a 'new start' in the priestly ministry of service.

What else can I bring? I have worked with the most fragile alcoholics, prostitutes, drug addicts. I have spent time in the service of the mentally ill. I have worked as a cleaner, a security guard, a factory worker, a service station manager and a teacher of English for migrants—so that I can pay the mortgage. At present, my wife and I care for migrants from Latin America as they leave migrant hostels to face life in the Australian community. As a family man, I know personally what it means to lose a child. I also know the health problems that go with having had two open-heart operations.

These years have been a hard but positive school for me. Hopefully, a more capable, or at least humbler, person has emerged.

Could I be a better pastor this time round? I have prepared many migrant children for the reception of the sacraments. I have sat and prayed with married couples, helping them to see the options facing them as they work through problems in their relationship. My Community Education Diploma, gained part-time over a number of years, would be an advantage. And I hope to begin a Master of Ministry course, with the prospect of spending my remaining years as a hospital chaplain—though, sadly, not in a Catholic hospital but in one run by the Uniting Church.

I do not regret leaving the priesthood to marry. I love my family, I love my church, and I belong. I have twice been invited to take up ministry in the Anglican Church, but I cannot leave the Catholic Church. So, after consulting my wife and family, and at the urging of concerned Christian friends, I apply to resume the priestly ministry again.

The gospel of Jesus is about service and love. He accepted Peter as the leader of his chosen, though Peter was more bruised and less gifted than the others. I believe that at this time there is room for the bruised man to be welcomed back to ministry in the Christian community. Nearly 100,000 priests have resigned from the church's ministry during the past 20 years. How many of them would return to it if they were allowed to do so? Why is the door bolted so tight? There is no question of setting a precedent, for there are already several married priests working as pastors in Australia.

I believe that among those priests who left the ministry to marry there are many who would return.

TERRY MONAGLE
My monastery is silver

The magazines of the past were often about prayer and carried prayers in their pages. Today's magazines have shifted the emphasis away from saying prayers to being prayerful. No subject interests Catholics more, as they constantly repeat the gospel question, 'Teach us to pray'. The magazines are full of this new experience of praying in one's own voice and at one's own speed. Terry Monagle's article in Australian Catholics *for October 1993 works on two levels. It situates prayer as a normal part of a normal day; thus needing the effort of winning time and attention for it to happen. It also shows how this personal daily discipline can be underpinned by the use of a traditional form of words. On the train to work he reads morning prayer from the Divine Office ('it takes four stations') and this becomes the nodal point around which the rest of the day spins. The Office is not an 'obligation'—and hence something to be got though—but a heartstarter for daylong attentiveness to God.*

My monastery is silver. It tracks through the suburbs from Surrey Hills to Melbourne. It is the 8.24.

Being husband, father, brother, office worker, mortgagee, smothers me with demands. God's powerful presence in prayer is equally insistent. Life consists in integrating and answering the demands of these two belongings.

How and where can I pray during the working day? How do all my activities as father, husband, son, brother, worker, interweave with this deeper belonging?

It starts: bring in the paper and the rubbish bin, put on the kettle, feed the cat, make the lunches, borrow train fare from the kids, sign that note, pull up the doona, shave, find a *pair* of socks, where's a hanky, pack that bag, put in those bills and cheques, defrost the sausages, rush for the 8.24, think up that agenda, remember to make those calls.

During the morning busyness, the ear half-listens to the news summaries: Bosnia, Cambodia, Burma, South Africa, Somalia, Tibet, Bougainville, unemployment. Between 6.40 and 8.10 the heart sinks lower and lower, almost to despair. There can't be a God in a world like that!

Life seems so frantic, the news so profoundly disturbing, the two so unconnected. The challenge to survive neutralises the challenge to respond to humanity. Our lives can feel shallow, our hearts despair.

These predicaments frame our spiritual lives. How do we, in busy urban Australia, worrying about two jobs, our children, the mortgage, the school fees, maintain an active spirituality? How do we satisfy our hunger for the infinite?

We all have our ways, expressive of our temperament, of preventing our profoundest instincts from being smothered. Here are some of mine.

Trains, planes, buses, trams. These, for me, are the best places for prayer. Rakes, brooms, spades, forks. These, for me, are the best tools for prayer. Hat, overcoat, walking shoes. Those are the best garments for prayer. Travelling, working, walking: in these are purpose but no straining of will. In these the heart can seek its goal.

I walk to the station in the morning. The air clears my head. The rhythm of the steps and the breath is a simple prayer, saying thanks for the morning.

On the train, the silver monastery, hiding in a corner with a small book, I read morning prayer from the Divine Office. It takes four stations. After that I just sit, half asleep, half praying a mantra, wondering about my fellow travellers, imagining how they live.

Work can be exhilarating, but often it is like gnawing on the same hard stones, meal after meal. The ache of boredom can become claustrophobic. Try as I might, many things I have to do are deeply frustrating. How can the boredom be transformed into prayer, made productive? How both to preserve a loving attitude to squabbling work mates and keep integrity?

You play the role, answer the phone, meet the deadlines. Lunchtime is a chance to make contact again. Sometimes I put on the jacket and walk to one of the nearby churches; sometimes Catholic, sometimes Lutheran, my favourite is Anglican. The emptier the better, and it is better to walk out of the city centre. I drop into a steady, comfortable gait. As I walk, I take it easy and let the feverishness of the brain fall away, concentrating on the mantra of the walk. I sit in a pew or follow mass. I think of Bosnia, Cambodia, Burma, South Africa, Somalia, Tibet, the people on the train, the unemployed who come to the city in the off-peak. In a small way, I enter into their suffering. Lunch hour is my great silence.

On the way home on the 5.59, I should say evening prayer. I don't, I'm too tired. The brain is empty, barely working. On Friday nights, in the winter dark, I wait forlornly on Richmond station for a connection, looking out across the lights of the suburbs, looking at my anonymous companions following their own trail of light to their homes. Each to their own, to a shared table, to those with whom they share it, to the space where everything allows them to name themselves, to be named by others.

At home, kids doing their homework, family meetings, doing the dishes, making phone calls, bringing in the washing, watching TV, the crabbiness, the relaxation.

The discipline of loving in the family: the core and test of our spirituality. That one has low self-esteem, that one is joyous, that one is likely to win 'bitch of the week', that one is cross because we are tired while she is wide awake, that one wastes money, that one gives lectures, that one is lazy. Each with her beauty of spirit, blooming and fragile. Each one needing nurture, and being nurtured. We sandpaper each other smooth.

'Thank you for this food, thank you for our guest, and God bless the cook.' The love of each, and the love of the group, give an inkling of the shape and hue of divine love. In the universe, we stand in that love. I pray that this love sustains those in Bosnia, Cambodia, Burma, South Africa, Somalia, Tibet, Bougainville, those on the 8.24, and those caught in all those wars in all those places whose names I can't remember.

How do we prove our solidarity for those in the news? Prayer is too easy. The causes to which we give money? (Making sure we get a receipt for taxation purposes.) It seems like tokenism. Does political commitment count? Maybe, but that, too, is mixed up with self-interest. Later in our lives, when the children are independent, perhaps there will be a chance for some full-time service. Time will test our genuineness.

Last thing at night, the jog or the walk. The final mantra of the step and the breath. Sometimes with the partner, sharing the day, our first conversation of the day. Put out the rubbish bin, the paper stack, the bag of bottles. Sometimes, in the bath, I finally get around to evening prayer.

Set the alarm for the 8.24. Try again.

BARRY OAKLEY
Reflections on evil

Here is a passionate, articulate Christian response to the horror of the Holocaust. Barry Oakley is famous for his comic novels and plays. He has edited The Australian's *literary pages and written a weekly column in* The Australian Magazine *for some years. His columns are often wry, whimsical, self-mocking and written in flawless prose—Oakley is one of the best writers of prose in Australia. On Saturdays some readers (myself included) turn first to his column as to the peak of that day's reading. It does not get better than this. In this column, which appeared in May 1994, Oakley confronts his readers with the outer limits of human behaviour, sin in the 20th century. The column was difficult to select because there were many other great pieces of writing under his name. Isn't it time some publisher gave us the best of Oakley's* Australian Magazine *columns?*

One of the drawings in the *Children of the Holocaust Exhibition* at the Australian War Memorial in Canberra shows the world from a different perspective. A dark-blue Europe stains the top of the globe and Africa and the Americas, light-blue, lie below and around it. Australia is out of the circle altogether, floating away on its own. The boy who sketched this map on the cover of his exercise book wrote across it When The Rains Came. This is clearly why so many Jewish refugees came to this country before the war. The further they could go from the spreading stain the better. The exhibition, which is approached through a pair of concentration-camp-style gates, is dimly lit. The drawings, on loan from the State Jewish Museum in Prague, shine out of a gathering twilight—they were done in Terezin, a garrison town in Czechoslovakia converted by the Germans into a ghetto, a halfway house to Auschwitz. The 70 drawings are unexceptional in themselves, the kind done by children everywhere. They show circuses, clowns, animals, toys, flowers. Very few reflect the atmosphere that surrounded them. In one, a peaceful village has a burning hill behind it. In another, a scene of princesses and clowns and flowers is invaded by a reptilian creature that breathes orange fire. The others belong to the untainted world of the imagination, a psychic cubbyhouse where children can hide and play games.

The Italian writer Primo Levi once said that he had a recurring nightmare when he was at Auschwitz, in which the survivors would not be listened to. They would find freedom but remain alone. They would tell their story and no-one would believe it. It was because of this fear that the survivors of Dachau, Buchenwald and Belsen made crude memorial towers from the debris of their camp. The English writer Ian Buruma, reviewing a book about Holocaust memorials in the _Times Literary Supplement_, and doing so with profound compassion, ends his review like this: 'And yet—and yet. I cannot help feeling that with all the talk of martyrdom and common remembrance, too much meaning is heaped upon the millions of victims. For the awful truth is that the Jews who were exterminated, in Himmler's phrase, as though they were vermin, died for nothing. There was no higher meaning attached to their deaths. They were killed because they were denied the right to live. And that was all'. If these deaths had no meaning, then life has no meaning. The Holocaust, in fact, overpowers one with meanings. It's a subject not so much for history (that has largely been done) as for contemplation. It is, in Philip Gourevitch's phrase, 'the heart of the absolute'. Like goodness, evil has depths beyond the reach of meditation. The most unfortunate phrase the philosopher Hannah Arendt ever coined was 'the banality of evil'—in relation to how ordinary Adolf Eichmann looked as he stood in the dock during his trial in Israel. Hitler, Himmler, Heydrich, Eichmann are not banal figures. Their wickedness has an oceanic depth, almost a hideous majesty. They are powerful and emblematic figures in their realm just as Mother Teresa is in hers.

This is why Thomas Keneally was wrong when he said, in an interview about his book _Schindler's Ark_, 'I've got to be frank. I've always felt that the Holocaust is a European problem and that anti-Semitism is a European disease and it's still a disease'. But the Holocaust can't be confined in space any more that it can be confined in time. Despite the horrors of World War I, there's a sense in which we retain an innocence about the nature of evil. Mass killing was done only by armies when they fought one another. Civilians died only when they were caught up in it. This was our innocence, an adult equivalent to that of the children of Terezin. But the Holocaust swept that away. This was something nobody had considered possible:

industrial deaths, organised by a government department, on a scale that defied comprehension. But even if it defies comprehension, maybe it's not all that hard to explain. European states in previous centuries had treated the peoples of Africa, America and Australia as if they were beyond and below the law; why shouldn't this imperialism turn inward? What Jürgen Habermas calls the 'deep layer of solidarity among all that wear a human face' had been ripped away before, but in the past those that had suffered had been peoples considered exotic, primitive, not fully human. Nazism succeeded in putting Jews into this category.

In a recent TV documentary, four young neo-Nazis were taken, un-willingly, to Auschwitz, to see the evidence for what they denied ever happened. There they met a remarkable woman, a cheerful lady in her late 60s called Kitty Hart, who told them what she had once seen—hundreds of people going to their deaths, day after day—from her barracks window. She became emotional, and as the young men turned away, not wanting to hear, she called out after them, 'Where did they go? The people that waited over there in that wood? Where are they? Did they just disappear?' When the young men had gone she was asked whether she found it unbearable to come back to Auschwitz like this. 'No', she said. 'This place is my home.' Like Rome or Mecca, Auschwitz is a holy place, a place of pilgrimage, one we should all try to make. These ordinary, simple drawings, shining like diamonds in a coalmine, help take us there. You can see them at the Sydney Jewish Museum from Monday.

JOHN HONNER SJ
Echoes of origins

Some Christians feel threatened by the theory of evolution because it challenges their way of reading the Bible. Similarly, some Christians think that to say that the universe began in a Big Bang is derogatory of the Creator. In his science column in Eureka Street *for November 1992, John Honner* SJ *addresses both anxieties. This is a clear piece of writing about science as well as a compact account of biblical interpretation. It does not demean those about whom he is writing, but nor does it water the truth as Honner sees it. The opening paragraph is surely a model for those who attempt to write simply about complicated subjects.*

A bird is singing high up in the branches of a tree. I can hear it, but I cannot see it. So, keeping my ear on its song, I move around at another angle, and then another angle, until I am fairly sure where it is. And then, if I look hard enough, I catch a glimpse of it.

So also, when the Russians were doing their underground nuclear testing, the Americans used listening devices in seismological stations around the world. By getting the direction and intensity of a number of signals, they were able to fix the point at which the explosion occurred and to estimate its intensity.

Every explosion has its echoes. The sounds reverberate for quite some time. The larger the explosion, the larger the reverberation. Now the Big Bang, if there was a Big Bang at the beginning of our universe, was a very large explosion with tremendous heat and energy being given off. The 'sounds' of this explosion are not so much noises as huge amounts of electromagnetic radiation. This radiation has been stretched out by the universe as it expanded. No matter what direction we tune our sensitive detecting devices towards, we find traces of a common 'background radiation'. Recent data from listening devices in space, however, gives us another ear and the possibility of being more certain that there *was* a Big Bang, and where and when it might have occurred.

The Big Bang is just a theory, of course, but the latest evidence brings scientists closer to confirming the theory. Some Christians may object to the idea of the universe beginning with a Big Bang, just as some have objected to the theory of evolution. Such scientific theories, however, should never be seen as problematic, for the accounts of creation in the Book of Genesis are not intended to make a precise point about the mechanics of creation.

You will note that I have written 'accounts of creation'. If you look at the opening paragraphs of the Bible you will see in fact two separate and in some ways contradictory accounts of how this God-made and God-cherished world came to be. The first account of creation (Genesis 1:1–2:4a) tells the story of how God made everything out of the void in six days and rested on the seventh day. The second story (Genesis 2:4b–24) tells the story of a single day on which the Lord made earth and heaven, on which Adam was formed from the dust and Eve from the side of Adam, and everything else was made.

These are quite different stories if they are read as scientific accounts. But if they are read as revealing that creation is good and God-made, they are in total agreement. And that, surely, is the point of these stories, Big Bang or no Big Bang.

LEO DONNELLY
Living with fear

When the Columban Fathers started The Far East *in 1920, it was meant as a support magazine for their missions. To keep it going they developed a school of writers who became the most skilled writing group in Australia and New Zealand. Other religious orders had individual stars whose erudition and literary gifts lent distinction to their magazines. There were talented individual lay people who won recognition in the Catholic press. But as a group it was the Columbans who stood out. Their reports home from the mission fields always made good reading, which ensured high circulation figures for* The Far East *(in 1962, 63,000). Over the years the style of missionary work has changed radically. But* The Far East, *as this story from its June 1994 issue shows, maintains its reputation for good reading. Three years earlier, Shining Path guerrillas executed an Australian Josephite sister, Irene McCormack, in the village square where Leo Donnelly's mission is.*

'I don't want to die, no, not even for the gospel. Trying to live for it is okay, but I'm not too pushed about dying for it, at least not for quite a while yet.' That is the prayer I make to the Lord every day. There have been occasions recently when death seemed close to being a reality for me. There was the somewhat doubtful consolation of it being swift—a bullet in the back of the head!

Up until now it seemed easier to confront the possibility of sudden death. A bullet from a rifle held close to the back of the head needed no second shot. Now, however, the terrorists here have changed their tack.

In this central highlands area, over 50 people have had their throats slit recently. Two of these were women belonging to our Columban parish. This is a less pleasant prospect, by comparison a bullet in the head would be welcome.

Thoughts of self-defence enter my head. Once, tempted to get a gun, I visited a gun shop in Lima. Later, in a dream, images of Peter pulling his sword to defend Jesus came to me. I didn't get the gun, but in the context of throats being slit, I'm mentally back in that gun shop. So I've settled for a heavy broom handle, about 75 cm long. Swinging this, and given half a chance, I reckon I could make things difficult for a man with a knife. There is something about a knife that angers me!

I loathe, too, the idea of having a gun. If I killed a terrorist in self-defence my missionary days would be over. Other terrorists would take pleasure in tracking me down and killing me in broad daylight.

Once a Columban home from Korea was caught up in similar violence (1950). With a 'lucky shot' he had picked off an assailant coming at him over the wall. Lying in his bed in the darkness he had spotted the sheen of the blade as his would-be murderer came in, knife between his teeth.

What was impressed on my heart was not that a brother Columban had killed a man, but rather the terrible effect this tragedy had had on him. I have no wish to carry such suffering.

Should I even have to wield my shillelagh I can only hope Irish ancestors and more recently the 'Bungaree Savages' in my blood line, will guide my arm. I would rather not do even that, but guns are out for sure. Such musings come to one in reaction to the thought of a knife near the throat!

I convince myself to stick it out because I am here solely for the gospel's message of universal love. This is my greatest source of strength. But it is a support that is often sabotaged by the seeming futility of so little love, against such a great wall of enmity. My witnessing to the values of the gospels appears indiscernible, lost in massive fires of hatred that are fanned by injustice.

I am being given the chance to live out the gospel to a depth that I never thought would be my lot. I don't kid myself. I am not doing anything extra special in the history of Columban missionaries; many have been in similar situations. As a seminarian I recall being proud of belonging to a group who then boasted that one in seven members was jailed or had died for the gospel.

Solidarity expressed by fellow Columbans written from forgotten corners of the world is a great help. Sisters who are unknown to me have chipped in with letters and prayers. Personal friends, out of their genuine concern, tend to be unhelpful. They want me to leave—the sooner the better.

Another thought that sustains me is the fact that I am a willing member of St Columban's Mission Society. We continually re-state our 'option for the poor', our 'solidarity with people in their suffering, their deprivation and their marginalisation'.

Circumstances demand that I am the one called to put flesh on these words. I know I am not alone, I have lots of Columban company in this. The Columbans in Lima, in Pakistan and the Philippines are never sure whether or when they will be embroiled in similar situations.

The Peruvian people themselves have opened me to the God of Life, not of death. Death is God's enemy, even as it is ours (Isaiah 25), even as it is my own. It is up to us, as witnesses of the gospel of love, to turn our world around. Only the gospel has power to do this. It is useless to look elsewhere.

As a preacher of the gospel, I am duty bound to push death back as far as possible. There is no way I will mindlessly give terrorists an opportunity to take my life. I will give them no pretext.

I have a sense of shared hope with the people of Huasahuasi. It is certainly important for many that a priest or religious stay with them and share their risk. They have no other option, their only home is here. Growing potatoes is their only source of livelihood.

The story of Peter comes to mind: 'Lord, to whom shall we go?' And for an updated version of this conundrum my own father once put it: 'Son, it is just as well you are going to be a priest, because if you had to earn your bread by the sweat of your brow you'd bloody starve to death!'

So, between Peter and the 'old man' it seems I have little alternative.

VERONICA BRADY
Between towns

Early in 1994, 250 people came to Sydney from around the country for a 'people's' National Catholic Conference. Self-consciously a meeting of the laity, it was emblematic of the kinds of groupings now common among Australian Catholics. Confident in their personal Catholicism, they set their own spiritual agenda. Although at times exasperated by the church's formal leadership, they exhibit a strong sense of family. These Catholics are at home in the church. They draw sustenance from a variety of sources, not all of them Catholic. Often they find powerful voices of consolidation among women, notably religious sisters. For some these are the real leaders of contemporary Catholicism. Sister Veronica Brady IBVM is one of the best known witnesses to this development. A teacher in the English Department at the University of Western Australia, she has become a significant figure in national intellectual life. This address to the National Catholic Conference appeared in Eureka Street, May 1994.

Being a non-Aboriginal Australian has always meant living in a kind of in-between. We live a long way from where we came from but also from where we want to be. Christopher Brennan called such a person the 'wanderer on the way to self'. Our unofficial anthem is *Waltzing Matilda*.

As Christians, too, we know ourselves to be a pilgrim people. Our upbringing pointed in the opposite direction, to fixity 'Full in the panting heart of Rome'. Cradle Catholics were brought up in a clear and coherent world, where bells rang for the consecration, the blessing at Benediction, for the Angelus and to call the priests, nuns and brothers to prayer. Fridays were special and we were proud of being different, eating fish. But we are a long way from there now, in time as well as place. We are between 'the God who was and the God who is yet to come'. It is as if we were in a tunnel, ambiguous, without fixed points of classification, passing through a domain which has few of the attributes of the past or of what we are looking for ahead—and this is true for the men among us as well as the women, perhaps even more so.

That may sound negative. It also sounds individualistic. But of course it is not. In the first place, to be Catholic is to be part of a community, or better, a communion which stretches across time as well as place. Our situation throws new light on the idea of purgatory on which most of us were brought up.

There is, inevitably, a tension between the church as an institution and as an occasion of grace. For some people, the church has become a counter-sign, more concerned, it seems, with property and narrow propriety respectful of the interests of the rich and powerful, than with prayer and the needs of the 'little ones'.

More temperately, you could say that we need and want to relate to the promise of Vatican II. The church is God's gracious gift, at the heart of 'the joys and the hopes, the griefs and anxieties of [people] of this age, especially those who are poor or in any way afflicted'. But the promise remains: God is still alive. We are on the way to Vatican III.

That brings us to the crux of the problem, to the three key questions we need to reflect on. First, what do we mean by 'church'? Second, what is the nature of its authority? And, third, what are we called to do?

First, the meaning of 'church'? Vatican II, is clear: The church is the central mystery of God's love for this world, communal not merely individual. It is the community of those called by his grace to live by faith, in hope and with love for all people and all of creation.

But it is not merely an inner mystery. Since none of us is merely an individual but exists in relation to others and to the rest of creation, our worship of God also involves obligation to others. As Karl Rahner notes, 'the doctrine of the church is not the central truth of Christianity', though listening to some Catholics, and to some of the moral trumpeting of Catholic officials especially, you would think it was. Rahner writes: 'Jesus Christ, faith and love, entrusting oneself to the darkness of existence and into the incomprehensibility of God in trust and in the company of Jesus Christ, the crucified and risen one, those are the central realities for a Christian'.

I have a feeling that lay people have always known this, obliged as you are to live what you believe without the defence of the institution or of religious labels, titles, language and pronouncements. But that brings us to the next question, that of authority. What authority constrains us as Catholic

Christians? We know, of course, what conservatives say, that it is the authority of the pope. That alone, however, intensifies the problem—as well as being bad theology. The pope, too, stands under the authority of God and of her/his revelation in scripture.

So often the question becomes rather 'Why stay?' Why not cut all official and visible ties with the institution? But that only intensifies the question, as many of you will know, since it means cutting off from the sacramental life and from the visible community of faith. This may be possible, of course, since God does not work only in, through and by the church. But it's difficult for us in our faith, our sense of God's logic. It also poses profound problems when it comes to passing on that faith to the new generation. As Catholics, we do not believe in scripture alone. Tradition matters, and tradition involves the dead who still speak in the language of the liturgy, in which they also worshipped, suffered and found their meaning. The church belongs to them, to all of us. To leave may mean denying the prophetic grace given to us here in this community. Authority is ultimately *God's*.

The best image is the one most profoundly scriptural. The church is the people of God. Indeed, I would like to argue that the crisis of the church is most intense among the 'professional guardians of the sacred', who find this inclusive and non-hierarchical vision difficult. But, if the church's centre of gravity is the majesty of God's love for this world, then to be worried by changes in political, social and economic structures is to miss the point. What Schillebeeckx calls 'God's essential reserve' remains: 'God can never be reduced to one of the forms in which she/he is manifested'.

So, in our time the surprise may be that the church is the people, not just the clergy. Indeed, the maturation of the people of God, their realisation of their prophet role, may be the great unfinished task of the church. We need to put an end to exclusion, denial and hierarchy, and move to the inclusiveness and community and love of life of the gospel. God, after all, does not live in any one 'holy' place but everywhere. Nor does she/he only share her/his gifts and power with the rich, powerful and educated. Indeed, as scripture insists, God's deepest concern is for those who are victims of power.

The beginnings of Vatican III in Australia at least, may be here where we are on the vulnerable edge between belief and unbelief, truth and error.

What, then, might be some of the appeals being made to us here by the Spirit of God, the God whose being is in her coming? What should we do? The awareness we spoke about initially of being in between, on the margins, I think, forces us to the kind of openness, to a proper humility and thus to the beginnings of grace. Humility means knowing our place before God. The great danger of Christianity today, J. B. Metz observes, is probably banality rather than naïveté, a lack of humility and a readiness to duplicate what has become the social, political and economic consensus,.

It may be then that in God's plan we in this country, already one of the most mixed in terms of the cultural origins of its people, will become a model of a truly universal church drawn together in the Spirit. From these others, too, we may learn about simplicity and joy, both of which are the basis of worship, reverence and a sense of stewardship of our bodies, the earth and all living creatures which lie at the heart of the gospel of Jesus.

To conclude, then, we are making for a town, for the heavenly city. But it is not out there but in here, among us, in the most unexpected places, especially in our pain; need in grace. The City of the Merely Human, as St Augustine said, is built on love of self at the expense of the other. But the City of God, the true church, is built on love of the others/Other at the expense of self.

UNSIGNED

Pray for those going home

This unsigned piece appeared in the Winter 1993 issue of The Holy Family Newsletter, *a St Vincent de Paul Society publication for those working in the migration field. Its crowded syntax conveys the intensity of the experience, both physical and emotional. At the same time the simplicity of style allows the drama of mass to impact with a wallop. Whoever wrote this is a talented writer: 'On the table was a candle, a glass of wine and two pieces of sliced bread'. The sliced bread fixes the reality in the reader's mind. I wish I knew this writer's name; and whether he/she has written other things.*

Eight storeys up, above bars and karaoke discos, a simple table was set in a small apartment in Hong Kong.

On the table was a candle, a glass of wine and two pieces of sliced bread.

At the gathering were three priests, a number of nuns and all together about 20 people from a number of countries.

Some barefooted, sitting as close as possible to the small air conditioner and fan, no one winning against the heat and humidity of a summer night in Hong Kong.

The candle was lit and the singing commenced. God was in the room because mass had started.

Cushions on the floor became hot, so, crouched against the walls, people prayed for the Hong Kong boat families who were in detention, prayers were said for the 14 children commencing their return journey the next day, prayers were said for the forced repats and those just arriving, private prayers were offered for the Australian-held boat families.

Each person at the mass could remember a name, a face, a cry from all those in detention.

The hymn 'Be Not Afraid' was sung, an appropriate war cry for each of those people, so depleted of hope.

The communion of bread and wine was distributed and readings were shared. A more sincere and moving mass could not have been held in St Peter's, Rome. Everyone at the mass believed in the sharing of love for 'the least of my Brethren'—the stranger, the rejected, the political throw-away.

ANGELA DUNNE
Jesus' People

Irish-born, Sister Angela Dunne FMM *worked for many years among the Aboriginal people of Mt Isa in Queensland. Something of her rich experience is caught in this short article on the death of a didgeridoo man, including her second baptism in waters behind Ayers Rock and the commissioning of five Aboriginal elders of the Catholic Church of Mt Isa. But it is Arthur Peterson, the didgeridoo man, who dominates this article. It appeared in* Nelen Yubu, *no. 55 (1992/3).*

I remember him dancing over the sand dunes in the creek bed, immersing us in his didgeridoo music, Bible in hand. I remember him emerging from beneath Uncle Bill's house, quietly dignified, coming from his cramped living quarters, left of a sheet of corrugated iron. I remember him graciously responding to any greeting he received, impelling respect through his innate dignity, simplicity and grandeur. I remember him enthralling the young children, black and white, with his didgeridoo, his dance, his love for them and for his culture.

Arthur Peterson, Uncle Arthur, Old Man, whatever we knew him by, was a friend to every one of us. Each of us who knew him hardly realised the privilege it was to share part of life's journey with him. He inspired us with such a sense of courage and, yes, joy too, that we hardly knew where to turn when he passed away so suddenly the same evening he suffered a heart attack and struck his head as he fell, 28 June 1992.

I had been baptised by him in the waters behind Ayers Rock, baptised a second time into the land, into the mystery of Uluru: made a 'friend of the whole place', to use Arthur's words, accompanied by a big, expansive gesture, as he described the significance of what he had done for me.

Arthur was a dancer. He danced into the lives of many of us. Dance was the cultural expression he used most often. He opened doors through this medium. It was a profound expression of himself as an Aboriginal man, in love with his own cultural heritage. For us it was a powerful vehicle. He danced across denominational boundaries, looked for, and made us look towards Christ in a way that was coming from the root of his being. He was above the tensions and the debates, and for the most part avoided the pitfalls of syncretism.

Arthur Peterson, elder of the Wanyi tribe, communicated in several Aboriginal languages from Mt Isa through Doomadgee out towards Alice Springs. He made many journeys down the east coast and out into the Territory but he always returned to his adopted home at Yallambee in Mt Isa. This man always travelled with his didgeridoo and his Bible—it was the voice of God for him; and his didgeridoo was wisdom. The haunting music was the breath of wisdom. With intense reverence he told us, 'When the didgeridoo is played, *that* is Wisdom'. What did he mean? We never questioned the truth of what he shared with us, but accepted it reverently and gratefully, and indeed the haunting music in the hands of Uncle Arthur was an experience to treasure. The music enveloped us.

Several times Arthur Peterson came to the AICC (Aboriginal and Islander Catholic Council) eucharist in the bush. Our favourite bush setting is the dry river bed. On these occasions, Arthur would dance around the site. He would play his didgeridoo as he danced and would make the area safe from all evil before our celebration. It was always so moving: this man from an ancient culture, performing an ancient ceremony in his ancient land in preparation for the sublime moment of Christ's presence among us.

Arthur's sense of theatre was never more finely displayed than on the day our five Aboriginal elders of the Catholic Church of Mt Isa were commissioned some four years ago. Fr Alan Sheldrick and Elder Arthur Peterson of the Wanyi tribe had been invited to commission these chosen leaders. Our ceremony borrowed heavily from the Uniting Church ritual, but a more ancient ritual inspired Uncle Arthur as he leaped out from behind each elder, challenging, inspiriting and admonishing them in his language and in English. He danced around galvanising them one by one into enthusiasm, commitment and courage for what lay ahead.

But Arthur no longer dances among us. The elders he had commissioned were called by his friends and family to lay this wonderful man to rest.

With what sensitivity elders Peter Smith, Nola Archie, Colleen Muckan and Dolly Hankin prepared that final celebration with Arthur's friends and family. Traditions to be respected, requests to be granted, desires to be adhered to, all had to be included. The silent procession came forward in our spacious parish church. Elder Peter Smith announced that certain permissions had been granted for this funeral. Arthur's name could be mentioned, and the didgeridoo, normally not permitted at funerals, could be played. The remains came to rest at the sanctuary and a little procession of his friends came forward to touch the coffin, to place a flower, to say a word. People were invited to speak about his life. They did so with pride and sorrow at his going. With prayers and hymns and didgeridoo we finally came to the last commendation and the committal to the cemetery.

The prayers around the graveside were simple and dignified. One man sat close to the grave calling out, 'My friend is going, my friend is going'. He would have been surprised to know how his words echoed in each heart. Then, with the slightest nod from a silent, tall, bearded man, dancers came forward. They danced precisely and deliberately around the grave, and as the coffin disappeared from view the didgeridoo the dancers carried was dramatically lowered vertically into the earth. It would not be played again on this earth by our friend Arthur, Wisdom Man of the Wanyi people.

I thank God for him, for his great spirit, for the great gift of having known him, for our Aboriginal council of church elders who carried out the sacred trust of his burial with sensitivity and dignity. Some say, 'We hear that Jesus walks among us and we do not recognise him until he is gone'. How often that is each one's life-experience.

PETER THOMAS

On prayer

Much Catholic writing about prayer has been done by those who could be called religious professionals: monks, nuns, priests or theologians. One of the signs of the laity's coming of age is that lay people now feel more comfortable in speaking of their own prayer life. Theirs is often a domestic prayer, as this article by the director of the Catholic Communications Office, Melbourne, shows. Peter Thomas takes the reader inside his own family and shows how he and his wife have tried to make their praying together a realistic activity. The unforced honesty of this article make it a notable piece of writing. It appeared in Australian Catholics *for February 1995.*

When my 10-year-old daughter, Katie, fell and fractured her skull, it gave me some anxious moments in the hospital casualty rooms. While Katie was being transferred by ambulance to the Royal Children's Hospital, I drove close behind muttering prayers for her recovery. Katie was unconscious and my wife accompanied her in the ambulance. I was upset and the only prayer that surfaced was my childhood Hail Mary. Such was my anxiety at the time that the rote prayers taught to me by my parents and the nuns was all I could utter.

Prayers taught at our parent's knees and often repeated as part of the ritual of family life enrich our religious culture beyond measure. Although the rosary is not normally my favourite prayer, I sank to my knees and prayed the beads with older members of my family when we learnt of the death of a close uncle.

At home we have tried to imbue a sense of prayer not as an 'add-on', but as integral as meals, TV viewing and feeding the dog. It's a delicate balance, particularly as children grow older, to have prayer and prayer ritual as routinely part of family life. I suspect that if it has always been there it's not nearly as intrusive or, in some circumstances, embarrassing.

In case you have the wrong idea, I should say at this point that my children, who are now adults, are not perfect or entirely at peace with the church. I don't know any grown-up children who fit that category! Mine, like almost everyone's, have difficulty with Sunday mass attendance and with doctrine and structure. But I have found that their attitudes to these matters are quite different to their attitudes to prayer.

Prayer, at least in my home, is as much a part of family identity as it is a part of institutional religion. Prayer is at every meal and every crisis. It's part of family bonding, and it is my belief that it plays an important role in keeping them identifiably Catholic, even if they choose to skip Sunday mass. Prayer forms, occasions, issues and references to Dorothy Day, Oscar Romero and other contemporary 'saints' help maintain their Catholicity, for this is the religious culture in which they have been nurtured.

For more than 20 years, we have lit a candle or lamp at every meal except breakfast. The light is a reminder that it is a special and sacred time. It focuses on the importance of this precious moment. The table is always covered with a cloth, and the TV and radio are never on. A certain generosity, a willingness to communicate, is the principle at the heart of this action. As children grow older, of course, things are more difficult to organise; but it is never impossible.

Every morning I have called my children from their sleep and gently blessed them with the sign of the cross on their foreheads. Sometimes they have been grumpy and mildly embarrassed, but never have they turned away. My 'baby', now 18, is the only child still at home. She still responds to my wake-up calls and daily blessing. But it is important to be sensitive and never to embarrass her. A blessing must be freely accepted. If there is any hint of resistance, it is better to find some other form of affirmation.

On holiday, when mass may not be available, we have had some of our best experiences of family prayer. By the sea or high in the mountains, the backdrop of nature is much appreciated by children and parents alike. It allows us to keep Sunday sacred. One takes the risk that this becomes the preferred ritual, even when mass is available. This has happened many times. But each time must be dealt with individually, respecting the circumstances of each family member.

To let our children observe their parents at prayer is an example *par excellence*. Not to parade piety or to intrude on their space to make a point, but to be seen, as a matter of family life, to be persons of prayer.

I don't know whether my children will retain the practice of their faith. No parent can make that claim. Life is different today! I'm reasonably sure that my children have a sense of prayer and therefore a sense of the sacred. Prayer cannot be 'done' in total isolation. It contains no magic, and its power emerges from the experience of living generously in the human communities we call families.

GRAHAM ENGLISH
Many parts, one Body

Graham English is an adult cartoonist whose work delights readers of
Women-Church. *He teaches religion at the Australian Catholic
University and before that was a resource person at Sydney's Catholic
Education Office. In the latter job he ran a religious education
newsletter for teachers which was notable for its book reviews. Anything that Graham English writes is thoughtful, witty and stimulat-
ing, as readers of his books know. This honest autobiographical account
compels the reader through the simplicity of the writing. It appeared in*
National Outlook *in September 1993.*

Like the sperm in the Monty Python song I have been a Catholic
from the start.

It seems longer. I was conceived with a long Catholic memory
and I lived in a Catholic milieu. My grandfather, who died five years before
I was born, spent his last years wandering around the farm mumbling the
litany of Our Lady; my aunt regaled me with stories of the old women at
Murringo who spent all of All Souls' Day at the church praying for those in
purgatory. Catholicism pervaded my life. I was in my twenties before I
discovered other faiths among my forebears and a neat row of skeletons in
the family cupboard.

Mum always said that she took me to mass from the day I came home
from the hospital and I never cried or played up in church once. I was the
eldest child, the first of seven pregnancies that netted three live children
and four who perished before they could be baptised and so tortured my
mother until her old age lest they be in Limbo, unable to see God.

Besides being taken to mass every Sunday from birth I was taught to
pray very early. My father knelt beside his bed every night for a long time.

As soon as we could we said the rosary each night after tea, kneeling
round the kitchen. On Sunday nights we went to the church for Benediction and sometimes on other weeknights as well. And we attended the
processions, special feasts and church celebrations. My father added more

and more prayers to the nightly list. We were pleased on the nights he was out and Mum let us off some of them.

But I lived in ambiguity. I remember a day when I was lying on the ground near the apricot tree in our backyard. There was a pale afternoon sky, I was seven and I was thinking of God and eternity. I was distressed. Why had God made me and condemned me to last for all eternity? I had not asked to be.

Some time about then I was lying in bed unable to sleep. The same thoughts, the same distress. I went out to my mother who was ironing and told her. She replied that she wanted to live long enough to rear us then she would be happy to go to God. In those days I think she did not relish life. I think she hoped that we would all join a religious order and be safe.

My father drank too much. He was not an alcoholic. He was a Catholic working-class man of his time who had a feeling for words but no-one to point him in the direction of poetry. He had felt little affection in the large family in which he was the second youngest and he had little confidence in his own ability.

When he was drinking he was unreliable and I was deeply embarrassed and angry. When he was not drinking he had a large store of common sense, a hatred of gossip and a skill for picking phonies. He would have been a fine teacher.

My mother had a bit of the larrikin in her, though I think almost no-one else knows that. She grew up in real poverty. At 16 she resigned her job as a domestic at the Catholic hospital when another girl was falsely accused and dismissed. She spent from then until I was born, 15 years later, as a domestic in hotels.

Though very religious, she was tolerant of other people, though not of my father when he was drinking. At some stage before she was married she had a breakdown and I remember her as nervy. From the ectopic pregnancy that nearly took her life when I was six months old until the last still birth when I was 11, pregnancy was the Banquo at my parents' feast.

I never saw my mother naked. I seldom saw my parents show affection. We were told nothing about sex. As an adult I asked Mum about their apparent coolness. 'I wasn't game', she answered.

Beside what I have said already about my parents, these fragments shaped my childhood religion. At night in the church the stained glass went black and the altar was a magic cave with flowers, lights, incense smoke and colours. I lived in the country where most people I knew were poor and where the winters were desperately cold. I yearned for spring. When my father was drinking I, as the eldest child, took on my mother's feelings.

A month before I was five we went to visit my grandmother's grave; she had died a few weeks before. It was the feast of the Assumption, 1949. I remember my mother saying to her sister: 'I am haemorrhaging'. The brothers telling us that drunkenness was a mortal sin then I'd see my father going to communion on Sunday after coming home drunk on Saturday. Acting as an altar server at mass. Eternity. The distress of that still touches me at four o'clock in the morning. White daphne, jonquils and wild spring flowers, especially Paterson's Curse. Death. In country towns there is always someone dying, and you usually know or know of them. They are often young people. Catholics were preoccupied with dying. Getting up on cold mornings to do the First Friday devotions. Saying at age 11 that I wanted to be a Christian Brother.

At the age of 15 I left home to become a brother at Strathfield. Seventeen years later I left the brothers. When I left, I told a lie, something I regret as I try very hard to tell the truth. I signed a document from Rome, written in Latin, that said my reason for leaving was that I could no longer keep up celibacy. That was not the reason. I left because, for the first time in my life, I realised that I had a choice, and mine was to get married.

My adult religion has been shaped by my childhood and by so much more. I entered the brothers at an opportune time. The liturgical revival in the Catholic Church was in full swing. The brothers introduced me to poetry and to the Bible. They taught me to teach. They also introduced me to John Ogburn, who later taught me something of seeing and so opened me to painting and sculpture. And the Vatican Council was on and I learned to be a thinking Catholic.

Some of the finest human beings I have known were or are Christian Brothers. And they taught me to tell stories. They also took some things from me and denied me some opportunities. But in my limited 15-year-old way I chose to be there and for 17 years I chose to remain.

Many people at my age did a lot worse. Then in 1973 I was sent to study religion in Melbourne. Someone who knew me at university, which I attended part-time after teaching all day and coaching football and doing all the other things we used to do in those days, told me lately: 'You said the secret was, don't get involved'. In 1973, for reasons I cannot explain, I ignored my own advice... It was a great year, my adolescence, and I fell in love three times. The last time it stuck.

Leaving the brothers was the most miserable experience of my life. This process took me two years. The most significant moment in it was the day I said to myself: 'I can leave if I want to'. That was probably the most important moment in my adult life.

When I was a child I believed nearly everything, though I was not very old when I began doubting the existence of Limbo. Now I believe very little. I believe that God delights in creation, including me, and that this delight led to God becoming incarnate in Jesus Christ who was executed. Lenny Bruce's question to the lady with the cross on a chain, 'Hey, lady, would you wear an electric chair round your neck?' struck me when I read it and still does. I believe that Jesus was raised and that we are saved. I believe in the existence of evil. That's about it, and that is the basis of anything I teach, write or draw...

I also pray for the dead, because I need to. I don't know if purgatory exists. I feel that death is a journey that I want to help others finish when they reach God, and I need to pray for them as I grieve. My favourite prayers are the Magnificat, the psalm that begins 'He who dwells in the shelter of the most high...', and any number of hymns. I love 'Virgin wholly marvellous' and had a friend play it at my mother's funeral.

Benediction as it was has disappeared from Catholic devotion. I still need what it gave me and I find whatever that is in Zen meditation. My favourite pope so far is Paul VI. He, like me, was ambivalent. I wonder how anyone alive now could be otherwise.

My favourite virtue is hope. My practice as a Catholic is centred on the eucharist, though I find it hard to be a member of a parish. I go to 11 o'clock mass because there is singing and I can sit quietly at the side. I usually try to avoid listening to the homily because I seldom find it nourishing. Now and then I am nourished, and surprised. I am not a joiner nor an ideologue nor am I a natural activist. Someone told me that I should stop being choosy and muck in with everyone else. It is too late for that.

RAY CASSIN
A shout for the Jug Girl

When Eureka Street *hit the newsstands first in March 1991, it carried a column, 'Quixote', written by someone called Ray Cassin. The bottom of the page said that Cassin was production editor of the magazine. Whoever he was, here was a sparkling new wit in Australian Catholic writing. It was not that he told jokes or wrote 'funny stories'—Cassin's wit came from his side-on look at reality, it was truly quixotic. Subsequent columns revealed him as a comfortable presence in unsmart pubs, a friend to old journos and an eater of junk food whose lodgings were, to say the least, downmarket. Yet he also knew enough to write the magazine's obituary of the French theologian Yves Congar OP. In 1994 he won the Walkley Award for the three best headlines published in the Australian print media. The 'Quixote' column closed after four years, leaving readers like me bereft at the disappearance of such good stuff. Choosing only one column from all that richness has been the hardest part of editing this anthology. 'A shout for the jug girl' appeared in January/February 1992.*

Don Quixote raised his voice, and called out in an arrogant tone: 'Let the whole world stand, if the whole world does not confess that there is not in the whole world a more beauteous maiden than the Empress of la Mancha, the peerless Dulcinea del Taboso'.

The merchants stopped when they heard this speech, and saw the strange figure who made it; and from his appearance and his words they divined that the speaker was mad. But wanting to know more fully what this confession he required of them really meant, one of them, who was a bit of a joker and very sharp-witted, said: 'Sir Knight, we do not know who this good lady is that you speak of. Show her to us and, if she is as beauteous as you say, we will most willingly and without any pressure acknowledge the truth demanded of us by you'.

'If I were to show her to you', replied Don Quixote, 'what merit would there be in your confessing so obvious a truth? The essence of the matter is that you must believe, confess, affirm, swear and maintain it without seeing her. If you will not, you must do battle with me, monstrous and proud crew. Now come on! One by one, as the law of chivalry requires, or all together, as is the custom and evil practice of men of your breed' (*The Adventures of Don Quixote* by Miguel de Cervantes Saavedra, trans. by J. M. Cohen).

'She's just the jug girl, mate', snickers the man seated next to me. He is referring to a thin blonde who stands behind the bar with a beer jug in her outstretched hand. There is no beer in the jug. It contains coins, mostly 10c and 20c pieces. She smiles. 'Do you want to put in for an extra show?' We add our contributions to the jug and she moves on down the line of drinkers. The man next to me is not my mate. I have never seen him before and, although I do not usually object to 'mate' as a general term of address, I decide that I do not wish to hear it from him.

But I do not pursue the matter. Instead, I ask about the blonde: 'The *jug* girl? Yeah, she's not part of the show, y'know, but she tries to work the pubs anyway. They let her strip here if she can fill the jug with coins, and she gets paid what's in the jug'. He paused, and added, 'She's a real bitch— she hit me last week'. I say nothing. I do not think it is necessary to ask why the jug girl hit him. Or to ask why, if he finds her so objectionable, he still tosses coins into the jug.

She is now standing in the middle of a school of drinkers at the end of the bar, where the new landlord and his brother are bolting together sections of what will become a catwalk. Evidently, the prospect of an extra show is not sufficient to persuade them to part with their loose change. One of them appears to be demanding more. He sways towards her, gesturing with his glass. Still smiling, she shakes her head, shrinking back against the bar. She turns and appeals to the landlord, who shrugs and returns to his unfinished catwalk. Well, the landlord is paying for the show, not for her. She's just the jug girl.

He hopes that the show will lure enough drinkers to compensate for his folly in buying the pub at all. It is the kind of small inner-city pub that is not quite in the right place to become gentrified and attract a yuppie clientele. Its patrons are what they have always been: mostly male, and mostly on their way home from work. Tonight, there is a large group of youngish males who are obviously from the same workplace. They are all drunk, one of them very drunk. He is dressed as a clown, with a plastic nose only slightly redder than the rest of his face. It is evidently a bucks' party, the clown is the prospective groom, and the landlord is very pleased. He has just the show for them.

The official stripper arrives. Unlike the jug girl she is not nervous. The jug girl, perhaps striving for professional solidarity, greets her eagerly. The greeting is ignored. Two policemen arrive and speak to the landlord and the official stripper. The landlord does not expect trouble; he is a former policeman himself, and the two policemen are old friends.

The show begins. Many of the drinkers move to the side of the cat-walk, and the official stripper begins to sway to the music. Every few minutes the music changes tempo and she removes an item of clothing, sometimes inviting the men near the catwalk to remove it for her. There are cheers and whistles, and she taunts the men as they taunt her. She is a professional. As the music grows louder the throng around the catwalk gets bigger, and the buck's party push the clown on to the catwalk. The stripper knows he is the star of their show. She is lying on the catwalk now, legs apart, wearing only a G-string. She orders the clown, who is very drunk, and crawling along the catwalk, to remove the G-string. There is loud applause from the onlookers when this operation is accomplished. The bucks' party pick up the clown, who now wears the G-string as a necklace, and carry him out into the night.

The jug girl is on next. She has filled her beer jug. She hands the landlord a tape of the music she will use and steps on to the catwalk. She cannot dance as well as the official stripper, and is not sure what to do about the groping hands of the men. She slaps them away, whereas the professional had made it all part of the tease. When the jug girl is naked, it is obvious that she is very thin. And there are bruises on her body. I look away.

'Bitch!' roars the man seated next to me. The landlord grabs him and marches him out the door of the pub. When the landlord returns, he switches the music off and says to the jug girl, 'If y'can't control the punters you'll never get a regular job'.

I leave. I am ashamed. My feminist credentials were never very good, and my chivalric credentials aren't much better. I decide I will not return to the pub. I wonder what the jug girl will do.

MICHAEL McGIRR SJ
Eyeball to eyeball with the Pope

Michael McGirr is a Jesuit priest whose short fiction is beginning to attract attention. He is also editor of Australian Catholics, *a mass circulation free magazine distributed through parishes and schools in Australia. This article appeared in the* Canberra Times *and the* Age *to coincide with the beatification of Mary MacKillop on 19 January 1995. Its honesty and humility are typical of the best Australian writing about the modern papacy. Father McGirr is aware of the difficulties of belonging to the papal church but he can see its advantages too as a herald of uncomfortable gospel truths.*

I was in Year 11 before it dawned on me that popes came and went. That year, 1978, we had three popes.

I suspect that one of the priests at school was secretly pleased by this uncommon turnover. He was a comic talent and a conclave specialist. After a 15-year moratorium, he was able to present his classes on the making of popes twice in a single semester. He offered odds against the election of an Australian pope, the kind of gimmick that secured the interest of even the most world weary 16-year-olds. One of these was a Pole who was repeating the year because, he said, he could earn more at school than elsewhere. He supplied cheap records, magazines, cigarettes and ran an occasional cocktail service from his locker. On the day that his fellow countryman, John Paul II, was elected, he put on free cask wine at the morning break. It was something to celebrate and most of us entered the spirit of the occasion. The conclave priest told us that after two John Pauls the next pope was sure to be Pope George Ringo.

Now, however, people are beginning to take seriously the pontificate of John Paul II. I have grown up in and committed myself to a church which has been radically shaped by him. It hasn't always been easy. But it still makes sense.

Religion at school was always sugared by bizarre personalities. It was possible on one day to sit at the back of our cavernous chapel while an elderly priest swept the place with incense. On other days, we had mass sitting around coffee tables and school desks. Our English teacher, who wore a green suit with a greasy collar, read religious poetry with a finger hooked into his collar to allow room for the emotions that filled his throat. But other times he removed his jacket, and, with his armpits pouring sweat, he launched into a full-blooded rendition of 'good clean Shakespearian bawd'. Our somewhat chaotic religious education embraced, in season, both the wonders of the Shroud of Turin and the iniquities of American foreign policy. My recollection is of a spacious church. There was plenty of room for all shapes and sizes. Religion itself seemed to me to work less like sugar and more like salt. It brought out the subtle flavours of the human personality. It could put a mad glint in the eye of people who'd been hard at it for fifty years. Done to excess, it hardened the blood vessels around the heart.

Even now, it's impossible to prise apart the mixed bag of motives that prompted me, in the year after I left school, to join the novitiate of the order that taught me. As many of my contemporaries were making in the opposite direction, I started to walk around backstage in the church. Ironically, I'm sure that I went my way for much the same reason as they went theirs. I had an appetite for life. I saw the church as a big wide world.

There were three or four elderly brothers living with us in the novitiate. Brothers had effectively spent most of their lives as servants, a situation which the charismatic leader of the order, Father Arrupe, had tried to humanise. Fr Arrupe was largely credited with taking the fear out of religious life. One of the brothers had hunched shoulders from years spent binding books in an ill-equipped room. His masterpieces were shelved when Vatican II changed the reading habits of the generation before mine.

One day, the novice master announced at breakfast that a community meeting was to be held immediately. Even the novices were to be present. This was unprecedented. The novice master opened a sealed envelope and read a solemn letter announcing that the pope had removed Fr Arrupe from office, together with his assistants, and replaced him with somebody else. Only the most perfunctory reasons were given. At the same time, Jesuits around the world were hearing the same news. Nobody knew quite what to make of it. We were asked to keep the matter confidential for the moment and to respond with loyalty to the Holy Father.

'La, la', said Brother Bookbinder, no stranger to weighty impositions from above. 'Will this affect the brothers, father?'

We all left that meeting with hunched shoulders. It was my first experience of the pope acting in any way differently from a media superstar. Along with Princess Diana, whose wedding was on most peoples' minds at the time, he was one of the most photographed people on earth. This was something different. His authority sat uncomfortably. But it sat.

It became clear that the new pontificate was to grind exceeding fine. The pope seemed to recover with amazing speed from an assassination attempt and, if it wasn't apparent from his writings, it was obvious from this that he was no delicate flower. He travelled tirelessly and became known as 'the pilgrim pope.' Many Jesuits felt they were living a precarious existence within the church. I was astonished sometimes when outsiders credited us with great power.

Soon after turning 21, a friend and I decided to make a pilgrimage of our own. It was more like a spiritual adventure. Over a number of weeks, we hitchhiked and walked from the east coast to the west. We travelled anonymously, without provisions or money. We knocked on doors and asked for food. We met all types. The most generous always seemed to be the ones with least.

Once we were offered a lift towards Renmark by a bloke who ran a nursery. After a few kilometres he turned on us, unprovoked, and demanded to know if we knew anything about 'The Black Pope'. The Black Pope is the nickname that used to be given to the head of the Jesuits in mock recognition of his influence on the Holy Father. The nurseryman told us the Jesuits were diabolical. Servants of Satan. The Black Pope was plotting with the real pope to overthrow the United States and commandeer the nuclear arsenal of the Soviet Union. The invective went on and on. I thought of the Black Pope, Fr Arrupe, who was at that stage languishing from the effects of a stroke. Towards the end of his life Fr Arrupe wrote, 'more and more I find myself in the hands of God'. It's not a bad caption for a life spent on pilgrimage, dependent on the uncertain hospitality of others.

I have only once ever come eyeball-to-eyeball with John Paul II. The context was another pilgrimage. In late 1986, a group of us drove 5000 km to celebrate the centenary of a Jesuit failure, our attempt to establish a community among Aboriginal people in the Northern Territory. Eight celibate young men travelled the distance in a minibus. It was the kind of thing we did. When we got to Uluru, we attempted to have a simple mass at sunset in the sand some distance from the rock. We were overrun by busloads of tourists who were inching forward to get better photos and trampled right over our makeshift altar.

A few days later, the pope came to Alice Springs to 'meet' with Aboriginal people. A path had been arranged for him to walk along at the showgrounds. I stood behind the rope. On my left, a group of Aborigines from Townsville were trying to set themselves up in such a way as to attract the pope's attention when he went past. They were not part of the official program but they wanted to present him with a message stick. They were in desperate earnest. On my right were some young German tourists. They had dressed a doll up as a baby and were hoping to trick the pope into taking it from them and kissing it or blessing it. For them, the whole occasion was a joke.

The pope arrived. He came to where we were. He ignored those nearby and looked straight at me. 'Hello,' I said feebly in the second before his attention was swept away. Of all the people on my right and left, I probably had least to communicate to him.

Eventually, with painful slowness, he delivered a speech. He said that long before Christians came to Australia, the Spirit was alive and active in Aboriginal culture. Next day, he was reviled as a red ragger in the Northern Territory press. Reading that paper, crammed in the minibus, was one occasion on which I felt enormously proud of the pope. I felt the same pride when he was attributed with a role in the revolutions of 1989, first in Poland and then elsewhere. I felt proud when he stood out against the Gulf War and was intrigued by a report, some time later, in which Saddam Hussein was said to be first off the mark in sending his good wishes to the pope on one of his increasingly frequent visits to hospital.

I can't say the last 18 months have always occasioned the same reaction. We've had a restatement in a papal letter, *Veritatis splendor*, of the kind of difficult sexual morality which showed many churchgoers the door when it appeared in *Humanae vitae* in 1968. We've had a statement trying ingenuously to end debate about the possibility of the ordination of women. We've had a Catechism which was initially translated into inclusive English. This was unacceptable. The version that was finally released speaks of 'men' when it presumably means 'all of us'. We've had a letter saying that those who divorce and remarry should come to church but may not receive communion. These publications have lined the walls of my first year as a priest. They haven't dominated it.

Australians don't mind getting gooseflesh out of religion. I was in the novitiate when Michael Chamberlain looked into a camera at Uluru and said 'the loss of our baby is the will of God'. Lindy Chamberlain's trial was a cruel witchhunt. It was triggered by the fact that nobody believed in a God who could so easily negate a parent's grief. Michael's statement, repeated for a voracious newsman, flew in the face of any common sense of God. Lindy Chamberlain was turned into a freak. Stories were conflated about sacrifices in the wilderness and God knows what else.

My deepest fear for Catholicism is that whilst our people are becoming predictably middle class and our leaders admirably safe, it is our beliefs which are now eccentric. I grew up with it the other way round: the religious people I knew at school cultivated their oddities on a bedrock of common sense.

Not so long ago, I attended an occasion of prayer about the ordination of women. It was held outside the cathedral gates on a Friday afternoon and had been well publicised in the media. Nevertheless, only a small group turned up to pray for change. A slightly larger, younger and better-dressed group turned up to pray against it. Meanwhile, tens of thousands of people went past in trams and cars on their way to another great Australian weekend. For one terrible moment, I thought we were fighting over a bone that few people cared about.

By way of contrast, I remember sitting in a living room in Alice Springs and watching footage of lunchtime crowds in Sydney turn out to see the popemobile. When he comes to Randwick Racecourse in January for the beatification of Mary MacKillop, he will most likely be part of the biggest gathering in Australia since the bicentenary celebration. I just hope there's more to it than a freak show. The pope puts the question of God to vast numbers of people in a way that no advertiser could invent. Ideally, the pope also holds together the plural religious culture of the Catholic Church. He reminds world leaders of their responsibilities for justice. It is a position which is undeniably rich in potential. The next pope may be a John Paul or a George Ringo. Hopefully, he will also be ready to listen and to celebrate with us the godly variety of human life.